D1382883

*The publisher and the University of California Press Foundation gratefully acknowledge the generous support of the S. Mark Taper Foundation Imprint in Jewish Studies.*

*Food and Power*

CALIFORNIA STUDIES IN FOOD AND CULTURE

*Darra Goldstein, Editor*

# Food and Power

A CULINARY ETHNOGRAPHY
OF ISRAEL

*Nir Avieli*

Drawings by Heimo Wallner

UNIVERSITY OF CALIFORNIA PRESS

University of California Press, one of the most distinguished university presses in the United States, enriches lives around the world by advancing scholarship in the humanities, social sciences, and natural sciences. Its activities are supported by the UC Press Foundation and by philanthropic contributions from individuals and institutions. For more information, visit www.ucpress.edu.

University of California Press
Oakland, California

Library of Congress Cataloging-in-Publication Data

Names: Avieli, Nir, author.

Title: Food and power : a culinary ethnography of Israel / Nir Avieli.
Description: Oakland, California : University of California Press, [2017] |
    Series: California studies in food and culture ; 67 | Includes bibliographical
    references and index. | Identifiers: LCCN 2017023348 (print) | LCCN
    2017026871 (ebook) | ISBN 9780520964419 () | ISBN 9780520290099
    (cloth : alk. paper) | ISBN 9780520290105 (pbk. : alk. paper)
Subjects: LCSH: Cooking, Israeli—History. | Cooking—Social
    aspects—Israel. | Israel—Social life and customs. | Kosher food. | National
    characteristics, Israeli.
Classification: LCC TX724 (ebook) | LCC TX724 .A925 2017 (print) |
    DDC 641.595694—dc23
LC record available at https://lccn.loc.gov/2017023348

Manufactured in the United States of America

24  23  22  21  20  19  18  17
10  9  8  7  6  5  4  3  2  1

*To my children: Zohar, Gilad, Noam, Itamar, and Hadas*

# CONTENTS

# ILLUSTRATIONS

# ACKNOWLEDGMENTS

It is impossible to acknowledge the contribution, help and support of the hundreds, perhaps thousands, of professional chefs and caterers, domestic cooks, food writers, diners, and eaters who shared with me their food and recipes and confided to me their thoughts and emotions. I tremendously enjoyed their food and company, learned so much from our conversations, and was humbled time and again by their generosity. I hope my text is as palatable as the food and food for thought they offered me so generously. I also hope they understand that this book, just like the food parents sometimes insist their children eat because "it is good for them," is meant to do good.

I am grateful to my colleagues and students in the Department of Sociology and Anthropology at Ben-Gurion University who have read or heard earlier versions of the chapters. Their questions, comments, and critique were extremely valuable and helped me fine-tune my arguments, acknowledge my biases, shortcomings, and mistakes, and improve the text.

This book was written while I was on sabbatical at Middlebury College, where my family and I enjoyed the hospitality of the faculty, staff, and students. Thanks are due to Timi Mayer, director of the Rohatyn Center for Global Affairs at Middlebury, who supported the writing of the book and made sure that my year was fruitful and pleasant. My sabbatical was supported by a generous fellowship from the Israel Institute.

Special thanks are due to Josh Berlowitz, a Middlebury senior appointed to be my research assistant while I was compiling the text. His editing of the text was very helpful, and his critique and suggestions were extremely significant. A scholar in the making, Josh was a great asset, and anyone should be so lucky to have an assistant and friend like him.

The staff at UC Press were supportive and professional. I would like to thank Darra Goldstein, Melissa Caldwell, Kate Marshal, Bradley Depew, Cindy Fulton, and Genevieve Thurston for accepting my manuscript and preparing it for press. I am especially grateful to Michael Herzfeld, Ellen Oxfeld, and an anonymous reviewer for their positive reviews of the manuscript and their valuable comments. The publication of the book was supported by the Israel Science Foundation.

I talked about many of the findings and ideas presented in this book with my late parents, Elyakum Avieli (1937–2004) and Aviva Avieli (1943–2015). They were not always convinced, but I think that they shared my concern about Israel and understood my attempt to make sense of some of the difficulties and problems Israeli society is facing. My sisters, Merav and Hila, were supportive and amused.

I discussed every observation, interview, idea, and argument presented in this book with my spouse, Irit, who is my best friend and partner, my most valuable commentator, and my companion in life. How can I thank her for what is essentially hers? Irit, this book, too, is yours as much as it is mine.

# Introduction

ON MARCH 14, 2006, New York–based Sabra Foods, partly owned by Strauss-Elite, Israel's leading food producer, set a Guinness World Record for the largest plate of hummus ever, 3.5 meters in diameter and 400 kilos (800 pounds) in weight. Sabra's American CEO, Yehudah Pearl, explained that this publicity stunt was aimed at expanding Sabra's market share and increasing the popularity of hummus in America.[1]

The brand name Sabra (*tzabar* in Hebrew) evokes notions of national and ethnic identity. *Tzabar* (or, colloquially, *sabres*), means prickly pear, but it is used in modern Hebrew to denote a Jew born in Israel—that is, a native Israeli Jew. Israeli Jews often describe themselves as prickly on the outside but sweet within (Almog 2000, 4)—tough at first but sensitive and kind once you get to know them. Paradoxically, the cactus is a recent arrival from the New World, a diehard, drought-resistant plant used by Palestinian farmers under Ottoman rule to delineate their fields. As a consequence, *sabres* grow nowadays mainly on the ruins of Palestinian villages (Ben Ze'ev 2011). This culinary symbol is therefore multivocal and evokes both an endorsing self-perception of Israeli Jews *and* the memory of the displaced Palestinians and their 1948 ruin. In this sense, the brand name Sabra exposes the ambiguity embedded in the "Israelization" of hummus: both prickly pears and hummus are conceived by Israeli Jews as symbols of their own localness, but since both are actually pre-Zionist, they uncover a continued Palestinian presence.

Returning to the evolving Hummus Wars, the 2006 Guinness Record for the largest plate of hummus did not go unnoticed. In October 2008, Fadi Abboud, the president of the Association of Lebanese Industrialists and later the country's minister of tourism, announced that Lebanon would petition the Lebanese Ministry of Economy and Trade to request protected status for hummus from the EU: "By marketing Lebanese national dishes such as hummus and tabbouleh[2] as its own, . . . Israel was costing Lebanon tens of millions of dollars per year." Abboud explained that Lebanon's case would rely on the "'feta cheese precedent,' whereby a European court granted Greece the sole right to use 'feta' in the name of the cheese it produced."[3] Abboud and the Lebanese government never did end up requesting such protected status for hummus, but the issue was important both economically and symbolically as it was deeply enmeshed in perceptions of Lebanese national identity and pride. The Lebanese therefore decided to respond to the challenge made by Sabra by setting their own Guinness World Record with a dish containing no less than 2,000 kilos of hummus in October 2009 (Ariel 2012). The response was swift: in November 2009, just a month after the Lebanese set the record, Israeli chefs prepared 80 kilos of meat and 12 kilos of fresh vegetable salad and stuffed it all into a giant pita, 3 meters in diameter, setting the record for the world's largest *meorav Yerushalmi* (Jerusalem mix), a dish of chicken meat and internal organs grilled with onions and seasoned with turmeric, garlic, and cumin, and served in a pita with salad and tahini. This dish, reputedly invented during the 1970s in Jerusalem's Mahane Yehuda municipal market, is a classic market "leftovers dish" and an iconic modern Jerusalem local specialty.

Mahane Yehuda market, where the record was set, is a well-known hub of vociferous Israeli right-wing nationalism and anti-Arab sentiments. The media often depicts the market's traders and customers as supporters of right and extreme-right political parties and as verbally and physically violent, especially when it comes to Jewish-Arab relations. While this may not be the case for many of those who sell and buy there, the media depiction of Mahane Yehuda is so defined that the market has become a testing ground for politicians, especially for would-be prime ministers, who perceive their short visit to the market, usually in the presence of dozens of bodyguards and policemen, as a litmus test of their popularity among the "real population" (*am'ha*). It was therefore an obvious location for a reaction to the Lebanese challenge.

Though Jerusalem mix is not hummus, Israeli media reports made it clear that this was yet another maneuver in the ongoing Hummus Wars. Hadshot Arutz 2 (Channel 2 News), Israel's leading news broadcaster at the time, began its report of the event by stating: "While the Lebanese 'stole' our Guinness record for the world's largest hummus plate, Israel decided to fight back [*lehashiv milhama*] with a feat that the northern neighbors can hardly duplicate: the world's largest Jerusalem mix."[4] A headline on the popular *Walla News* website was even blunter: "Another Victory for Israel: Record in Jerusalem Mix."[5] The futility of the ploy, however, was noticed by an *Al Arabia* (a Palestinian news website) reporter, who wrote: "They should have no trouble getting their concoction of 200 kilograms (440 pounds) of mostly chicken innards recognized by the *Guinness Book of Records*—no one has ever attempted it before."[6]

As such, the Guinness World Record for the largest Jerusalem mix could hardly count as an Israeli victory in the Hummus Wars. In a surprising twist, Jawadat Ibrahim, a Palestinian of Israeli citizenship from the village of Abu Gosh and the owner of the popular Hummus Abu Gosh restaurant, announced that by doubling the Lebanese record and preparing a plate containing no less than 4,000 kilos of hummus, he could "restore the state's honor"[7] (see also Hirsch and Tene 2013, 39).

The Palestinian-Israeli village of Abu Gosh is an interesting place. Located some 15 kilometers to the west of Jerusalem on Highway 1, which links the capital to Tel Aviv and the densely populated central coast, it boasts dozens of restaurants specializing in hummus and other Palestinian/Arab/Middle Eastern foods such as falafel, tahini, and tabbouleh. These food venues cater mostly to an Israeli Jewish clientele, making Abu Gosh one of the Palestinian villages most frequented by Israeli Jews and, as a consequence, among the most prosperous. Though many Israeli-Palestinian villages feature similar restaurants, Abu Gosh is exceptionally popular among Israeli Jews because its dwellers are considered "good Arabs."[8] The first reason for this is historical: in 1948, the village head (*mukhtar*) cut a deal with the Hagana (the prestate Jewish defense organization) leaders to keep his village neutral in the Jewish-Arab conflict in return for Jewish protection. Abu Gosh villagers maintained the agreement and even assisted the Jews, but, unbeknownst to most of the Israeli Jewish public, once the war was over, many villagers were deported, along with dwellers of neighboring Palestinians villages that had been conquered by the newly established State of Israel. The Abu Gosh deportees were allowed to return only because of a civil campaign headed by prominent Jewish figures. In her ethnography of Abu Gosh, Rebecca Stein (2003) quotes several villagers who recount bitter memories of their relations with the Jews and stress the fact that, despite their collaboration with the Jews during the war of 1948–49, most of the village lands were confiscated. Her informants made a point, however, of concealing these negative sentiments from their Jewish customers to ensure the long-standing image of the village as welcoming and safe for Jewish customers.

The second reason for Abu Gosh's popularity among Israeli Jews is the widespread belief that Abu Gosh is a Christian village and as such is safe, or at least safer, for Jews than Muslim Arab villages. Abu Gosh's Christian image is constructed around its Notre Dame Church, large Benedictine monastery, and popular annual Abu Gosh Festival of Liturgical Music, which attracts thousands of upper-middle-class Israeli Jews. The Central Bureau of Statistics of Israel indicates, however, that 99.9 percent of the village residents are Muslim.[9] Abu Gosh's popularity as a hummus hub is thus based on a set of incorrect assumptions made by Israeli Jews about the religion of the village dwellers and their relations with the Israeli state and its Jewish citizens.

Jawadat Ibrahim, the Israeli Palestinian who decided to challenge the Lebanese record and "restore the state's honor," is interesting, too. According to media reports, he left Israel as a young man, possibly because of financial debts, to join his brother in the United States. But after winning millions in the Illinois Lottery, he returned to Israel to establish his restaurant and became a successful businessman.[10] Ibrahim is one of those Abu Gosh Palestinian Muslims that Israeli Jews incorrectly believe to be Christian, pro-Zionist, and "good." Naturally, I found the whole event extremely captivating and headed, along with my colleague, sociologist Rafi Grosglik, to Abu Gosh on January 8, 2010, to witness Ibrahim's attempt at setting a new Guinness World Record for the largest plate of hummus.

While the media rhetoric in the Israeli Hebrew broadcasting was statist (*mamlachti*) and even nationalistic, using terms such as "us," "the Lebanese," and "our national dish," the atmosphere in Abu Gosh had a local, not national, flair. The village was decorated with its own municipal flags rather than Israeli flags, and localness was the main theme in the day's speeches, a point to which I will return shortly.[11]

We reached Abu Gosh early, just prior to the arrival of a large truck labeled "Salatey Miki" (Miki's Salads—Ibrahim's Jewish business partner). Boxes of prefabricated commercial hummus were unloaded from the truck, and their contents were poured into a huge satellite dish borrowed from the neighboring satellite farm of Neve Ilan. The dish was placed on a weight located on a high ramp above the parking lot of Ibrahim's restaurant. Standing next to the workers, we could not help but notice the acrid odor of the hummus, which smelled spoiled.

As the day progressed and the temperatures rose, the hummus in the satellite dish was exposed to the blazing sun and increasing heat. Coincidentally, January 8, 2010, was the warmest day ever recorded in an Israeli winter, with temperatures soaring to 30°C. Because January is usually cold and cloudy, the organizers had not devised a plan to deal with the heat with shade or refrigeration. Judging from the initial smell, it was clear to us that the hummus was rotting under the hot sun. In fact, although spectators had been promised free samples once the record had been set, the hummus was not apportioned, and no explanations were provided. Although no one admitted to me that the hummus had not been fresh to begin with or that it had spoiled due to exposure to the elements, it is quite clear that this was the case. The fact that, to my knowledge, none of the thousands of spectators made a fuss about the unfulfilled promise of free food suggests that I was not the only one aware of the state of the hummus.

Dozens of men clad in chefs' apparel moved busily among the crowds during the event. One of them told me that they were not chefs but waiters from the local restaurants and had been invited by the organizers to walk around wearing cooks' outfits. He admitted what we had already guessed, that they hadn't prepared the hummus. We even identified some of them as being the same men who took part in the construction of the stage earlier on.

An important and unusual feature of the event was the fact that it was trilingual. Although Hebrew, Arabic, and English are the official languages of the State of Israel, Arabic is often overlooked at events that are not explicitly Arab oriented. But here, the hosts made a point of using the three languages. The event was led by Zuhair Bahloul, a Palestinian sports broadcaster of Israeli citizenship who is often ridiculed by Israeli Jews because of his highbrow Hebrew and heavy Arab accent.[12] Bahloul, speaking in Hebrew, Arabic, and English, began by declaring, "Abu Gosh is on the map."[13] He was followed by Miriam Toukan, the first Palestinian to make it to the finals of *Kohav Nolad,* the Israeli version of *American Idol,* in 2007. She sang Israel's Eurovision-winning song "Halleluiah" in Arabic and Hebrew.

Jawadat Ibrahim's trilingual speech further highlighted the "Abu Goshness" of the event. He repeatedly stressed that the event was taking place in Abu Gosh but did not mention the State of Israel as he had in interviews in the national Jewish-dominated media. He also pointed out that hummus was a traditional local specialty (that is, that hummus was a Palestinian or Arab dish, not an Israeli one). But his main argument was that "the dwellers of Abu Gosh [i.e., Palestinians of Israeli citizenship] were the bridge for peace in the

Middle East." He recounted how Jewish, Arab, and other world leaders had met at Abu Gosh on several occasions and negotiated peace over plates of hummus, and he called for further meetings and peace talks between political leaders in Abu Gosh. In an interview conducted a couple of months after the event, Ibrahim commented further: "We at Abu Gosh know that we bridge all cultures. In my speech at the record-breaking ceremony, I even said that I was willing to make the next plate [i.e., set a new record] together with a Lebanese chef. Unfortunately, they said no, and we all know why."[14]

Once the record was confirmed by Jack Brockbank, the Guinness representative, the song "Od Yavoh Shalom Aleynu (Salam)" (Peace shall be bestowed upon us [salam]), which includes the Arabic word *salam* (peace) and is thus bilingual to a certain extent, was played while blue and white balloons were released into the skies to the sound of cheering and clapping Jewish and Palestinian onlookers. Blue and white, the colors of the Israeli flag, had, until that moment, been absent from the event.

As the event concluded, we approached Brockbank to determine whether he knew that the hummus was industrial. He responded swiftly: "Of course I know, but it was the same in Lebanon. . . . No claims were made that the hummus was homemade." He thus confirmed our observation that the claims for cultural authenticity were asserted while using mass-produced, globalized merchandise, adding yet another paradox to this incident.

Driving home, I couldn't help but reflect on the irony of the event: A Palestinian of Israeli citizenship set out, in his own words (in Hebrew), "to save the nation's honor" by preparing the largest plate ever of hummus, a dish of his own ethnic culinary heritage but one that is also a contested marker of identity and a desired economic asset claimed by the Lebanese, Palestinians, and Israeli Jews. He did it in a village whose Palestinian-Muslim identity is purposely blurred for political and commercial reasons, and he achieved his feat with industrial hummus produced by his Jewish business partners, beating Lebanese contesters, whose culinary heritage is similar, if not identical, to his own, and who also used industrial hummus for their feat.

Most disturbing, however, was the metaphor itself: Ibrahim suggested that peace in the Middle East was best negotiated over a dish of hummus in the liminal setting of a Palestinian-Israeli village, and he urged for further dialogue in the same location and over the same dish. The hummus he used, however, was smelly and rotten, thus reflecting accurately, although unintentionally, the state of peace in the region: foul, putrid, and unappetizing.

1. *Hummus for Peace*

## FOOD AND POWER

The maneuvers in the Hummus Wars touch on many of the issues, relations, and dilemmas discussed in this book. While the strained relations between Israeli Jews, Palestinians, and Middle Eastern Arabs were the explicit motivation for the Hummus Wars, other issues, ideas, and social groups were involved in the events at Abu Gosh and are discussed throughout the book. Ownership and power, for example, were defined in the Hummus Wars in terms of quantity, an important topic discussed in this book. The Hummus Wars are also a great example of the kind of internal debates that pervade the culinary sphere, where members of a given social group negotiate different aspects of their identity—such as ethnicity, religion, gender, and class—among themselves over the dining table, a process that is evident in each and every culinary setting explored in this book. The process of culinary globalization and attempts at transcending the local, which were evident at Abu Gosh, are also negotiated in various sections of the book. Yet the main theoretical thread that weaves the different cases, contexts, and processes into a coherent text is that of the interface of food and power.

"Power" means different things to different people, and its relationship with food and eating is complicated. In what follows, I present some of the seminal definitions of power by social scientists and then apply them to the culinary sphere. As very little has been written on the interface of food and power in Israel, much of the ethnographic examples I discuss are from elsewhere, especially the United States, mainly because much of the existing research focuses on American foodways.

Max Weber originally conceived of power as "the chance of a man or a number of men to realize their own will in a communal action even against the resistance of others who are participating in the action" (2009, 180). According to Weber, power is a probability of successful action—not a certainty—and, at least when it comes to states, is derived from their monopoly on the legitimate use of force (Uphoff 1989; Nash 2009).

Although Weber's work focused on the power of nation-states, his theories apply more broadly to all relationships because power derives from imbalances in a variety of resources, including legitimacy, prestige, access to economic resources, and violence. These imbalances present themselves on interpersonal, national, and international scales. Importantly, Weber distinguishes these bases of power—traits affecting the probability of an individual's successful action—from power, which is the action itself. As these resources fluctuate, so do the probabilities they affect. Thus, Weber saw power as a dynamic balance of one's own means against those of others.

Although he agreed with Weber's dynamic conception of power balances, James Scott expounded on the power those on the bottom exert on the social order, which he referred to as "resistance," in his book *Weapons of the Weak*. He posited a Newtonian dimension to power—that is, for every action, there is an equal and opposite reaction—and argued that attempts to change power balances "operate against entropy," creating friction (Wolf 1990, 590). Furthermore, he rejected the idea that "subordinate groups acquiesce to economic systems that are manifestly against their interests" because they are persuaded by the ideas of the ruling elite unless they chose to revolt (Gal 1995, 407).

Instead, Scott documented the everyday forms of resistance employed by peasants to defend their interests against those who wish to extract resources from them, including sabotage and foot-dragging. These acts substantially yet nearly imperceptibly challenge the ability of the ruling class to exert control. Unlike Weber, Scott believed that power could be found both at the top and at the bottom of the social order because, except in a case of complete destruction, no person's agency can be completely dominated. Even prisoners in a prison (as we will see in chapter 5) and social groups located at the bottom of the social power structure, be it the poor, different kinds of minorities, or those subjugated, conquered or enslaved, can and do resist the power inflicted on them from above.

Scott was, in part, reacting to Antonio Gramsci's theory of hegemony, which introduced into the power discourse the idea that a state secures its power by securing superiority in the marketplace of ideas and culture. Hegemony is power derived from "cultural or spiritual supremacy," and it often works in tandem with a state's coercive power (Femia 2005, 342; H. Katz 2006). When a ruling class achieves hegemony, it rules with consent of the governed, which is "secured by the diffusion and popularization" of its worldview (Bates 1975, 352; Scott 2005).

Gramsci suggested that new elites take control over civil society with coercive power. Because they lack cultural domination, new elites, especially those who come to power by revolution, tend to resort to dictatorial methods of control until, once they have cemented their hegemony, they are able to rely on popular acceptance and identification. Although hegemony may extend beyond borders, especially from developed countries to developing countries, a "proper hegemonic culture" is most likely to occur in a specific and united national cultural context (Femia 2005). Hegemony, thus, can be defined as the acceptance by lower classes within a society of the opinions and beliefs produced at the center of society—that is, by the social elites. Hegemony's success is therefore based on the fact that it is taken for granted and perceived as natural.

In a series of essays on diverse topics such as the arts (Bourdieu 1996), the media (Bourdieu 1996), the economy (Bourdieu 2005), and gender (Bourdieu 2001), Pierre Bourdieu complicated Gramsci's understanding of hegemony and explored the processes that produce and maintain it. Bourdieu argued that different groups compete for hegemony in different *fields* of cultural production, which are themselves set in a dynamic hierarchy. Social agents active in the fields produce and reproduce sets of bodily practices and dispositions that are internalized by members of different classes, forming what Bourdieu called the *habitus*. It is the embodied nature of these practices, rather than an intellectual or cognitive pursuit, that transforms hegemonic ideas from abstract notions into general beliefs that are perceived as natural and primordial. Bourdieu's emphasis on embodied practices is highly relevant to the sociological and anthropological analysis of foodways and their importance: the food people eat and the modes of food consumption are among the clearest expressions of the habitus.

In contrast with Gramsci, Scott, and Weber, who theorized about the power of people at the two extreme ends of the social ladder, Michel Foucault posited that power was a complex system of relationships touching all people and that it connected all members of society in a more diffuse web. Foucault's power "organizes and orchestrates" social settings by affecting the "distribution and direction of energy flows" (Wolf 1990, 586). According to Foucault, power is the ability to shape an environment so as to create the possibility or the impossibility of another's action. Power does not act *within* a system; it acts *on* the system. Unlike other theorists, Foucault considered power to be expansive and productive, not a zero-sum game (Nash 2001). Power is a renewable resource exerted and harnessed by all participants in a system and affects the way each of them views the system itself. Thus, despite accepting the dynamism of power suggested by other theorists, Foucault differentiated his theory by rejecting the ability of any single person to collect it. In her recent book *A Taste of Power,* Katharina Vester (2015) applied Foucault's theory to a critical rereading of American cookbooks of the nineteenth and twentieth centuries. Vester showed how power in these texts works in different directions, at times reaffirming existing power structures and at other times subverting them.

In a similar line, Peter Farb and George Armelagos (1980, 4) suggested, "Once the anthropologist finds out where, when, and with whom the food is eaten, just about everything else can be inferred about the relations among society's members." Vester (2015, 196) noted that "food-expert discourses" affect how, why, where, when, and with whom we eat as well as the means of production for our food. Power relations are always fluid and being challenged, and food provides a key forum for that contest.

Scholars have theorized at length about the application of Gramsci's theory of hegemony to food discourses, surmising that societal elites use cuisine as a manifestation of their elite tastes and attitudes and as a method of distributing values and ideas to the lower classes (De Vooght and Scholliers 2011; Gvion 2009). Cuisine is essential to nation-building, as it allows a people to define themselves by what they eat in contrast to what others eat, but it can also be a tool of nation-destroying when one culture seeks to impose its will on and eradicate another. Which foods people eat, and which other people eat those foods, defines a nation and a culture in contrast to its neighbors. Israeli cuisine intentionally straddles the Mediterranean and the Middle East, allowing Israelis to anchor themselves to modern, Western, "superior" Europe when convenient and to prove their connection to the soil they inhabit when necessary.

As an element of public art, food expresses the values of societal elites and connects citizens to the state. Usually, the richer, ruling class can afford to purchase more expensive foods and subsequently develop more sophisticated tastes. Through private chefs, cookbooks, television shows, and cooking demonstrations, the culinary tastes of these elites are then disseminated through society, reinforcing this class's hegemonic control (Albala 2011; Vester 2015). Often, these culinary preferences reinterpret nostalgic pasts by modernizing traditional dishes and aligning them with current elite sociopolitical positions, which, after being polished, are disseminated to the masses.

Recent literature proposes that minority groups use cuisine to resist hegemony and to assert their own unique culture within a broader culture just as much as elites use cuisine to create the broader majority culture. Minorities see cuisine, essentially, as another one of Scott's weapons of the weak. Just like elites, minority groups connect with their pasts through food, demonstrating their worthiness for rights in society based on the longevity and uniqueness of their culture (Barabas 2003; Gvion 2009).

Minorities also "stage authenticity" (McCannell 1976) in their restaurants, which helps them shape their public image, sometimes by challenging prevailing stereotypes, and allows them to survive economically. In Israel, Liora Gvion contends, Palestinians of Israeli citizenship use food to challenge their marginalization while also taking pride in the Arab and Palestinian identities that differentiate them from the hegemonic Israeli Jewish foodways (Gvion 2009). Similarly, Mizrahi Jews (originating from the Middle East and North Africa) have attempted to assert their right to political and social inclusion by emphasizing their Jewish identities while simultaneously capitalizing on their unique cultures and cuisines for economic survival, cornering much of the Israeli fast-food industry.

In the United States, too, food discourses have often been defined by their resistance. For example, Americans first distinguished their cuisine as American by using egalitarian terms that contrasted with aristocratic British tastes (Vester 2015). Women have used food throughout American history to assert power in a patriarchal culture, and recently food has become a medium for queer women to protest the hegemonic heteronormative culture (Vester 2015). The Nation of Islam, an African American emancipatory movement that sought empowerment in radical Islam, similarly grew as a movement by adopting Marcus Garvey's message of racial empowerment and reclaimed dignity, which specifically included the rejection Southern soul food as a legacy of slavery and white supremacy (Rouse and Hoskins 2004). Later, as the Nation of Islam adopted a more mainstream version of Sunni Islam, practitioners of the faith reappropriated soul food to connect to American identities and shift the religion from a racial and political movement to a more spiritual and religious one. Throughout American history, then, newly defined and growing interest groups have used food to challenge existing power balances and cultural norms.

Beyond preferences of taste though, power dynamics have also been contested through the supply of food, a necessity of life. In times of scarcity, the value of food increases to such an extent that it becomes the most valuable resource in a community (Phillips 2009). In rural and poor communities, villagers use food like currency to purchase both other material goods and immaterial political support. The ability to provide or deny food thus grants the Weberian state immense power over citizens.

In theorizing about revolutions, Anthony Oberschall and Michael Seidman (2005, 376) suggest that the principal means of competing factions to attract support is control over the food supply because "who will be fed and who will starve—the power of life and death—is the ultimate form of coercion in human affairs." In revolution and in civil war, the winner is more often the side that most effectively controls the food supply rather than the side with the largest arsenal or army. This "economy of predation" leads to decisions based on shortage and security, leading people to barter their support for resources, especially food.

Following the 1972 international food crisis and 1973 OPEC oil embargo, scholars sought to expand Weberian conceptions of power with respect to food to the international scene through discussions of American agripower as a diplomatic counterbalance to Middle Eastern petropower. Agripower is exercised through coercive control over the international food supply, though it is much more difficult to deploy due to the difficulties in food storage and exportation (Paarlberg 1978; Rothschild 1976; Tuomi 1975). Somewhat sadistically, agripower is premised on exerting control over other nations through physical starvation, similar to the way that the deployment of petropower seeks to coerce other states by starving them energetically and, as a consequence, economically.

On a national scale, Weberian state power is most keenly discernible in confined institutions like prisons, where power hierarchies are extreme and policed and control over "personal experiences of consumption" is a weapon of dominance (Smith 2002; Godderis 2006). Prison guards can and do assert their power through arbitrary decisions, especially concerning the necessities of life. Providing or withholding food, especially for seemingly random reasons, reinforces the power imbalances inside the prison. Providing low-quality food—even, or perhaps especially, when prisoners serve as kitchen staff—demonstrates lack of concern for the prisoners' health and well-being, a further sign of how little the guards value their wards as well as a show of the extent of their control over them. Rebecca Godderis concludes that surveillance and control of consumptive practices is one of the most noticeable and hated manifestations of power imbalances.

Hunger strikes, by contrast, allow citizens, and especially prisoners, to challenge their inferiority to the state by rejecting this reliance narrative (Anderson 2004). Hunger strikes, if they manage to receive sufficient media attention, draw awareness to the position of the disadvantaged by publicizing their lack of choice in their extreme circumstances. Furthermore, hunger strikes create martyrs, around whom coalitions of supporters rally (Passmore 2009). Even as I write this book, hunger strikes by Palestinian prisoners in Israel protesting their indefinite detentions without indictment or trial have rallied a coalition of supporters against Israel's security apparatus.[15]

While the state wields immense power over citizens in its ability to manipulate and disrupt the food supply, ordinary citizens still possess some power to resist the dominance of the state by rejecting their dependence. This form of resistance is necessarily self-destructive, but it can also be an effective way of proving the independent power of the weak to, at the very least, inspire dialogue about their plight.

Indeed, the powerful *and* the supposedly powerless can manipulate food supply, taste, and cuisine. The state seeks to maintain a Weberian control over the supply, and its elites assert their Gramscian hegemony over cuisine. Marginalized groups, however, resist both dominant cuisines and state control over supply through both moderate means, such as capitalizing on their own unique culinary traditions, and more extreme measures, such as hunger strikes. The power over food thus belongs simultaneously to all in society and to no one in particular.

Following Foucault's theory, when it comes to food, power constantly ebbs and flows throughout society according to circumstance. Every application of food systems' power is met with resistance as some seek to define the food systems of all and others fight that definition. Food is a weapon and a blanket, a means of control and of protest. Most of all, food is power.

## RESEARCHING ISRAELI FOODWAYS

This book is based on a long-term ethnographic project that has been conducted in various settings and contexts in Israel since the late 1990s. The project engages with the ways in which power is produced, reproduced, negotiated, and challenged in different culinary realms day-to-day in Israel. In some of the chapters, I deal with prominent culinary phenomena, such as Israeli Independence Day barbecues or the debates over the definition of Israeli cuisine. In others, I touch on subtler issues, such as why Italian food is so popular in Israel and the privatization of kibbutz dining rooms. At times, I discuss specific events, such as the Hummus Wars or a conflict that occurred over meat allocation during my own period of service in reserve duty in a military prison.

*Food and Power* is not a classic ethnographic study bound in space and time, conducted by an outsider, and based on temporary immersion in a local community. In order to discuss my methodological approach to this long-term project, a few words are due regarding its nonconventional qualities and the processes by which it was conceived and developed.

First, I am an Israeli citizen, born and raised in Israel, and certainly not a stranger to Israeli culture and society. And though "ethnographic homework"[16] can be executed in cultural contexts that are as alien to the ethnographer as any site in a remote culture and society (and in a culturally varied country such as Israel—such settings are not hard to find), much of the research for this book was done in the spaces that form (or could form) my "natural habitat." This complicated the process of estrangement (Maso 2001) and required constant awareness to the "taken for granted" that constitutes my own experience and worldview.

Israel is a small country (roughly the size of Vermont or Slovenia), and though some research realms and issues were beyond my everyday territory, I rarely experienced the sense of awe and wonder I have felt so often in Hoi An, a small town in central Vietnam where I have been conducting ethnographic research since 1998. I also didn't experience the same kinds of misunderstandings and mistakes that, as I came to learn in Vietnam, signaled the gap between my own cultural perceptions and those of my Hoianese friends and meant that I was on the right ethnographic track (see also Avieli 2012, 249–268).

This is not to say that I was Mr. Know-It-All in Israel. Pursuing the interface of food and power in my home country had its surprises, discoveries, and insights, and every now and again, its mistakes, misunderstandings, and frustrations. My long-term engagement with Israeli language, culture, and history facilitated my awareness of minute details and intimate nuances that are well beyond my language capacity and cultural sensitivity when conducting research in Vietnam. So while I gave up what Michael Agar (1996) calls "the professional stranger's perspective" when conducting "homework" in Israel, my native understanding and awareness facilitated the production of nuanced ethnographic knowledge.

What further removes this project from classic ethnographies is the width of its thematic and spatial scopes. The trajectory of multisited ethnography was defined by George Marcus (1995, 97) as pursuing the "circulation of cultural meanings, objects and identities in diffuse time-space . . . that cannot be accounted for ethnographically by remaining focused on a single site." However, as Ghassan Hage (2005, 464) notes, "It is not enough to be doing an ethnography that involves flying between two or three locations for people to call it multi-sited ethnography." Hage points out that multisited ethnographies tend to focus on specific groups of people (e.g., immigrants from a single village or members of specific ethnic diaspora) that move to—or are scattered in—different locations but share cultural conventions and understandings and maintain social networks and relations. He therefore argues that with time and immersion, as research becomes "thicker and stickier," his study was not multisited anymore but rather focused "on one site, occupied by transnational families and/or communities" (465).

My study was conceived and executed in a different way and is multisited in the sense that each chapter deals with a specific culinary site or phenomenon. Components of the Israeli culinary sphere, these sites and phenomena may interact with one another to a lesser or greater extent, but I approached each of them as an independent case study that called for its own research questions, methodology, and theoretical background.

At this point, I must also state that *Food and Power* is not a coherent or holistic culinary ethnography of Israel, nor does it pretend to be one. Thinking about the process in which the research was conceived, I must admit that I never really chose the different research sites and themes—they very much chose themselves. When I returned home in 2000 after fourteen months of fieldwork in Vietnam, I started teaching a course at the Hebrew University of Jerusalem on the anthropology of food, and I have taught it ever since in a variety of formats. Teaching this course in Israel meant that I had to think of Israeli examples that would add a comparative dimension to class discussions and readings. A strong believer in field trips, I had to consider where to take my students and what to show them. I assigned them their own ethnographic projects, and they came up with many wonderful observations and insights. So while I was developing my ethnographic study on Vietnamese foodways, another ethnographic study was evolving, one that I never planned to execute.

It was only in 2010, when I convened a conference on "Food, Power and Meaning in the Middle East and Mediterranean" at Ben-Gurion University, that I realized that I was actually conducting some sort of multisited ethnographic study of Israeli foodways that was theoretically engaged with the ways in which power and power relations take part in culinary phenomena in Israel. Choosing research sites was therefore a gradual and, at times, unconscious process. News reports and articles that I observed, heard, or read; colleagues, students, and friends who came up with observations, suggestions, and questions; and everyday life events led me up and down the country. I was constantly facing intriguing phenomena and puzzling questions, and, being a food anthropologist, I felt I had no choice but to pursue them.

The field trips I took my students on turned out to be great successes, and all of a sudden I started to be contacted by people I didn't know. Some were students' parents; others had just heard of these trips somehow and asked me to take them on culinary tours. In 2011, I developed a set of tours that I titled Comfort Food in Zones of Conflict. This was a politically motivated project: observing my students, I realized that much of the violence and hatred in Israel is based on the fact that conflicting social groups (Jews versus Palestinians; secular citizens versus members of religious communities; citizens versus refugees and migrant workers; etc.), who are deeply scared of each other, hardly interact. And when they do, it is often in conflictual contexts. As always, anger and hatred are based mainly on ignorance and prejudice.

It turned out, however, that the food of "the others" was often perceived as an attraction, and food-focused tours allowed participants to shift their attention from the conflict to more pleasant aspects of the interaction. And just like in Vietnam, people failed to see the political edge of food and were therefore willing (and even eager) to explore the culinary realms of "the others," feeling that this would be nonpolitical and therefore a safe zone of interaction.

But the culinary sphere is inherently political. I was deeply touched as I watched the interaction between retired Israeli Jews and retired Palestinians at a coffee house in the depths of Old Jerusalem's Muslim quarter during January 2011. Members of both groups told me that this was the first time in their lives that they had interacted with people they would normally perceive as "the enemy" as equal human beings rather than enemies, conquerors, terrorists, or so forth. It was amazing to see how fear dissolved with the sweetness of tea and anger was forgotten when *knafe* (a Palestinian cheese pastry) melted on their tongues, and how "the others" became human when they shared their cooking secrets in the privacy of their kitchens. These tours were both products of my ethnographic project and sites where further research was conducted and data collected.

The elastic and evolving nature of this research called for the collection of data through additional methods that were beyond ethnographic participant observation and the incumbent interviews with interlocutors or informants. I relied on a wide network of relatives, friends, and friends of friends (interviewees located through the more professional-sounding process of "snowball sampling"). All ethnographers know that this is exactly how fieldwork is done, but my Israeli networks were much wider and intensive than those I had in Vietnam. As a native Israeli and a native Hebrew speaker, I was also able to make use of all kinds of media, including television and radio reports, news articles, and webpages. However, I did not consider such media reports to be ethnographic observations, which form the empirical backbone of anthropology. I approached these visual, oral, and written texts in a similar way to the interviews and conversations that I held, taking them not as forms of observed phenomena and certainly not as the objective truth, but rather as stories people tell themselves about themselves.

The study of the Hummus Wars is a good example of this methodological process. It began with a short news report that caught my attention, continued with me following the verbal and practical reactions of different participants as presented in the media, and culminated in my attending the event in the village of Abu Gosh, where the bulk of my ethnographic material was collected. This event lasted for several hours, but as I always do with such culinary events, I arrived early in the morning to observe the preparations and talk to the people involved in the cooking before the crowds of spectators arrived. During the event, I took notes and photos, talked with participants, and recorded the speeches. I remained in Abu Gosh when the event was over to observe the dismantling of the installation and the cleanup. In Vietnam, I learned that this was an especially fruitful moment ethnographically because the hosts relaxed once the guests were gone and were often happy to discuss the events and comment on them. During the following days, I collected media reports of the event and followed the reactions that these reports elicited. Once I developed my own framework for the analysis of the Hummus Wars, I talked to various people in different contexts and asked them about their perception of the occurrences at Abu Gosh and of hummus in general. These people were not involved directly in the events at Abu Gosh but were Israelis who had their own opinions on hummus and on the Hummus Wars. Talking to them helped me fine-tune my understanding of the meanings of the Hummus Wars and the event at Abu Gosh.

Due to the multisited nature of this project and to the very different contexts in which it was conducted, I further elaborate in each chapter on the specific methodological approaches I employed for each case. Chapter 1 has an extended methodological section, which sets the ground for much of the research presented in the book. In other chapters, I address and explain specific methodological choices, implications, and dilemmas.

## THE DRAWINGS

Another unconventional feature of *Food and Power* are the drawings by Heimo Wallner. When conducting ethnographic research in Vietnam (as well as in India, Thailand, and Singapore), I used a large reflex camera and collected thousands of images. Taking pictures was both exciting and easy: I was surrounded by scenery that was unfamiliar and exotic and by human practices that were new, intriguing, and, at times, strange and even bizarre.

Focusing on the salient, unique, and unfamiliar is an essential part of the ethnographic condition: ethnographers travel far and wide and conduct their research in cultures and settings that are significantly different from their own so as to bypass the constraints of the "taken for granted"—the familiar daily practices that make up much of the human experience but are so hard to notice and analyze precisely because they are so familiar and taken for granted. We therefore study other cultures and focus on the practices that *they* take for granted, which for us are nothing but familiar and mundane. Taking pictures under such circumstances is easy: things are almost constantly new, strange, salient, and intriguing.

As mentioned earlier, this was not the case with the ethnographic projects presented in this book: I was conducting my research in my home country and culture, often in very familiar settings, and attending mundane and, indeed, taken-for-granted events and activities. I found taking "good pictures"—images that capture the mystery and perhaps revelation of the "ethnographic moment"—very hard as everything was so familiar. At the same time, everything in anyone's home country is complex and multilayered, and thus an image with a clear message is hard to come by. Add to this the fact that I wasn't even carrying a camera when I attended many of the events described in the book—either because I didn't expect anything to happen or because I felt awkward carrying a camera into settings in which I was not "the anthropologist" but rather a relative, neighbor, or friend—and you'll realize why, in stark opposition to my study in Vietnam, I didn't have many good images for the book.

But when I saw Heimo's work, first at an exhibition and then at a seminar at Middlebury College, I felt that his Zen-like line drawings managed to capture very complex ideas and present them in a very powerful way. I asked Heimo if he would create drawings for the book, and he liked the idea. The working process was such: I sent him the chapters, and he read them and then drew some images. I chose the images that I felt worked best—that is, those that captured the main ideas I was trying to convey—and these went into another round of fine-tuning (for instance, I asked Heimo to make the person roasting meat for chapter 2, dedicated to Israeli Independence Day barbecues, fatter and to add an Israeli flag over the hamburger for chapter 1, "Size Matters").

It would also be possible to fine-tune a photograph in this way using sophisticated photo-processing software, but I suppose that most ethnographers would be reluctant to manipulate a photograph they took in the field to such an extent: this would equate to manipulating the data, something that is perhaps done, at least to a certain extent, by all scientists but is usually nonreflexive. When done intentionally, manipulating data is akin to cheating.

But in this case, I was not dealing with images from the field but with Heimo's interpretations of my own interpretations. Furthermore, drawings, unlike photos, are not ethnographic statements of being in a particular place, a quality that is often attributed to images presented in ethnographic monographs and articles (and crystallized in some of Bronislaw Malinowski's images of himself in the field). They are clearly the outcome of the artist's imagination and do not posses the scientific power of a picture, which is supposed to be an accurate representation of some aspect of the field.[17]

The reader is therefore invited to bear in mind that the drawings are not meant to be direct representations of some social reality. They are Heimo's readings of my text, shaped in his own artistic style and at times negotiated and reshaped following my comments. In a sense, the drawings are meant to do the work of a caricature: they capture the essence of a complex social event in an almost abstract form. Come to think of it, ethnographic writing as a genre is somewhat reminiscent of caricature: it is an attempt to extract an idea and present a clear argument out of the messy, noisy, and complex setting of everyday life.

## CHAPTERS AND ARGUMENTS

My culinary ethnography of Hoi An (Avieli 2012) was concentric: I started with the analysis of daily, home-eaten meals and gradually expanded my attention to festive, public, and extraordinary meals, with the emphasis shifting from private events where food was shared by a small number of intimately connected people, to culinary events where increasing numbers of people shared their food, and finally to moments when the entire Vietnamese nation was eating the same foods at the very same moment.

*Food and Power* is a very different project, not only because of its multisited design but also because its scope is much wider. As stated earlier, this is not a comprehensive ethnographic study of Israeli foodways. However, each of the chapters is engaged with a question, an issue, or a dilemma that reflects on Israeli society as a whole. This book begins with chapters that deal with the widest and most inclusive topics and gradually moves into more peripheral and remote sociological and ethnographic zones.

Beyond the introduction, *Food and Power* is composed of six thematic chapters and a conclusion. The first chapter, "Size Matters," deals with a question that haunts Israeli chefs, journalists, academics, and diners alike: How do we define Israeli cuisine? Based on interviews with dozens of chefs, restaurateurs, and food critics, and defying existing conventions of Israeli cuisine as an amalgam of diasporic Jewish cuisines, local produce, and (according to some) local Palestinian cuisine, I argue that a defining element of Israeli food is large portions of "satisfying" dishes made from mediocre ingredients. Satiety is exposed in this chapter as a cultural rather than physiological trait. The implications of this tendency for excessive portions are discussed in personal, social, and national contexts.

The second chapter, "Roasting Meat," deals with the meanings of what is clearly the most prominent and most "Israeli" food event on the Israeli calendar: Israel's Independence Day barbecues. Based on ethnographic research conducted on Independence Days from 2002 to 2009 in Jerusalem's Sacher Park, this chapter analyzes the two main practices in this salient food event: the roasting of meat and the managing of space. I show how these practices reflect age and gender hierarchies, express the masculine myth of Israeli independence, and reveal the Israeli mode of grasping space. These practices also expose the ambivalence characteristic of the sense of power Israeli Jews have when it comes to their strained relations with their Palestinian and Middle Eastern neighbors.

In the third chapter, "Why We Like Italian Food," I try to understand the extreme popularity of Italian food in Israel, second only to Mizrahi food. My argument, based on observations from a study conducted in a dozen Italian restaurants, is that Italian food is so popular because the portions are very large, the food is dairy-based, and the restaurants are family-friendly, all of which correspond to specific sociological trends in contemporary Israel. The most intriguing finding, however, is that cooks and diners repeatedly asserted that the popularity of this cuisine stems from ecological and cultural affinities between Israel and Italy. I argue that Italian restaurants allow Israeli Jews, and especially members of the socioeconomic Ashkenazi middle class, to imagine themselves, even if only for the duration of a meal, as belonging to Mediterranean Europe rather than to the Middle East. I also show how pizza is "orientalized" in the Israeli periphery in a counterhegemonic culinary trend.

The fourth chapter, "The McDonaldization of the Kibbutz Dining Room," deals with the unexpected consequences of the privatization of these iconic kibbutz institutions. The dining room was always the heart of the kibbutz, the main hub of social life, and the outmost expression of the communal ideology. Based on ethnographic research conducted in the dining rooms of three kibbutzim in different stages of privatization, or "McDonaldization," this chapter follows the contested meanings of the dining room experience. The food and eating patterns that prevail in these dining rooms are presented as expressions of hegemonic power structures, and their modifications reflect changing values within and beyond the kibbutz. My findings challenge the common understating of the "kibbutz crisis," or the understating of failure in general as a consequence of the rise of individualism in contemporary Israel, and suggest that the main competitors over kibbutz members' loyalty are primordial and nonegalitarian social institutions such as the family, ethnicity, class, religion, and gender, which socialist ideology wished to eradicate.

The fifth chapter is titled "Meat and Masculinity in an Israeli Military Prison." Based on a study conducted in an Israeli military prison for Palestinian detainees, this chapter engages with what is probably the most complex, controversial, and problematic feature of contemporary Israel: the strained relations between Israeli Jews and the Palestinians living in the territories occupied by Israel during the 1967 war. The reserve soldiers charged with guarding the prison insisted that their poor military performance and their sense of weakness within the prison power structure were due to a lack of meat. A discourse of victimization evolved among the soldiers in which their apparent weakness—which they claimed to be a result of their meatless diet—became the justification for institutional and personal abuse inflicted on the Palestinian prisoners. This chapter sheds light on the intimate realties of the Israeli occupation of the Palestinian territories and exposes some of the implicit mechanisms that maintain a sense of victimization among Israeli Jews, which facilitates the maintenance of the occupation.

The sixth chapter, "Thai Migrant Workers and the Dog-Eating Myth," deals with the prevailing total social fact that the Thai migrant workers who make for the bulk of the agricultural workforce in Israel systematically hunt and eat Israeli pet dogs. Despite extensive media accusations and widespread public consensus regarding the Thai penchant for Israeli dogs, my ethnographic research reveals that Thai migrant workers do not hunt or eat dogs in Israel or in Thailand. I follow the emergence of this culinary stereotype in the mid-1990s and decode its meanings. I argue that Israel's constituting socialist ethos conflicts deeply with the notion of migrant labor, especially when it comes to agriculture in the "working settlements"—kibbutzim and moshavim—that are the iconic manifestations of socialist Zionism. Following the official Israeli policy of racial division of migrant labor, which allocates migrant workers from specific cultures into singular occupations, there emerged a culinary myth that has very little to do with the Thais and their culinary preferences but rather that evolved around the cultural meanings and social position attributed to dogs in Israeli Jewish society. This culinary myth defines a particular kind of negative exoticism that facilitated the dehumanization of the Thai migrant workers and justified their ongoing exploitation.

In the conclusion, "Food and Power in Israel—Orientalization and Ambivalence," I point to two culinary trends in contemporary Israel that emerge at the intersection of food and power. First, I argue that the Israeli culinary sphere has been very much "orientalized." Earlier in the book, I point out that Mizrahi ethnicity is an Israeli creation, the outcome of the forceful fusion of members of diverse cultures and socioeconomic classes and their demotion to the Israeli socioeconomic and spatial periphery. In the conclusion, I argue that while the process of *mizruah* (orientalization) involves fierce conflicts in the political, socioeconomic, and cultural arenas, Mizrahi food is embraced by members of all the ethnic groups in Israel. In this sense, Israeli kitchens and food events celebrate *mizrahiyut*.

Second, I point out that power in the Israeli culinary sphere entails ambivalence and is treated with ambivalence. The meanings Israelis attribute to their food and foodways expose their take on their own power: they indulge in their power and celebrate their might but simultaneously perceive of themselves as the ultimate and eternal victims and as completely powerless. This ambivalence sheds light on many of the issues discussed in the book and is important when thinking theoretically about the work of power in the culinary sphere.

*Food and Power* is engaged with social processes that many commentators, both Israeli and foreign, perceive as radically departing from the original Zionist attempt at balancing between democratic governance and Jewish identity. Some argue that the Zionist project was colonial, brutal, and unjust to begin with and that the Holocaust was only a pretext for justifying the mistreatment of the Palestinians. Others contend that the occupation of the West Bank and Gaza in the aftermath of the 1967 war was the point at which the Zionist project took a right turn toward messianic ethno-religious nationalism and became a conquering and brutal Goliath rather than the slender and beautiful-eyed David it claimed to be.

The debate regarding the moment when Zionism went astray notwithstanding, there is no doubt in my mind that the Socialist-Zionist ideology that made my grandparents leave their homes and families in Bukovina in 1930 and immigrate ("ascended" is the term they used) to Israel to take part in the radical attempt to change the Jewish condition and fate, and the Religious Zionism that motivated my wife's grandparents to leave Kurdistan and move to Jerusalem in 1921, have very little to do with the prevailing ideologies in contemporary Israel. Let me be clear: I worry that the Israeli occupation of the West Bank and Gaza, the deeply embedded cultural and cognitive militarism (Kimmerling 1993b) that affects all social realms and relations in Israel, and the way in which Israel treats its non-Jewish citizens and residents are all detrimental to its social fabric and democratic system. As an anthropologist, I study microprocesses and specific social relationships, but *Food and Power* exposes antidemocratic, xenophobic, and racist tendencies, as well as misuse and abuse of power, that plague modern-day Israel. In this sense, this book is a stern critique of contemporary Israeli society.

*Food and Power,* however, is not a post-Zionist critique of the State of Israel and certainly not a call for the country's demise. While the book is engaged with some of the negative features of Israeli society, such as greed, ethnocentrism, racism, patriarchal machismo, and other forms of abuse of power, which I find disturbing and harmful, I have dedicated this book to my children, hoping that the ethno-messianic ideology will eventually collapse due to its essential immorality, internal contradictions, and lack of practical solutions for the problems and difficulties Israel faces. Zionism has always been an unrealistically hopeful realistic project, and this book is my very humble contribution to the efforts to reorient Israeli society in a more democratic and humanistic direction and to make life in this country bearable, just, and perhaps even pleasant. The food, cooks, and diners I met while researching this book, some wonderful, other less so, are the strongest evidence for the potential of Israel to fulfill its original goal of redeeming the Jews from their diasporic condition and allowing them to live, for better and for worse, as a nation among nations.

# ONE

## *Size Matters*

WHAT IS IT THAT MAKES the foodways of a specific group of people unique and distinguishable from those of their neighbors? In other words, what makes a cuisine? This is one of the most complex and challenging questions that can be asked about a cuisine. Popular wisdom would have us concentrate on well-liked or emblematic dishes as the representatives of specific cuisines. Italian cuisine is therefore defined by pasta and pizza, Moroccan cuisine by couscous, and American cuisine by hamburgers. Such definitions however, essentialize cuisines, ignore spatial and social variations (Appadurai 1988), and disregard cooking and eating modes. They also lead to food stereotypes: the French are frogs, the Germans are krauts (from sauerkraut), the Ethiopians smell of injera (sour bread), and the Chinese, well, they eat everything.[1]

In a chapter titled "Eating American" in his book *Tasting Food, Tasting Freedom: Excursions into Eating, Culture, and the Past,* Sidney Mintz, the founding father of the anthropology of food, recounted how a comment he made during a lecture about the fact that he did not think that there was such a thing as American cuisine elicited vehement responses from his offended and angry listeners, who felt that denying American cuisine equaled denying the existence of American culture (Mintz 1996). He went on to explain that "eating American" is distinguished by traits such as mobility, ethnic variation, eating out, eating fast, and eating increasingly standardized, processed, and artificial food. Thus, he shifted the focus from the culinary realm to the *practice* of eating, pointing out that *how* people eat is at least as important as *what* they eat. Following this assertion, I argue that the defining qualities of Israeli cuisine are not specific tastes or seasonings or a set of popular dishes. Rather, contemporary Israeli cuisine is defined by very large servings. To be sure, other cuisines, such as the American, have a similar penchant for generous, if not humongous, servings. What I wish to explore, however, are the *meanings* Israelis attribute to their desire for large portions, which, as we shall see, shed light on hidden aspects of contemporary Israeliness.

## A LITTLE BIT OF EVERYTHING

Gastronomes and cultural critics have been struggling with the definition of Israeli cuisine for quite some time now. It is commonly argued that Israeli cuisine is the outcome of a dramatic meeting between different ethnic cuisines imported by Jewish immigrants, the produce of advanced Israeli agroindustry, Israel's ecology, and, according to some, the "native" Palestinian kitchen (Kleinberg 2005). The result is an extremely varied cuisine, which my interviewees often described as "mishmash" or as featuring "a little bit of everything."

Prominent Israeli food writer Ruth Sirkis responded to the question "Is there an Israeli cuisine?" as follows:

> This question comes up all the time. People find it hard to accept that national food can be as varied as Israeli cuisine. It is easier to argue that the Italians eat pasta, the Chinese rice, the Americans hamburgers, and the Israelis hummus, *mangal* [barbequed meat], and gefilte [short for gefilte fish, a type of fish ball]. But the definition is much wider and deeper. *Our food is the compound of ethnic cuisines, international influences, produce of the land, and the fast development of food culture.* Everything falls under the rubric of Israeli food. One could argue that Israeli cuisine is a kind of cholent or shakshouka.[2] Everything comes and mixes in, creating something new, different from its ingredients. For me, Israeli cuisine is multifaceted, intriguing, tasty, colorful, both traditional and modern.[3]

Sirkis's famous cookbook *Mehamitbach Be'ahava* (From the kitchen with love) was first published in 1975, and it remains Israel's most popular cookbook, having sold over million copies, making it the best-selling book in the nation's history, second only to the Bible.[4] Its cover reflects Sirkis's definition of the Israeli cuisine. It features a picture of chicken with oranges and grapes, a dish that was never popular in Israel but exemplifies the culinary fusion Sirkis champions, combining local produce ("traditional" grapes and "modern" oranges) with Jewish Ashkenazi fare (boiled chicken) into an original and innovative dish.[5]

Omer Miller, chef of the "successful Tel Aviv restaurant Chadar Ha'ochel [meaning "the dining room," a reference to Israel's socialist culinary past and kibbutz culture, see chapter 4] and author of the recent cookbook *Mitbach Israeli* [Israeli cuisine],"[6] also highlights fusion as the main quality of Israeli cuisine. He points out that his favorite recipe is "sea fish over vegetable salad, served with fried pita shreds and *labane* [strained yogurt cheese], because this is . . . a combination of sashimi and Arab salad. It is exciting to take something from the gentle Japanese cuisine and serve it over a spicy salad. This combination is only possible in a young cuisine, which is cheeky. . . . It's Israeli, just like us."[7]

Erez Komorwski, another trend-leading gastronome, followed suit. While recounting the early stages of his culinary career, he recalled: "During those days, we were still debating whether an Israeli cuisine exists at all. But suddenly I realized that the melting pot of the Israeli cauldron isn't different from the American one, only that instead of mixing in Chinese, Mexican, and Japanese, we are dealing here with food from Morocco, Turkey, Tripoli, and the Caucasus."

While this definition of Israeli cuisine as a combination of Jewish dishes with different origins fused with the local produce and local culinary traditions into a highbred entity is historically accurate, it doesn't really tell us much about the specific characteristics of Israeli cuisine or about its meanings. Indeed, one of the main contributions of the anthropology of food to our understanding of the culinary sphere was the assertion that all cuisines are the outcome of historical processes of cultural immigration, exchange, and fusion in specific ecological contexts (see, e.g., Goody 1982; Mintz 1985, 1996; Counihan 1999; Ashkenazi and Jacob 2000; Sutton 2001; Wilk 2006), and therefore, fusion, as central as it is to Israeli cuisine, does not distinguish it from other cuisines.

### RESEARCHING ISRAELI CUISINE

The findings presented in this chapter are the outcome of an ongoing ethnographic research that was launched during the late 1990s when I decided to interview prominent players in the Israeli culinary sphere and ask them about the Israeliness of their cooking. At that time, even the most respected Israeli chefs and restaurateurs were not the celebrities they are today,[8] so they were easily accessible.

Due to the reputation of those involved in the restaurant industry as busy, nervous, and short-tempered, I expected them to be reluctant to meet with me, but I was surprised to find that most chefs were eager to be interviewed and happy to spend a few hours talking to a researcher. I was pleased by their willingness to talk yet also somewhat intrigued: Why would these busy, hardworking, and often stressed people want to spend so much time talking to me? One of Israel's most prominent chefs-turned-celebrities made a comment that shed some light on this unexpected willingness. A couple of hours into the interview, conducted at his restaurant, he suddenly said: "You know, it's amazing! People always ask me how to cook this or that, but no one has ever asked me what I think." Through the years, I have learned that this comment holds true for many people working in culinary professions: they amass endless knowledge and insights about food over the course of their careers but are usually asked only about their recipes, so they are happy to share their thoughts with anyone who is willing to talk about the *why* of their cooking rather than the *how*.

I conducted a dozen interviews with prominent chefs, including Israel Aharoni, who single-handedly introduced Chinese food to Israel and had a central role in the development of Israeli elite cuisine; the late Hanoch Bar Shalom, praised by many as Israel's "chefs' chef"; and Boaz Zairi, Israel's pioneering sushi master. I also interviewed salient culinary innovators, such as Nechama Mousayof, who was involved in establishing Israel's first Italian-style espresso bar (Espresso Bar, opened in Tel Aviv in 1992) and Spaghettim, a successful Italian-food franchise. I approached the first interviewees through personal contacts and then continued by applying snowball sampling using the interviewees' recommendations and contacts that I made over the years.

My initial research question was simple. I started each interview by asking, "So, what is Israeli about your cooking?" From that moment onward, the interview usually flowed, and I was mainly concerned with writing down the cascade of observations and insights. The interviews lasted one to three hours and were usually conducted at the interviewee's restaurant, which allowed me to further expand the scope of observation and data collection.

The content of the interviews, however, turned out to be quite different from what I had expected. I anticipated that these chefs would talk about ingredients, spices, cooking techniques, and dishes, but they actually talked about sociology and anthropology. They defined social categories, discussed cultural tendencies, and described power structures. Yet the most intriguing, and also most common, comments they made addressed the quantitative dimensions of Israeli foodways.

Over the years, I continued to collect data on the ways in which Israeli cuisine is defined, practicing participant observation in various sites (the HaCarmel and Mahane Yehuda markets, the Taam Ha'Ir [Taste of the City] yearly food festival, military and kibbutz dining rooms, etc.), interviewing culinary practitioners, and following the ever-increasing influx of media publications on food in Israel and on Israeli food.

While writing this chapter, I browsed dozens of websites, food portals, blogs, and readers' responses (called "talkbacks" in Israel). These virtual sources notwithstanding, the data, ideas, and analysis presented in this chapter are based primarily on ethnographic participant observation and on interviews that I conducted or that were published in printed media. This chapter is therefore not a "netnography."[9] I have used these Internet sources to enrich the ethnography in the Geertzian sense. I do not treat web texts as accurate manifestations of some external and independent reality but rather as ideas that chefs and customers have expressed regarding various aspects of the food they cook and eat.

Finally, the interviews and texts mentioned throughout this chapter were all conducted or written in Hebrew. I translated relevant excerpts into English.

## LARGE AND CHEAP

While the chefs and entrepreneurs I interviewed suggested various definitions of Israeli cuisine, I gradually realized that the most prominent markers were the quantity of food, the size of portions, and, more implicitly, the issue of value for money. Israelis like their portions large, and they like them cheap.

One of the chefs recounted his experience with a salad bar that he set up in the mid-1990s at a restaurant in a fancy shopping center targeting upper-middle-class clientele in Tel Aviv:

> We decided to offer a salad bar, just like in America, where customers fill up their own plates. To price it, we consulted the professional literature, which suggested that the average customer would dish up some 750 grams of salad. But since we wanted to make sure that we were pricing correctly, we weighed each salad plate at the register during the first week of operation. The average weight was almost 1250 grams, some 70 percent over the international standard. We had to reprice the salad bar, and it became so expensive that we realized there was no point in offering it.[10]

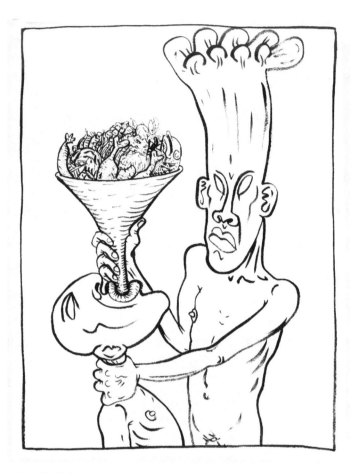

2. *Israeli Chefs*

One of the founders of a successful franchise that specializes in pasta explained the culinary logic behind the success of his enterprise, which distinguishes itself by serving huge, moderately priced portions:

> In Italy, pasta is either a starter or an intermediary course, between the *antipasti* [before the pasta] and the main courses. They serve portions of roughly 80 to 100 grams of cooked pasta on small plates. So we decided to offer portions of 150 to 200 grams of pasta. Do you know how much a 10-kilo bag of dried pasta costs? Maybe 25 shekels.[11] ... And the sauce is also quite cheap, even if you use high-quality ingredients. So we could offer very large portions, which cost only a few shekels, and sell them for less than 30 shekels. The portions were so big that we had to order special plates that would be large enough.[12] ... The customers loved it!

He later pointed out that the same logic of serving culinary items marked as foreign and of high quality led to the success of the espresso fad, which he introduced in Israel: "A cup of espresso is extremely cheap to make, less than a shekel, so even when you sell it for three, the profit is very high. Add to that the fact that our espresso bars had no kitchens and no kitchen expenses, offering only dry cookies and sandwiches. This allowed us to sell imported coffee and snacks for a moderate price with a large profit margin."

A prominent Israeli food journalist suggested while we were discussing the issue of portion size that the main reason for the failure of French *nouvelle cuisine* in Israel was not kashrut Jewish dietary laws, as is often argued by Israeli food experts, but the fact that this cuisine features small portions of expensive dishes that require a lot of skilled work: "The Israeli clientele demanded larger portions at a cheaper price, and chefs had to either enlarge the dishes, which made them ridiculously expensive, or use cheaper ingredients, which resulted in inferior food. In any case, these places were eventually unsuccessful."

Some French restaurants, however, have done well in Israel, but only once they deal with portion size. Shaul Ben Aderet, chef-owner of the well-established Kimmel restaurant, located in one of Tel Aviv's trendiest neighborhoods, is reputed in the food portal *ROL* for changing "the well-known French concept whereby small and expensive portions are served in huge utensils. He adjusted the serving mode to the Israeli audience by serving large portions with large dishes for a moderate price."[13]

## ISRAELI BREAKFASTS

Israelis boast about and indulge in the so-called Israeli breakfasts[14] served at hotels and restaurants in Israel. It is important to bear in mind that hotel breakfasts are included in the room's price and are, therefore, "free" in the sense that guests may eat as much as they like for no additional fee. However, the quality of the products and dishes is often mediocre.

Consuming huge amounts of food at Israeli hotel breakfasts is an established Israeli culinary cliché, often ridiculed by Israeli comedians. A classic example is Shaul Biber's classic 1950s skit "Ochel, Kadima Ochel"[15] (Food, charge forward [for the] food), which depicts the atmosphere at an Israeli Workers Union guesthouse in the 1950s where the guests were encouraged to eat as much as they could day and night.

The practice of stuffing oneself at hotel breakfasts when traveling, however, is condemned by Israeli tour leaders, who caution their Israeli customers to avoid gluttony at hotel breakfasts abroad and to refrain from preparing sandwiches for the rest of the day, a "custom" tolerated in many Israeli hotels but considered theft in other countries. In some Israeli hotels, however, signs in Hebrew boldly point out that no food can be taken out of the dining room.

Food critic Tahel Blumenfeld neatly summarizes the overindulgence embedded in these Israeli breakfasts:

> There is no doubt that breakfast at an Israeli hotel is a constitutive event in the life of the country's dwellers. This meal, in which impossible amounts of food are stuffed into the digestion system at impossible hours, encapsulates everything that makes us "The Chosen People": Size does matter to us; we love salted herring when we don't have to pay for it; cottage cheese is great, but we like to have some three hundreds kinds of cheese next to it; and, of course, we prefer to fill our plates many times with a lot of food that we shall never eat.[16]

In an article she wrote about Israeli hotel breakfasts, journalist Shoshana Chen adds:

> Those interested in witnessing the encounter with the Promised Land after forty years of wandering in the desert are invited to stand at the entrance of a dining room in a typical Israeli hotel, preferably in Eilat, the gluttons' capital of the nation, at 9 a.m. Multitudes of vacationing men, women, and children charge in as if they have never seen food. Mountains of herring, sweetened yogurts and puddings, cheeses, vegetables, salads, and croissants are loaded on to plates. Grab as much as you can. . . . [At Jerusalem Sheraton Plaza,] at least 700–800 eggs are cracked in accordance with guests' requests, whereas Dan Eilat offers a 60-meter-long breakfast buffet, out of which 18 meters are devoted to a minimum of twenty-five kinds of baked items.[17]

Chen quotes David Fattal, CEO of Fattal Hotels, on the quantities of food consumed at Israeli breakfasts: "Guests in a fully occupied hotel of some 300 rooms (600 guests), exterminate [*mehaslim*] 700–800 croissants and cupcakes in a single breakfast, along with some 500 rolls, 40 bread loaves of different kinds, and several good kilograms of various breakfast cereals."[18] Anat Shaul, food and beverage manager at Hotel Daniel Herzliya, confirms that her breakfast plan is based on two and a half croissants, two and a half to three rolls, and two eggs per guest, along with four to five kinds of bread, twelve kinds of vegetables, a warm food counter, a baked items buffet, a fresh

3. *Israeli Breakfast*

and dried fruit counter, a selection of natural yogurts, and cornflakes. Shaul concludes: "Israelis like to eat with their eyes, take twice as much as they really eat, and walk at least three times to the food serving area in a single breakfast to refill their plates."[19]

These huge amounts of food call for specific utensils. Haim Spiegel, food and beverage manager at the leading Dan Hotels network, recounts that when Dan Eilat was opened, he had to replace the breakfast plates that measured 18 centimeters in diameter with ones measuring 25 centimeters (the size of large dinner plates commonly used in Israeli homes), but "guests still fill them up a few times in a single breakfast."[20]

Yet Israelis like their portions big and cheap not only for breakfast and not only in Israel. One of the main reasons for the extreme popularity of Turkey as a tourist destination for Israelis (that is, up until the souring of diplomatic relations between the two countries in 2010) was the *hakol kalul* (all inclusive) plan at Turkish hotels, which meant that guests had a virtually endless supply of food throughout their visit. Other hotel services such as spa treatments or motorized water sports were never included in these packages, but the unlimited flow of food was the main lure, attracting some five hundred thousand Israeli visitors to Turkey in 2009. Obviously, the luxurious hotels, their swimming pools, and their beaches were important factors, but these can be found in other destinations. It was the cheap price of the packages and the included food that made Turkey Israelis' top vacation choice during most of the previous decade.

After a stay in one of these hotels, my still-confused ten-year-old nephew told me that when he approached the dessert buffet and took a slice of watermelon, an Israeli women, a stranger to him and his parents, approached him, added two large watermelon slices to his plate, and told him, "Take more, take more, abuse them [*dfok otam*]."

Israelis seek out large portions at home and abroad. In the early 1990s, while I was having lunch with a group of male Israeli expats in California, one of them was asked by the waiter how he wanted his steak (referring to the roasting grade). The Israeli man answered: "Big!" The waiter was visibly uncomfortable, but the rest of the group burst into laughter. They found this remark so witty that they still mention it whenever we meet, almost thirty years later. Most intriguing, however, was the fact that even in the United States, where restaurant portions are generally very large, this response made the American waiter uncomfortable, while the Israelis found it amusing and smart.

In a different context of dining abroad, a classic Israeli "backpackers' myth"[21] recounts how four *moshavniks*[22] went to a famous *parilla* (grill house) in Quito, Ecuador, that specialized in all-you-can-eat roasted meat. After a couple of hours of nonstop meat devouring and quite a few refills, they were approached by the proprietor, who said that he was reluctant to serve them more meat. "In that case," they responded, "we won't pay." "Fine," said the proprietor, "just leave!" Whenever I recount this story, Israelis burst into laughter. Non-Israelis, however, find it vulgar and disturbing. The underlying messages of this story are that Israelis like large portions of cheap food and they feel that achieving such meals demonstrates their wit and sophistication. For non-Israelis, such stories demonstrate Israeli greed and gluttony.

## TASTE OF THE CITY

The preference for large, cheap portions in Israel is not static and certainly not a thing of the past. In fact, it is on the rise. Despite increasing affluence, the emergence of elite cuisine, the introduction of foreign foods and eating styles, and growing attention being paid to health and weight, portions are constantly increasing while quality is often declining. This process is most clearly evident at the Taam Ha'Ir (Taste of the City) food festival, celebrated each year in the nation's cosmopolitan cultural center, Tel Aviv, since 1996.

The founders of this festival, reputed to be the second-largest food festival in the world,[23] wanted to introduce elite restaurants to persons of lesser cultural and/or economic capital by offering small portions of gourmet food for a fraction of what they would cost at the restaurants and serving them in the informal setting of a street festival: "13 years ago, a small food festival was launched in Ha'Arba'a Street that included twenty gourmet restaurants. The goal was to allow the public the possibility to taste gourmet dishes at an affordable price."[24] This has remained the festival's stated mission to this day. Thus, an article dedicated to the 2011 event that was published in the festival's sponsoring magazine, *Achbar Ha'Ir* (*City Mouse*), stated: "Dozens of food stands of leading restaurants will offer especially cheap dishes (30–35 shekels)."[25]

While conducting participant observation at the festival over the years, I realized that the culinary arrangements and the food on offer were changing. Small bites of gourmet food, such as a quarter-portion of Aharoni's famous foie gras for 25 shekels, were gradually replaced by hamburgers and other kinds of grilled meat—food that can hardly qualify as gourmet. The portions became much larger, making each dish a whole meal rather than a sample. The portion prices also increased (to 40–45 shekels), becoming similar to those of a main dish at a medium-range restaurant.

These changes were noted and endorsed by the customers. In the early years of the festival, despite the cheap prices, people I interviewed often complained that the portions were too small and that they had to purchase four or five dishes to feel *sveim* (full or satisfied). As portions grew, these remarks disappeared, and the festival attracted increasing numbers of participants, eventually becoming "the second-largest food festival in the world."[26]

Professional chefs and journalists, however, have been critical of this change. Restaurateur Zahi Bukshester commented in 2011: "Sadly, in the last couple of years, I didn't participate [in the festival] because I didn't like the fact that the event had turned into a food market and stopped being a festival of quality restaurants."[27] Journalist Orna Yefet was blunter: "Gourmet restaurants, and even simply good restaurants, . . . were replaced by much simpler venues. . . . The gourmet dishes became the kebabs and hamburgers that one can find on any street corner."[28] Bukshester and Yefet commented on the declining quality of the food, but this change was directly related to the enlargement of the portions. During the 2008 festival, one of the chefs told me, "We push [me'ifim, or "fly," in the original Hebrew] 300 kilos of meat daily," indicating that it was all about selling quantities of food for a profit. Also that year, I noticed that a well-known chef was advertising his hamburgers with loud yells. When I asked him why he was yelling, he responded, "This is a market, therefore I yell," suggesting that this was a market-style event rather than gourmet festival. When I was discussing the shifting size preferences at the festival with food journalist Hila Alpert, she sighed and commented: "Israelis are the biggest pigs ever."

### ENLARGING FOREIGN DISHES

Boosting small portions and emphasizing quantity over quality is also evident in the processes by which Israelis have incorporated into their cuisine global culinary trends such as tapas, dim sum, sushi, and other dishes originally served in small portions. Yet even dishes that are not that small or that are supposed to adhere to universal size standards, such as McDonald's hamburgers, have been enlarged in Israel.

In Spain, tapas are small, cheap portions of finger foods that accompany drinks at bars—the Iberian version of the eastern Mediterranean meze. While the variety of tapas is endless, depending on region, season, and location, the portions are always small. The verb used for eating tapas in Spanish is *picar* (peck) rather than *comer* (eat). In northern Spain, tapas are sometimes called *pinchos,* another reference to their small size, as diners "pinch" them with their fingers.

Tapas served at Israeli tapas bars, however, are different: they are much larger and are quite expensive. According to the owner of one of the trendiest tapas bars in Tel Aviv, the first tapas bars in the country (opened around 2005) were established by young culinary entrepreneurs who became acquainted with tapas in Spain or, in most cases, in the United States, where tapas were a recent trend. These pioneering establishments served mostly tapas made with imported Spanish ingredients and fresh seafood, which were therefore small and expensive. The entrepreneur pointed out that such portions elicited substantial hostility among Israeli customers, who felt that they were being cheated. This can be easily discerned in the readers' responses to a very positive journalistic review of a newly opened tapas bar in Tel Aviv in 2009:

> Y.: Everything looked really inviting and good until we got the food. Each portion was literally bite-sized. The prices, however, are of main courses, 60–70 shekels. We were cheated once; we won't fall for it again.

> A.: No need to endlessly discuss the issue. There were five of us, we paid 845 shekels [over US$200] and left hungry. . . . Plain stinginess! And I am positive that [the chef] understands the lack of proportion between the size of the dishes and their prices.

> N.: We were looking forward to get to this new place and trying the tapas but were so disappointed when we found out that the portions were tiny [*ktantanot*]. The average portion was no larger than a bowl of peanuts served for free at bars, except here they will charge you a fortune for it. . . . We left hungry and with an inflated bill. We will never return. . . . However, [another] tapas bar is most recommended: cheaper, bigger portions, and much tastier.[29]

While some readers' responses were less critical and even enthusiastic, most commenters condemned the size of the tapas, especially in relation to their price. Food critic Sagi Cohen, in a review of a tapas bar that he crowned "the first real tapas bar in Israel," argued that the large tapas served in Israel are hardly tapas at all: "All the restaurants who called themselves tapas bars to this day are actually restaurants serving diminished versions of large portions. With all due respect, 'a sixth of a steak' is not a tapa but five-sixths of a cheat, exactly like the fact that 'half a portion of gnocchi' is not a tapa but an outrageous pricing system."[30]

When my interviewee opened his own tapas bar, he decided to serve larger portions made with cheaper ingredients. He also shifted the emphasis from alcohol to food, "as there is no real drinking culture in Israel." He explained that his menu "is less varied than a Spanish tapas bar, but most customers order only one or two dishes per person, so there is no need for so many options."

Chinese dim sum went through a similar process of Israelization and enlargement. Dim sum is not a dish but rather an eating style: traditionally, it refers to a large variety of small dishes served with green tea in Cantonese teahouses, mainly for breakfast. Cantonese cuisine is among the most sophisticated Chinese cuisines, and dim sum is one of its greatest achievements, with a huge variety of fine, highly elaborate dishes. While steamed dumplings, stuffed and carefully folded, are emblematic of dim sum, an average Cantonese teahouse features dozens and even hundreds of other options.

According to sociologist Rafi Grosglik (pers. comm.) Israel's first proper dim sum restaurant was established in Tel Aviv in 1995 by a couple of young entrepreneurs who had had dim sum in China and thought that "it was cool and might work in Israel." They wanted to offer authentic dim sum but had very limited culinary knowledge and therefore simplified it to "classic fillings and four or five folds [this refers to the way in which the dough is folded into specific dumpling shapes]." The restaurant fared poorly and was eventually taken over by another entrepreneur, who had previously worked at a local Chinese fast-food chain. He tried to pursue the dim sum path and even hired Chinese cooks. But he realized that dim sum was not attractive enough to diners. So, according to Grosglik, he decided to also offer "noodles and stir-fries, which are very popular in Israel, as well as a variety of lunch specials." However, he did keep a few dim sum items on the menu to distinguish his restaurant.

These remaining dumplings were adjusted to the Israeli market in several ways. First, Grosglik pointed out, the fillings were adapted: "All the 'strange' ingredients were removed. For example, the classic combination of pork, spring onion, and ginger was removed from the menu. . . . Shrimp, however, was okay. They also invented a filling of frozen spinach mixed with shredded roasted peanuts, seasoned with artificial oyster sauce. It was sweet and salty and had spinach in it, and Israelis loved it."

Grosglik explained that the most important change had to do with the dough for the shells. Cantonese dumplings are often made from rice or tapioca flour, which makes for a fine and translucent pastry, but Israeli customers wanted only wheat-flour shells, which creates thick, coarse pastry similar to Italian pasta: "Instead of the tiny, sophisticated dim sum served at Cantonese teahouses, they ended up serving huge portions of cheap, easy-to-make street foods such as fried *gioza* and steamed *bao-dze,* which are intended to stuff poor, hungry workers rather than please members of the sophisticated, urban elite."

Sushi was also adjusted to the Israeli taste through a similar process. According to a colleague who conducts ethnographic research in Japan, Japanese sushi are served in bite-sized portions to allow the diner to experience the combination of flavors, aromas, textures, and colors all at once. He estimated that Israeli sushi, however, is 40 percent larger than the Japanese equivalent. We should bear in mind, though, that sushi was originally devised to accompany alcoholic drinks, just like tapas and dim sum, and is therefore a finger food rather than a main dish. As Boaz Zairi, a leading sushi master told me, because "Israelis don't drink and don't have a drinking culture, sushi is considered a dish, and Israelis expect it to be as large and as filling as any other dish."

Sushi arrived in Israel via the United States, where it had already been adjusted to American preferences. The American website SushiNow.com points out that

> American sushi is larger in general [than Japanese sushi]. The individual pieces are usually too big to eat in one bite. . . . In the same way that other cuisines are altered in the United States, more emphasis is put on the quantity of sushi and less on quality and eye appeal. . . . Meal proportions have expanded to rival meals available at other restaurants. The traditional Japanese reverence for good quality food in small portions has dissipated in America, with sushi bars deferring to the American-sized appetite and attraction to colorful food in big portions.[31]

Some of the American modifications—such as the enlargement of the sushi units and the inclusion of ingredients such as avocado (in California rolls) and other vegetables, canned tuna (in Hawaiian rolls), and salmon and cream cheese (in Philadelphia rolls)—were in line with Israeli culinary preferences. However, the Israeli version differs from the Japanese original and the modified American variety in that Israeli sushi is not only larger than the Japanese original but also more substantial. Israeli food portal Sushi4Me. com explains: "'Inside out' sushi is identical to 'conventional' sushi. The only difference is in the rolling technique. . . . Many [Israeli] cooks and diners prefer this rolling technique over classic rolls because one can squeeze much more filling into the sushi."[32] Similarly, in a discussion group titled "Real Sushi" that took place in 2012 on the now defunct Israeli portal pkfight.com, a user by the name Yehuda pointed out:

> It appears that sushi preparation in Israel is done according to slightly different rules that adhere to the Israeli food culture. When preparing an Israeli

sushi roll, it has to be fuller and more compressed because this is how many customers like it. The Israeli diner, who likes his pita packed with goodies, might be turned off from sushi portions that look too humble; Israeli sushi had to give up some minimalism to adhere to Israeli preferences.

Beyond size and consistency, the proportions between the rice and the fish and vegetables have also changed in Israeli sushi. In Japan (and in other rice cultures), rice is the centerpiece of the meal, and the other ingredients only accompany or decorate it (Ohnuki-Tierney 1993, 1995; Ashkenazi and Jacob 2000; Avieli 2012). Israeli meals, however, adhere to the Western notion that animal protein is the centerpiece of the meal (Douglas 1972; Murcott 1982). Vegetables are not the core of the Israeli meal, but they are important and omnipresent.

It is easy to understand why Israeli sushi features larger, thicker, and heavier pieces of fish and larger vegetable bits. But the use of large pieces of fish also relates to the tendency of Israeli Jews to avoid raw flesh.[33] One of the main features of Israeli sushi is the emphasis on cooked fish, and it is harder to cut cooked fish thinly. Sushi has become popular in recent years as an appetizer at Israeli weddings, for example, but this sushi very rarely contains raw fish; canned tuna or smoked salmon are usually used instead. While caterers that I interviewed argued that they were restricted to these ingredients because of hygiene problems and the delicacy of raw fish, when I approached guests at weddings and asked if they would like to try raw-fish sushi, they often responded with disgust and even horror.

Not only are canned tuna and smoked salmon more durable than raw fish, but they also have a stronger taste and aroma and, as mentioned above, are harder to slice into fine slivers. Thus, the resulting sushi features thicker pieces of fish, which, as we have learned already, Israeli diners prefer. Add to this that canned tuna and smoked salmon are cheaper than fresh fish and cheaper to handle (in terms of transportation and refrigeration), and you'll understand why they are the most popular fish for Israeli sushi.

This taste for coarser sushi made with large pieces of animal protein has resulted in specific Israeli inventions. One of them is the Israeli version of tempura sushi (sushi fried in tempura batter). In a post in the "Real Sushi" discussion group, mentioned above, the poster Yehuda argues: "One can also find special sushi invented by Israeli chefs. An example is a sushi coated with breadcrumbs and fried in oil *so as to produce a dish similar to schnitzel,* Israel's most popular dish. It is sometimes prepared with chicken breast instead of the traditional sheet of nori, which makes it even more similar to the tradi-

4. *The Largest McRoyal*

tional schnitzel" (emphasis mine). The outcome, of course, is quite distant from the tiny, light-tasting rice balls topped by translucent fish slivers served in Japan.

It is important to note, however, that this augmentation of portions is not limited to foreign dishes that were originally small. The best example of this tendency is the enlargement of McDonald's McRoyal hamburger in Israel. This makes for an illuminating case precisely because McDonald's claims that it practices strict universal standardization (Ritzer 1996).[34]

In 2001, some eight years after the arrival of the infamous fast-food chain to Israel, McDonald's Israel CEO, Omri Padan, announced that they would increase the size of the McRoyal by 25 percent, making it the largest hamburger at any McDonald's in the world and, for that matter, at any international hamburger chain anywhere. He explained that the decision was made after surveys carried out at local McDonald's branches indicated that Israelis prefer big portions and tend to "supersize" their meals.[35]

Cultural geographer Maoz Azaryahu, who studied McDonald's as an example of the "Americanization of Israel," addressed the enlargement of the McRoyal in an article, which he concluded by arguing: "The chain also developed a new type of hamburger to conform to Israeli preferences and tastes. As advertised, the McRoyal was more of everything: bigger, spicier, and juicier. Accordingly, even if the idiom appeared to be American, *both content and accent were unmistakably Israeli*" (2000, 62; emphasis mine). Thus, in an article whose main argument is that McDonald's takes part in the "Americanization of Israel," the author contends that the enlargement of the hamburger was an Israeli cultural transformation of the American original.

I would like to conclude the discussion of the Israeli tendency to enlarge foreign food by recounting the experience of a cultural critic who wrote an essay on the food at an experimental chef's restaurant in Tel Aviv, which, according to its website, featured "high-quality local ingredients," "innovative and creative local food," "an informal atmosphere," and "light meals, tidbits, and drinks."[36] The website clearly defined the atmosphere and food as "Western and modern."

The chef-owner agreed to be interviewed for the essay, but he asked to read the text before it was published. According to the author, after reading the text, the chef asked that his name and the restaurant's name not be mentioned. He explained that the essay might damage the planned remarketing of the restaurant, which was struggling economically: "We are no longer a restaurant that should be visited only when one is full but rather a place that accommodates low-budget and hungry customers." Thus, even at the most sophisticated bastions of imported food and style, portion size and satiety are seen as crucial features that attract or deter Israeli clients.

## CULINARY EXPERTISE AND FINE FOOD

I'll now depart for a while from the issue of large portions and suggest that the large fish slices and coarser sushi, thick-shelled dim sum, and simplified, enlarged tapas also have to do with a lack of culinary expertise or refinement among Israeli chefs. This might look like a trivial claim: If a cook is not well trained or doesn't really care about food, the dishes he or she produces will hardly be fine. However, my observations and interviewees hinted at a tendency among Israeli chefs to disregard and even mock the culinary training and expertise necessary for producing fine food. This inclination is in line with my argument regarding the Israeli preference for quantity over quality.

One of the country's leading chefs complained during our long conversation, "Nowadays, young people with big dreams take a three-day cooking class in Paris and immediately set up a French restaurant." Later in the interview, I asked him about his own training. He told me that after working for a year or so as a kitchen assistant for a leading chef and gastronome, he went to France and took a couple of short cooking courses before setting up his first restaurant in Israel (which was very successful and made him famous).

In another interview, a leading Israeli sushi master argued that sushi preparation is an art that can only be acquired through long years of training under experienced Japanese sushi masters. Later in the conversation, I asked her about her own training, and she explained that she had worked in a sushi restaurant in Europe, where she developed her passion for Japanese food and specifically for sushi. When I wondered if this was enough, she responded: "I had a Japanese spouse." She later explained that she made repeated visits to Japan and to Japanese restaurants in other countries and was constantly learning and improving her knowledge and skills, yet the discrepancy between her definition of the proper training for sushi masters and her own (limited) training loomed over the rest of the conversation.

It should be noted that both chefs are talented, experienced, and have been very successful in their various culinary ventures over the years. I am by no means dismissing their cooking abilities. In both cases, however, I found the gap between the long-term professional schooling they deemed necessary for chefs and their own limited training both interesting and baffling.

Food critics have also noted the lack of training and expertise among leading Israeli chefs, especially when it comes to foreign food. In a rave review of a newly opened tapas bar, Hagit Evron wrote: "[Yonatan] Roschfeld, a talented chef specializing in French cooking, studied Spanish cuisine, went back and forth [between Israel and Spain] a few times and consolidated a menu, . . . one that, as far as authenticity goes, gets a high score. True, in any other place in the world . . . *opening an ethnic restaurant requires years of contemplating, experiencing, and experimenting.* But Roschfeld is very talented and very self-confident" (emphasis mine).[37]

Though Evron admittedly loved the food, she couldn't help but point to instances in which the gap between the culinary pretensions of the restaurant and the actual food was too wide: "I really tried to avoid the electrifying atmosphere and concentrate on the food. For instance—the quesadilla. I love quesadillas! Even though this is a Mexican dish, one shouldn't be petty-minded. They speak Spanish in Mexico too, and Israelis love grilled-cheese sandwiches." Just like with her previous remark, she distinguishes between the food's taste, which she liked, and its culinary integrity, of which she is critical.

If leading Israeli chefs seem to be confident in their ability to produce high-quality foreign food despite their limited culinary knowledge and training, it seems that this tendency is even more common at the lower end of Israeli culinary landscape. The following vignette is an example: I once took my children to a sushi place that caters mainly to students at Ben-Gurion University, located in Beer-Sheva, a town with very limited culinary pretensions. My children wanted to see the preparation process, so we sat at the bar. The restaurant was operated by a young woman, who took our order and then turned to prepare the sushi. Before making the rice balls, she dipped her hands in a bowl of water. My son asked her why she did this, and she explained that it was so the rice wouldn't stick to her hands. I asked her a few questions about herself, and when she said that she was a student, I asked how she learned to make sushi. She responded: "What's the big deal? You take some rice, shape it into a ball, top it with some fish or vegetables, and that's it." She added that the owner, a student himself, had taught her how to make sushi a couple of days earlier. The sushi she served us was wet and inedible.

Here again, culinary expertise and refinement were simply dismissed, and sushi was reduced to rice balls topped with some fish. Once the quality of the ingredients and culinary expertise are so casually dismissed, it is hardly surprising that size remains the only attribute of value. If sushi is "just a ball of rice topped with some fish," if it is "no big deal" to prepare sushi, tapas, dim sum, or hamburgers, and if it takes only a couple of weeks in a cooking school or a few trips abroad to master a foreign cuisine, then the value of culinary knowledge is low. As a consequence, quantity and not quality defines the value of a dish for Israeli diners.


## WHAT DOES IT MEAN TO BE FULL IN ISRAEL?

Large portions define Israeli cuisine. But what meaning do Israelis attribute to these oversized servings? When I was discussing the large portions chef Haim Cohen's customers demanded at his first restaurant, he suddenly said: "Do you know what it means to be *saveah* [full, or satisfied] in Israel? . . . You sit at the table, your belt and upper pants button open, you sweat, you can hardly breathe, and you feel as if you are about to throw up. . . . Now that is what we call *saveah*."

Over the years, I have asked Israeli chefs, food entrepreneurs, and many other interlocutors to comment on Cohen's statement. The most common reaction was laughter accompanied by an enthusiastic nod of approval. Israelis are clearly familiar with this description of satiety. When I inquired about the reasons why Israelis define satiety as such, the explanations had to do with different moments in Jewish history.

First, it was argued, in contrast to anti-Semitic myths, most Jews of the Diaspora were poor and hungry. Living under constant threat of violence and deportation for two thousand years, they became accustomed to eating as much as they could whenever they had the opportunity because they were never certain when their next meal would be. Under such circumstances, a full stomach was the prime concern, and taste was less important. Indeed, Jewish cuisine throughout the Diaspora features substantial and hearty dishes such as stews, dumplings, fish and meat balls, pies, and stuffed vegetables, all made with cheap ingredients and seasoned with small amounts of animal protein. The emblematic Jewish food cholent (a Sabbath stew made of lentils, grains, root vegetables, eggs, bones, and a little low-quality meat), gefilte fish, and *kubbe* (Kurdish Iraqi bulgur balls) are classic examples of this culinary tendency. And as anyone who has ever had cholent knows, eating it results in the kind of satiety that adheres to Haim Cohen's definition of the word.

Different Jewish histories, however, define different kinds of hunger and satiety. The Holocaust trauma was often mentioned when explaining the tendency of Ashkenazi Jews (Jews of European ancestry) to stuff themselves. Israeli folklore and modern literature abound with references to the complex relations Holocaust survivors have with food. Large servings and the insistence that the diners finish every bit of food are common reactions to Holocaust deprivation, at least to a certain extent, among Ashkenazi Jews.

Mizrahi Jews (a loaded term that I will thoroughly discuss in the following chapters), it is often argued, approach food quantities differently. Mizrahi Jews were influenced by their Arab neighbors and the Arab custom of offering sumptuous feasts as an expression of proper hospitality and as a token of prestige. A friend of Moroccan descent once pointed to the colorful, dish-laden table at his parents' house during a Sabbath meal and told me: "In Moroccan Arabic, there is no word for *ktzat* [a little bit]." Another friend, who immigrated to Israel from Morocco as a young child, commented when discussing food amounts that he considers stinginess the worst of all character traits and that he finds the idea of doggie bags embarrassing because they express extreme stinginess.

I am not suggesting that generosity is an exclusively Mizrahi quality. Rather, I wish to highlight the Mizrahi perception of themselves as generous and to explain the large quantity of food they offer to their guests as an expression of this self-perception.

Obviously, poverty and deprivation also explain the Mizrahi tendency to prefer large amounts of food. The most significant childhood experience of my wife's late grandmother, for example, was the famine that hit the Middle East in the aftermath of World War I, in which three of her siblings perished. Throughout her long life, feeding her family members remained her greatest goal (see also Sered 1989). Her children and grandchildren became affluent (and plump) over the years, but she went on insisting that they should eat more, dishing up impossible amounts of food and demanding that they finish everything on their plates.

Two thousand years of the Diaspora, poverty, and hunger—which culminated in the Holocaust—and the sense of constant threat (real or imagined) felt by most Israeli Jews have created what Gad Yair (2011) defines as a collective Israeli posttrauma. My interviewees suggested that one possible consequence of this collective mental condition is unappeasable hunger. This hunger helps to explain why Israeli portions have to be so large and why Israelis need to eat so much to feel full.

## NOBODY'S SUCKERS

Collective Israeli hunger notwithstanding, the preference for large portions may also be explained by other Israeli cultural inclinations. Luis Roniger and Michael Feige (1999) discuss the extremely important Israeli principle of not being a *freier* (literally "a free gentlemen" in German but used in modern Hebrew to denote a sucker), claiming that while the desire to avoid being a sucker is not exclusively Israeli, the centrality of this sentiment in Israel calls for explanation because Israeli society has always emphasized collective goals and individual self-sacrifice and has been critical of individuals pursuing personal desires and profit.[38]

According to Roniger and Feige, the conventional sociological explanation for this attitude has to do with the erosion of ideological commitment in Israel (Almog 2000). During the years preceding the creation of the State of Israel and in the early years of independence, the prevailing ideology was collectivist, crystallized in the ideal of the pioneer who would sacrifice everything, including his or her own life, for the nation. In the context of local and global changes, this ideology gradually eroded as individualism was slowly acknowledged and eventually upheld and embraced by many Israelis.

Roniger and Feige argue that this reading is simplistic, and they describe a more complex process. According to them, the extreme reluctance to be seen as a sucker is the outcome not of a linear (that is, deterministic) shift from collectivist ideology to individualization but rather of the paradoxical coexistence of these two beliefs. The State of Israel still upholds collective goals and continues to make huge demands on its citizens, including compulsory military service and reserve duty. Indeed, Israelis must face the high personal risks incurred by the never-ending Israeli-Arab conflict daily. Life in Israel also means a heavy tax burden, a high cost of living, poor infrastructure, and overburdened bureaucratic, educational, and health systems. Life for Israeli citizens is extremely intense, demanding, and exhausting. In this sense, Israeli citizens take on the role of *frayerim*—they are the state's suckers day in and day out.

Roniger and Feige describe various instances in which Israelis acknowledge their sucker status and even take pride in it. A recent example is Ma'Ahal Hafrayerim (The Suckers Camp), a campaign launched in 2012 for the universalization of military and reserve service. The activists proudly described themselves as the nation's "suckers" for performing military and reserve duties and taking on the responsibility for the nation's security. By protesting and demanding that the military burden be shared more equally, the protestors exposed the ambivalence suggested by Roniger and Feige regarding suckerhood: while the dwellers of the improvised camp were proud to be the nation's suckers, they were reluctant to be the *sole* suckers.

Roniger and Feige argue that not being a sucker is a powerful mode of resistance to the hegemonic national ideology. At the same time, the meaning of this ideology is derived from its dialectical relations with mainstream Zionist ideology: "The non-*freier* . . . defines the meanings of Zionism by negating it. He does not define what should be done, but offers a model for what mustn't be" (Roniger and Feige 1993, 132).

Stuffing oneself for a low price is clearly an application of the "being nobody's sucker" principle: large portions, whether of Israeli or foreign fare, and whether consumed in Israel or abroad, indicate that the diner was not cheated or abused but rather received his or her share and perhaps even more.

Indeed, one of the most common reactions in many interviews and readers responses to a meal considered too meager or too expensive is the slang expression *frayerim lo metim* (suckers don't die; they only change), which indicates that the diners have been duped once but won't be fooled again.

Roniger and Feige further argue that the obsession with avoiding suckerhood is paradoxical: the State of Israel was created precisely to overcome the chronic "sucker condition" of Jews of the Diaspora, who were members of a weak and ill-treated minority group. But the State of Israel required individuals to sacrifice themselves for collective goals and hence become, as it were, the state's suckers. Once Israeli Jews began refusing to take on the role of sucker, the existence of the state was jeopardized, along with the "nobody's sucker" status of its citizens. Thus, Roniger and Feige conclude, any way you look at it, Israelis are suckers.

Within the culinary realm, this paradox has evolved in a different direction: Israeli Jews define a proper portion as being first and foremost large, which produces an extreme form of satiety. The quality of the food is a distant second. Israeli portions are therefore big but not necessarily of high quality. I have pointed to many instances in which the quality of food was ignored and even disdained and ridiculed. The outcome is that Israelis get large portions of mediocre food. Just like in other realms of social life, the Israeli obsession with not being anyone's sucker (by demanding large portions) results in a constant state of suckerhood (since the food quality is low).

Let me conclude by stressing that the various definitions of Israeli satiety, be it a response to Ashkenazi or Mizrahi history of lack and hunger, the Mizrahi ideal of generosity, or the Israeli "nobody's sucker" complex, are not physiological. Israelis do not feel full when their nutritional demands are satisfied nor once their digestive systems are stocked. Rather, they are satisfied only when they feel that they can face two thousand years of Jewish Diaspora, the Holocaust, the heavy demands of contemporary life in Israel, and the looming threats of the future. That certainly calls for a lot of food.[39]

# TWO

# Roasting Meat

YOM HA'ATZMAUT (INDEPENDENCE DAY) IS the most Israeli day on the Israeli calendar, when the nation's Jewish citizens recount their constitutive myth as a distinct people and celebrate their unique history (Handelman and Katz 1995). This is a Durkheimian ritual of cohesion, in which the community celebrates itself, exposing and reaffirming its social structure and cultural arrangements. Up until the 1980s, Israelis celebrated Independence Day in a variety of ways, such as going to public performances and local fairs, participating in *rikudei am* (folk dancing) and *shira betzibur* (public singing), going on individual and organized hikes, visiting Israeli Defense Force bases, attending military parades and weapon displays, and watching the World Bible Quiz on TV. While these activities have lost much of their energy and appeal since the mid-1980s, roasting meat *al ha'esh* (over fire) has become the main activity of Independence Day. Without it, Independence Day does not feel right, and beyond these barbecues, not much happens on the holiday.

Thus, on Independence Day 2006, while driving to Jerusalem for fieldwork, I overheard an enthusiastic Galei Tzahal (Israel Defense Force Radio) broadcaster reporting: "We combed the country, looking for people who don't barbecue. It wasn't easy, but eventually we found some. They are the graduates of the 1953 class of Hakfar Hayarok agricultural high school." He then interviewed one of the group members, who was hosting his former classmates in his backyard. The interviewee explained that the friends met yearly to celebrate Independence Day without a barbecue: "We sing, we light a campfire, . . . we remember days when grilling was not the only thing to do on Independence Day." Later in the conversation, though, he admitted, "Just to be on the safe side, we did hang a picture of a *mangal* [barbecue]."[1]

Grilling meat is so central to Israel's Independence Day that the holiday itself has come to be known as *Yom Hamangal*, or "Barbecue Day." Journalist Tahel Blumenfeld (2007) describes it as follows: "Plumes of smoke will rise from the parks and woods on Yom Hamangal, which some still insist on calling Independence Day." Under the headline "We Have Celebrated Independence," Journalist A. Katz (2007) wrote: "The Israelis did not remain at home. Masses of people went outdoors to celebrate Yom Hamangal."

A newspaper ad published on April 20, 2007, in *Ha'ir* for Mizrah-Maarav (East-West), an importer of Asian food products, went even further. It read: "For fifty-nine years we have been barbecuing with the very same spices— now it's time to become truly independent with new tastes." While the ad was about exotic barbecue sauces, it also implied that cooking meat *al ha'esh* on Independence Day had been a central practice of the festival ever since the establishment of the State of Israel in 1948, fifty-nine years earlier. This claim, however, runs counter to the statement made by the interviewee quoted above as well as to my own recollection of Independence Days during the sixties and seventies. However, it was very much in line with the feelings articulated by the many Israelis I have interviewed since 2001, who strongly associate Independence Day with roasting meat *al ha'esh*.

Grilling meat is therefore the most publically celebrated Independence Day activity, and the chunks of grilled meat are pieces of distilled Israeliness, symbolic and material representations of the way many Israelis experience their national identity.

## MEAT, POWER, MASCULINITY, AND NATIONALISM

Anthropologists have long noted the strong links between meat consumption, physical power, and social dominance. While nutritionists and material anthropologists (primarily Marvin Harris) contend that meat is exceptionally nutritious, Nick Fiddes argues that meat eating is, above all, symbolic: "Killing, cooking and eating other animals' flesh is the ultimate authentication of human superiority over the rest of nature" (1991, 65; see also Willard 2002). Mary Douglas (1975) and Anne Murcott (1982) also suggest that the centrality of meat in the Western meal derives from its symbolic status as emblematic of power and control.

Alan Beardsworth and Teresa Keil argue, however, that the physiological and the symbolic may be complimentary, with eating meat combining nutrition and symbolism: "Eating red meat is seen ... as the ingesting of the very nature of the animal itself, its strength and aggression" (1996, 202). Eating meat, they contend, has the potential of making the eater "as strong as an ox," with matter and spirit reinforcing each other. Carol Adams (1997) points out that the British Royal Guards were nicknamed beefeaters due to their diet of meat, which was designed to ensure their physical strength as members of a crack unit and reward them with a high-status food that was otherwise reserved for the aristocratic classes. The religious injunction against eating carnivores in Judaism and Buddhism may also be explained by a fear of assimilating the ferociousness and cruelty of these animals into the eater's body and mind.

Eating meat also represents socioeconomic and political power. Julia Twigg suggests that in Western societies, "meat is the most highly prized and culturally significant of foods" (1983, 21), while Norbert Elias shows that in Medieval Europe, members of the higher classes ate prodigious amounts of meat while peasants ate very little of it: "Cattle were expensive and therefore destined ... essentially for the ruler's table" (1978, 118). Pierre Bourdieu (1984) also argues that meat is indicative of economic wealth and high social status and that eating certain kinds of meat is a symbolic action that represents economic, cultural, and symbolic capital, designed to reproduce and enhance class distinctions. Meat was, and still is, relatively expensive, and the regular consumption of high-quality meat, especially beef, represents affluence.

Meat, however, is not only a means of social competition over power and status. Researchers who study the consumption of meat in so-called "primitive" or indigenous societies claim that the practice is characterized not only by social competition but also by cooperation and sharing within broad social circles and according to meticulous rules. Kristen Hawkes (1993) argues that men in such societies hunt big game and share the meat to gain social benefits, and Susan Kent (1993), Nicolas Peterson (1993), and Barbara Thiel (1994) claim that meat is shared primarily for social reasons. In more recent discussions, Kristen Hawkes et al. (2001a, 2001b) complicate this model by adding competition and struggle for social prestige as further dimensions that affect meat sharing. Indeed, in his classic article "Poor Man, Rich Man, Big Man, Chief: Political Types in Melanesia and Polynesia," Marshal Sahlins (1963) argues that pork sharing in public feasts in these nations constitutes a key physical and symbolic resource in the political game. Accordingly, far from being exclusively an act of generosity and cooperation, sharing meat is also a token in the social competition for status and prestige.

Claude Lévi-Strauss's contribution to the social meaning of the barbecue is seminal here. In his classic essay "The Culinary Triangle" (1966), he argues that grilling is the most wasteful form of cooking since a considerable portion of the meat's volume, weight, and fat are lost in the process. Indeed, one kilo of meat, when cooked in ten liters of water, would provide eleven kilos of soup, whereas grilling one kilo of raw meat would deliver only about half a kilo of barbecued meat. When meat is boiled, it is diluted; grilling, on the other hand, is a process of concentration. Grilling meat over a fire connotes wealth, abundance, and generosity, as it implies a willingness to waste a precious resource. Grilling also concentrates the meat, imbuing it with higher nutritional, economic, and symbolic value. Grilling is thus a cooking technique that increases meat's value as a symbol of power and wealth.

Eating meat, particularly red meat, is also a gendered practice. Michael Herzfeld (1985) describes how meat was central to the meal of every Cretan who considered himself a man, while Twigg (1983) suggests that the blood that gives red meat its color is expressive of power, aggression, passion, and sexuality—attributes that are desirable for men but considered disturbing and even offensive for women. Willard concludes: "Because physical power is historically associated with masculinity and virility, . . . meat has been perceived as a masculine subject" (2002, 12).

Feminist critics such as Twigg (1983) and Adams (1990) develop the discussion of the relationship between meat, masculinity, and power by proposing that specific symbols related to meat are situated in a concentric hierarchy: culture above nature, humans above animals, and men above women. While Twigg suggests that the association of vegetarian and dairy foods with femininity indicates weakness and passiveness (as in the use of the term "vegetable" to describe a comatose person), Fiddes argues: "What meat exemplifies, more than anything, is an attitude: the masculine worldview that ubiquitously perceives, values and legitimates hierarchical domination of nature, of women and of other men" (1991, 210).

Adams (1990) is the most outspoken in her feminist critique of eating meat, showing how men use similar language when referring to animals and to women and how they subject both to similar kinds of symbolic and physical violence. Men verbally butcher women's bodies as if they were made of different cuts of meat (breasts, thighs, buttocks, etc.) and use cooking metaphors (grinding, banging, hooking, skewering, etc.) when referring to sexual intercourse with women. Adams concludes that condoning violence toward animals legitimizes violence against women. She states that feminism is consistent with vegetarianism and therefore calls on all those who consider themselves feminists to avoid meat.

Sahlins's analysis of American barbecues and the relationships between grilled meat, power, masculinity, and space in his book *Culture and Practical Reason* brings us a step closer to the Israeli case. Sahlins (1976) points out that beef is an essential component in the American diet and is specifically crucial when it comes to power and masculinity. Without a steak, he argues, the American male is powerless and impotent. The American masculine emblem is the cowboy, the lonely tough man, the individualist who represents most distinctly the relationship between masculinity and power on the one hand and between cattle and beef on the other. The cowboy and cattle also define a spatial context: the American frontier was conquered by cowboys, who gradually moved westward with their herds and turned a region seen as late as 1890 as "a vast and desolate area populated by savages and wild animals" (Willard 2002, 108) into a productive area and one of the largest pasturelands in the world. Accordingly, American historian Frederick J. Turner stated that the migration to the West was "the greatest pastoral movement in recorded history" (quoted in Willard 2002, 108) and that cattle were the most important element in the subjugation of the West. In return, Willard argues, American culture endowed the frontiersman with the cowboy myth: the lone hero who overcomes the forces of nature, wild animals, and Indians and turns the wilderness into the area where Americans produce the most important ingredient in their diet—beef.

Naturally, the emblematic cowboy grills his steak over a campfire, under starlit skies. Willard argues that the American barbecue represents not only power and masculinity but also the relationship between masculinity, nature, and space. The American barbecue dinner is a celebration of masculine power, the subjugation of nature, and the conquest of space. Therefore, she argues, Americans celebrate Fourth of July with a barbecue. By eating grilled beef, the participants reenact the American formative myth of the conquest of an immense, wild space by tough, armed, individualistic men and their cows. Rebecca Scott (2010, 7) adds that American meat eating was as much a "nation-building project as it was food consumption," and she coins the term "meat heroism" to connote the relationship between "hero" meat sandwiches, North American masculinity, and nationalism.

Barbecuing is privileged also in other modern nation-states, such as Argentina, Brazil, Uruguay, Australia, New Zealand, and South Africa. As in the case of the United States, these are modern migrant nations where (white) men used immense cattle herds to occupy and colonize territory. Michael Symons (2007), for example, argues that the promise of plentiful meat ("three times a day") was one of the key factors that attracted British immigrants to Australia, while Rita Denny et al. (2005) emphasize the barbecue as emblematic of present-day Aussie and Kiwi identity. In her ethnography of Tucumán, Argentina, Ariela Zycherman states: "During my research beef was used on numerous occasions as a signifier of national identity and its consumption was one of the main differences between being Argentine and being from anywhere else" (2008, 33). The gaucho, the cowboy figure in Brazil, Argentina, and Uruguay, is the local emblem of masculinity, spatial domination, and domestication of the frontier (Bornholdt 2010).

A particularly extreme instance of barbecuing in a violent, colonialist context is described by Allen Feldman, who analyzes a series of events in apartheid-era South Africa in which white policemen interrogated and tortured prisoners while barbecuing meat:

> *Braai* is Afrikaans . . . for an outdoor barbecue, and *braaing* is a ubiquitous weekend recreational practice throughout South Africa. Associated with sports competitions, hunting, [and] the frontier geography of the bush, . . . it is also part of the political culture of white male dominance. . . . It is my contention that at the *Braai* and torture sites described above, consumption, commensality and violence were integrated, and that this synthesis seems to have become a convention. (2003, 245)

The literature clearly associates barbecuing with power, masculinity, and modern nationalism. It also points to the colonial context, in which the grilled meat represents the violent occupation of indigenous space, with cattle serving both as a means to take over the land (for pasture) and as a key resource for the energy required for occupying that space (as food). Grilled meat is therefore privileged in modern immigrant nations as representative of the historical processes of their colonialization.

The literature cited so far suggests an explanation for Israeli Independence Day barbecues: in Israel, just like in the United States and in other modern colonial nations, barbecues stand for masculinity, power, and the conquest of space. These ideas are especially important during Israel's Independence Day, which commemorates the ongoing conflict over territory and emphasizes the central role played by men in this struggle. Moreover, as in the other nations that celebrate the barbecue, grilled meat alludes to nation building, the conquest and settling of space, and the dispossession of indigenous populations. Just as in North America, South America, South Africa, Australia, and New Zealand, grilled meat is a key symbol of modern nationalism, holding a privileged position in national events, and above all in Independence Day celebrations.

However, Israeli Independence Day barbecues are very different from those celebrated elsewhere and feature unique characteristics that call for specific interpretation.


## FIELDWORK AT JERUSALEM'S SACHER PARK

This chapter is based on ethnographic fieldwork I conducted in Jerusalem's Sacher Park from 2002 to 2009. Every Independence Day during those years, I stayed at Sacher Park from early morning till late afternoon. I walked around the celebrators, spoke to them, asked questions, observed the variety of interactions taking place, and listened to the "public conversations" accompanying them (by this I mean loud vocal exchanges that were easily overheard, as opposed to private talks). Some years, I also visited the park on the evening before Independence Day and followed the various events taking place in preparation for the next day's barbecues.

I collected most of my material through informal conversations with the celebrators. When they were willing, I conducted nonstructured interviews, usually once celebrators expressed interest in my study and wanted to further discuss my observations. I was often invited to share food. In these cases, I spent more time (up to several hours) with my hosts.

Beyond participant observation at Sacher Park, I conducted semistructured and open interviews with Jewish Israelis of various socioeconomic classes, ethnic groups, and locations before and after Independence Day. These interviews focused on the individuals' participation in (or avoidance of) al ha'esh events, whether on Independence Day or on other occasions. I also followed media reports on Independence Day in general and on al ha'esh in particular, collecting written and visual texts about what is often referred to as "the Israeli mangal [charcoal grill] culture" (tarbut ha'mangal ha'Israelit).

It is important to note that I do not consider Sacher Park Independence Day barbecues to be accurate representations of Israeliness on any level of generalization or abstraction. As one of my interviewees (who was an MBA doctoral candidate from Ben-Gurion University) suggested on Independence Day 2004, "The people here do not make for a representative sample of Israeli society. . . . They are *mizrahi'im* ['oriental'], *masorti'im* [traditional in their religious observance], and of low socioeconomic status."

This observation was quite accurate and important for understanding the arguments in this chapter. I do not argue that *al ha'esh* events at Sacher Park are accurate representations of barbecues held elsewhere in Israel or that they constitute a microcosm of Israeli society. In fact, there is a huge variety of ways in which Israelis of diverse classes, ethnic groups, religious beliefs, or political affiliations celebrate Independence Day (including many activities other than barbecuing). Yet the link between these barbecues and Mizrahi cultural patterns in contemporary Israel is a central component of my analysis.

Independence Day barbecues at Sacher Park are representative, however, in two respects. First, they are salient and emblematic events that attract media attention and were perceived by many of my interviewees as key reference points for Independence Day celebrations in contemporary Israel. Second, they are similar in many ways to other public and extremely popular barbecue events held on Independence Day and on other occasions at Ben Shemen Forest, Tel Aviv's Charles Clore Park, or the Angels Forest near Kiryat Gat (all of which I also visited during the research period). I therefore think that the analysis of the Sacher Park events, although not strictly representative, is revealing and facilitates the exploration of key characteristics of Israeliness in the early twenty-first century.

### WHY BARBECUE?

In response to the question, "Why do you barbecue on Independence Day?" my interlocutors suggested a wide range of explanations, all of which can be traced to one of three common Israeli cultural scripts: the *kumzitz* bonfire, the American barbecue, and *mizrahiyut* (literally "orientalism").

### *The* Kumzitz

Expressing the view of many people I spoke with, one interviewee reminisced, "In the past, we used to light a *medura* [campfire] and sit till dawn, with coffee and potatoes and onions and singing. . . . Gradually, we added pita with hummus, and then meat." As a matter of fact, some of the elements of Independence Day barbecues, such as the importance of fire or sitting in a circle and drinking Turkish coffee boiled over the fire, are clearly borrowed from *kumzitz* (gatherings, often around a campfire), central to the Palmach[2] ethos. This was particularly true of those who held barbecues on Independence Day Eve, which often featured a campfire and a grill. Though Sacher Park was not designed for bonfires, when I got there on Independence Day, I would always find remnants of fires that had been lit the previous evening. Many interviewees mentioned these nighttime gatherings when discussing their barbecue experience. One of them noted: "They really can't wait. . . . At 6 p.m., right after Memorial Day, they rush to light bonfires and *mangals*."

Prestate cultural forms, shaped mainly by members of the youth movements and Palmach warriors, are discussed by Tamar Katriel and Chaim Noy, among others, in the context of Israeli youth trekking. Katriel (1995) argues that these treks are a kind of Zionist secular pilgrimage, while Noy (2006) suggests that the ideology of occupying the land by foot and defining the territory and its boundaries through symbolic spatial presence (along with the "Palmach style" of unkempt clothing and hair, rucksacks, bucket hats, and the so-called biblical sandals[3]) was adopted by formal and informal Jewish education systems after statehood and subsequently by young Israeli backpackers abroad.

The *kumzitz* was one of the emblems of Palmach culture, and it still serves as an important cultural script for a variety of outdoor activities in early twenty-first-century Israel. This script involves a group of peers leaving the urban space and traveling to a "natural" area such as a grove, a field, or an empty urban lot, where they gather wood, light a campfire, roast potatoes and onions, and boil black coffee. As indicated by the name, which comes from the Yiddish "come and sit" or "join in," the *kumzitz* is a social event that promotes commensality and celebrates sharing, equality, and team spirit, with participants sitting around a fire, partaking equally in the food and drink (often also using the same dishes), and singing together.

The *kumzitz* is a classic liminoid event (Turner 2017) that evokes a temporary sense of *communitas* among those involved. It is also associated with simplicity and the rejection of petit-bourgeois values, as participants sit flat on the ground and share food and drink in common utensils, using their bare hands to handle the food and eat. The smell of smoke clinging to their clothes and hair after the event and the ashes and dust that stain their clothes and bodies further communicate proximity to nature, simplicity, and abandonment of petit-bourgeois standards of cleanliness. Campfires, coffee, and smoke are also associated with Arabness and Bedouinness, emphasizing the participants' direct relationship with the land and representing some sort of (alternative) Jewish autochthonous style. The traditional *kumzitz* did not include roasted meat, but the mythology around it (immortalized in books such as *The Anthology of Fibs,* by Dan Ben-Amotz and Netiva Ben-Yehuda) refers to stolen chicken and even sheep, whose flesh was cooked over the campfire.

Sacher Park Independence Day events clearly echo the *kumzitz* script: the participants go outdoors (in this case to a man-made park, which, like most groves and forests in Israel, was constructed as part of the Zionist project), light fires, boil coffee, eat with their hands (or from a pita bread or from coarse, disposable dishes), share the food, and sit in a circle while eating.

The gendered division of labor characteristic of the *kumzitz* script is also very reminiscent of the gendered roles I observed at Sacher Park. The *kumzitz* is a masculine affair. Men play the dominant roles, while the women are perceived as guests, considered too delicate to handle the roughness of outdoor life and in need of special attention and accommodation; they partake in the food and drink but are not expected to gather firewood or light the fire. These are masculine practices, which, as suggested by Robert Connell and James Messerschmidt (2005), always involve intense competition: who can carry the heaviest logs, who can build the right bonfire and make it burn big and tall, and who can light it with the fewest matches.

Despite the practical and structural similarities of these events, Sacher Park Independence Day barbecues also feature material and conceptual elements that are very different than those signified by the *kumzitz,* primarily the absolute centrality of the family rather than the peer group as well as the conspicuous consumption of both food and equipment, which emphasizes middle-class values, economic inequality, and competition for status and prestige. The most salient difference, however, is the importance of roasted meat in Independence Day barbecues.

### The American Barbecue

While *kumzitz* was the most popular cultural reference among my interlocutors, American influence and specifically an emulation of classic Fourth of July barbecues were mentioned by many of the celebrators I spoke with at Sacher Park. Some of the people I interviewed in contexts beyond the park, particularly Israelis of higher socioeconomic status, tended to emphasize the difference between American and Israeli barbecues and often indicated their identification with the American model. This was epitomized by an interlocutor who said, "In Ramat Hashron [an affluent and stereotypically Ashkenazi and elitist town near Tel Aviv], we have barbecue, not *mangal.*"

At Sacher Park in 2006, I met two American sisters who appeared to be Orthodox. They were sitting with their family members among the trees so as "not to trample the grass."[4] They told me that Israeli Independence Day barbecues were "copied from the Fourth of July." When I asked how the Israeli version was different from the American event, they explained that in the United States, they used to grill the meat on a gas barbecue in their backyard, whereas in Sacher Park, they use charcoal. It is important to note that one feature of Israeli *mangal* and particularly of Independence Day barbecues at Sacher Park is the strong scent of smoke and of gasoline, which is commonly used to ignite the charcoal. American-style gas grills are often used by more affluent Israelis at home, and they express wealth and sophistication.

The American sisters also pointed to culinary differences: "Here, people eat hummus, tahini, and pita bread, while in America they have hamburgers, hot dogs, and marshmallows." They were just about to roast hamburgers, hot dogs, chicken wings, and marshmallows—all distinctly American barbecue items—but planned on eating them "in a pita, not in a roll."

A comprehensive discussion of US-Israeli relations and the Americanization of Israeli society and culture is beyond the scope of this chapter, but two key points are relevant here. First, Israelis view Americanness as the epitome of Western sophistication and modernization (Ram 2004). Associating Israeli Independence Day practices with the Fourth of July imparts status and prestige to the event, a perception directly conveyed by a celebrator who pointed out that American barbecues were "posh and always done over gas," distinguishing them from the local low-tech charcoal grills most common at Sacher Park.

At the same time, the United States is often presented by both Israeli and American politicians as "Israel's best friend." As Israel's main political and military ally, key trade partner, and aid provider, the United States has a major role in ensuring Israel's independence and prosperity. Moreover, the largest Jewish community in the world is found in the United States, which is also home to the largest Israeli immigrant community. The Israeli adoption of American customs on Independence Day was therefore almost obvious. Indeed, one of the most visible manifestations of the growing American influence in Israel was the hanging of the American flag right next to the Israeli flag on cars in the days leading up to Independence Day during the first decade of the twenty-first century. On Independence Days from 2007 to 2009, there were car flags that had the Star of David on one side and the Stars and Stripes on the other. When the American flag is hoisted on Israel's Independence Day, the relationship between the United States and the State of Israel and its independence is extremely blatant.[5]

From a different perspective, US-Israeli relations might be understood not as bilateral and friendly but rather as hierarchical—the countries can be seen as having a patron and client relationship organized by a postcolonial framework (Frenkel and Shenhav 2003). Baruch Kimmerling, for example, argues that, "politically, the United States tends to view Israel as an extension of American Jewry, thus rendering Israel a kind of ethnic frontier of the United States" (1989, 275). This approach casts Israel as a kind of fifty-first state (many Israelis refer half-jokingly to this idea as the perfect solution to the country's woes). In any case, these different conceptions all underlie the Fourth of July serving as the model for Israel's Independence Day barbecues.[6]

## *Celebrating* Mizrahiyut

Jews who immigrated to Israel from the Middle East and North Africa were, up until the 1950s, termed *Spharadim* (Spanish) because of their praying style, which distinguished them from Eastern European Jews, who prayed in Ashkenazi style. In a gradual process, Iraqi, Egyptian, Kurdish, Moroccan, Tunisian, and Syrian Jews, as well as Balkan and Turkish Jews (who prayed in Sephardi style) and Yemeni Jews (who had their own unique style), were grouped into the new category of *Mizrahiim* ("orientals").

This social category was invented and implemented by members of the hegemonic Ashkenazi elite in their capacity as professionals who ran the state apparatuses. Ostensibly a neutral spatial designation, *mizrahiyut* actually served to hierarchically organize ethnic relations in the young nation-state (Khazzoom 2003). By relegating Middle Eastern, North African, and Balkan Jews to the chaotic, sentimental, traditional, and primeval "orient," European Jews (most of whom immigrated from Eastern Europe, which is set geographically to the east of North Africa), redefined themselves as Western and hence rational, orderly, modern, and civilized.

*Mizrahiyut* was understood as a combination of personality traits such as short temper and emotionality; limited intellectual capacity; behavioral patterns such as violence and loudness but also warmth and hospitality; and cultural preferences such as making pilgrimages to the graves of *Kdoshim* (saints), kissing the mezuzah, preparing lavish meals, and having a taste for Arab language, music, films, and food. This included preferences for hot and spicy food, Middle Eastern meal structures, and roasting meat *al ha'esh* or barbecuing.

The structural, practical, and culinary features of the annual pilgrimage to Rabbi Shimon Bar Yochai's grave in Meron and Baba Sali's grave in Netivot and of the Mimouna[7] celebrations (held at Sacher Park on the day that follows Passover) are strikingly similar to Sacher Park Independence Day barbecues. The countless barbecues held by Jews of Moroccan descent for a multitude of social reasons throughout the year also follow very similar organizing principles and behavioral patterns. Thus, even though Sacher Park Independence Day barbecues are civil events celebrating the nation-state, they are molded more than anything by ethnoreligious and culinary Mizrahi celebrations.

Yoram Bilu (1988, 307) describes the Moroccan Jewish *hillula* (death anniversary celebration) of Rabbi Shimon Bar Yochai,[8] which is held on Mount Meron next to the rabbi's grave, as such: "Many of them spend several days at Meron, camping in a picnic-like atmosphere on the forested slopes surrounding the site. They gather there in groups of kin and friends of all age levels, males and females together, feasting on slaughtered sheep, consuming large quantities of spirits, singing [and] dancing.... The ascent to the tomb, the spiritual climax of the celebration [*hillula*], takes but a negligible part of their time."

Bilu further explains that the celebrators are mainly preoccupied with eating and drinking and that some of them purchase lambs, goats, and calves, which are slaughtered on the spot and cooked "for the rabbi." This meal is seen by the participants as the culmination of the entire event, since it forges an immediate link between the celebrators and the holy rabbi, facilitated by the meal they "share" with him.

Tal Alon-Moses, Hadas Shadar, and Liat Vardi (2009), who focus on the spatial aspects of Baba Sali's[9] tomb, also recount how during his *hillula,* animals are slaughtered and barbecued on the spot, while Haim Yacobi (2008) points to the importance of what he terms "the feast shelter," a large pavilion built within the tomb compound, where the pilgrims feast over roast meat. In recent years, I attended these two mega-events and observed how barbecuing plays a key role in both. In fact, a new grove of trees was planted near Baba Sali's tomb-compound in Netivot,[10] and a designated picnic area was constructed, complete with benches and public barbecue stands.

Independence Day is ostensibly a civil holiday, significantly different from the religious pilgrimages to the sages' tombs at Netivot and Meron, but apart from the prayers, the lighting of candles, and other ritual practices (which, according to Bilu, are relatively inconsequential for the participants), the centrality of the barbecue makes them surprisingly similar to the Independence Day barbecues at Sacher Park.

Outdoor barbecues are also extremely popular among Mizrahi Jews in many other contexts, such as weekend meals, family gatherings, and picnics. The fact that the term used in contemporary Israel for barbecue events, *mangal* (which refers to the grilling utensil and the act of barbecuing, or *lemangel*), is an Ottoman Turkish term further contributes to the Mizrahi nature of the practice. Barbecuing meat, just like participating in *hillula* events, is perceived as a Mizrahi custom, even though Jews from many other ethnic groups, including Ashkenazi Jews, and certainly Jews born in Israel, partake in the practice.

A celebrator from the town of Sderot,[11] whose parents immigrated to Israel from Morocco in the 1950s, responded to my query regarding the centrality of barbecuing at Independence Day celebrations in Sacher Park with: "It's nothing special for us [Moroccan Jews].... We always have barbecues ... and also on Independence Day." Other Moroccan Jews I talked to explained that grilling meat is how they always party (a similar argument was voiced by South African and Argentinian Jews I interviewed at Sacher Park on various Independence Days: "This is how we always celebrate"). Thus, just as the *kumzitz* constitutes an Ashkenazi outdoor cultural script that has shaped Sacher Park barbecues, Mizrahi-style celebrations represent another cultural model for the Independence Day barbecues at the park, one that is actually much more influential than the Ashkenazi model.

Mizrahi religious, social, and cultural events, patterns, and preferences were looked down on and ridiculed by Ashkenazi elites up until the late 1970s and were therefore practiced in private spaces or in the Mizrahi-inhabited peripheries. The political shift of 1977, in which the predominantly Ashkenazi Israeli Labor Party lost its political hegemony to the conservative, Mizrahi-backed Likud, and the ensuing recognition and legitimization of Mizrahi culture meant that Mizrahi Jews could finally publically celebrate their ethnicity. It is little wonder, then, that barbecues became the dominant way for celebrating Independence Day in the mid-1980s, when increasing Mizrahi confidence and self-esteem moved barbecues from the periphery right into the heart of the country and right into its national day. The way I understand it, Israeli Independence Day barbecues at Sacher Park are celebrations of *mizrahiyut* in contemporary Israel.

Interestingly, Israeli Jews associate roasting meat not only with Mizrahi Jewry but also with Arab culture. In Israel, Mizrahi restaurants are cheap establishments offering pita bread, Mediterranean salads, and grilled meat, and the term "Mizrahi restaurant" is used interchangeably with "Arab restaurant." The Ashkenazi claim that there is an affinity and similarity between Mizrahi Jews and Arabs contributes to what Khazzoom (2003, 481) terms "the great chain of orientalism"—a process whereby members of the Israeli Ashkenazi Jewish elite actively block social ascendance of new minorities by tagging them as "oriental" and hence cultureless and inferior (Gerber 2003).

Identifying grilling meat with Arabness is intriguing and even paradoxical in the particular context of Israel's Independence Day—a day that celebrates Israel's victory over the Arabs in the 1948 war and that is celebrated right after Yom Hazikaron (Memorial Day), which commemorates those who have died in the wars waged against the Arabs. On the other hand, eating the food of the enemy—grilled meat, in this case, along with the masculinity and power it entails, might also be understood as expressing the total victory of the Israelis over their Arab enemies.

It should be noted that these three cultural scripts—the *kumzitz,* the Fourth of July barbecue, and Mizrahi celebratory grilled meat feasts—do not contradict or exclude one another. In fact, when considered collectively, they help explain some of the popularity of these barbecues. They allow members of the various Israeli Jewish ethnicities and social classes to find a convenient point (or points) of reference without having to endorse all potential meanings. American celebrators at Sacher Park relate to their Americanness, point to the affinity between the United States and Israel, and enjoy the sense of superiority Americanness confers in Israel. A few meters away, a group of girls belonging to the Bnei Akivah religious youth movement describe the barbecue as an extension of the Palmach ethos. Next to them, some Moroccan Jews talk about "going outdoors" and "eating our food." It is the flexibility and multivocality (Turner 2017) that turn Sacher Park during Independence Day into an area that is particularly suitable for the articulation of diverse and even contradictory ideas and attitudes.

## GRILLING MEAT AT SACHER PARK

While the scholarly literature reviewed earlier refers mainly to red meat, and particularly beef, as the ultimate source of power and masculinity, the

5. *Grilling Meat*

celebrators at Sacher Park consume many types of animal flesh. Despite the large variety of meats and cuts, these barbecues retain a pretty consistent culinary structure and involve similar cooking and eating practices.

First, only men cook because, as I was told, "Only men can prepare meat properly." They ignite the charcoal, handle and fan the fire, and decide when to place the meat over the grill and when to remove it, season it, and serve it to the other celebrators. Many of the men I interviewed reported that they personally bought and prepared (marinated, skewered, seasoned, etc.) the meat for cooking.

Second, the order in which the various types of meat are grilled follows a simple logic: the cheaper and quick-cooking products (mainly processed fast-food items) are grilled before the slow-cooking and more expensive cuts. Sausages and chicken wings are put on the grill first, followed by hamburgers and kebabs. Skewered *pargiot* (spring chicken) comes next, and beef steaks and lamb chops are prepared last.

The common explanation for this culinary sequence is that the kids have to eat first "because they are hungry and cannot wait," and the women who must also be fed quickly, prefer skewered chicken or *pargiot* (which "the kids like too") because these meats are "soft." The men, who are busy barbecuing, serve meat to the children and women and are the last to join the feast, once the steaks are ready.

Thus, at Sacher Park barbecues, men take on the classic masculine provider role. This cooking and eating sequence reaffirms the Israeli tendency to prioritize children and reflects the predisposition of Israeli men to sacrifice themselves for their families—the master narrative of Independence Day and of Memorial Day, celebrated a day earlier. Both events emphasize the role played by the (predominantly male) soldiers who sacrificed their lives so that their wives and children could go on living in an independent state.

Yet this grilling order can be understood differently. First, the argument that children (and women) have to be fed quickly because "they can't wait" suggests that children and women are feeble and hardly able to control themselves. This would mean that men, who are able to restrain themselves and wait patiently for their share of grilled meat, are morally superior (see also Bourdieu 1984). Second, while beef is the symbolic and physical source of power and potency, women and children are fed chicken and inferior cuts of processed meat. So women and children are fed meat that is culturally and nutritionally perceived as inferior. And third, despite the claim that "children and women can't wait," the men barbecuing constantly eat bits and pieces of meat throughout the grilling process. Thus, in practice, the men at Sacher Park consume significantly larger quantities of meat than the women and children and hardly demonstrate any self-restraint or self-control, which are the proclaimed pretexts for their privilege when it comes to serving themselves superior cuts.

This culinary sequence expresses a hierarchy in which men are superior to women and children. Though it is a classic patriarchal hierarchy, it contradicts both the Israeli discourse that prioritizes women and children and the master narrative of Israeli Independence Day, which celebrates the self-sacrifice of male soldiers. The claim that children and women have privileged access to food because they eat first actually represents their social subordination: women and children cannot restrain themselves and therefore have to settle for inferior cuts, while the supposedly patient, upright men get the better meat.

Barbecued meat therefore represents masculine superiority in Israel, just as it does in many other cultures. However, the variety of meat types, including low-quality, mass-produced, processed meats and *pargiot*—the

6. *Steaks for the Men, Chicken for the Women, Sausages for the Kids*

most popular meat grilled at Sacher Park—hints at further layers of meaning when it comes to the power structures governing the event. If the power acquired by ingesting beef derives from the immense strength of the ox, consuming *pargiot* transfers weakness to the eater: chickens are small, vulnerable birds, and *pargiot* are young chickens that haven't laid eggs yet, almost hatchlings, extremely vulnerable and weak. As indicated by slang, the male cock stands for virility and potency (Geertz 1973), while "chick" is a term for a young girl considered easy prey for men who covet her soft flesh.

Although a preference for poultry can be explained by health considerations (chicken is less fatty and consequently deemed healthier than red meat) or economic preferences (chicken is substantially cheaper than beef), my usually explained the popularity of *pargiot* by arguing that it is a "soft meat"—that is, less muscular. Thus, if muscular red meat stands for power and virility, chicken's soft, white flesh articulates weakness and vulnerability. The fact that beef is reserved for men further supports my argument that the power hierarchy described in the literature reviewed above is also true for the Israeli case: beef is considered suitable for men, while chicken, specifically young chicken, is served to women and children because the flesh of this meat is "soft."

Although my interviewees didn't say that chicken is less fortifying or nourishing than beef, their actual eating practices chart a power structure made up of two parallel systems: children, women, and men versus sausages, chicken, and beef. Their references to masculine restraint and to women's inability to deal with steaks as well as their allusions to the masculinity and acted-out sexuality of women who insist on eating steaks emphasize the fact that beef is empowering while chicken is not.

*Pargiot* also represent Israeliness in another intriguing way. Yehuda Avazi, a famous Israeli restaurateur, started the practice of using the term *pargiot* for the large, deboned thighs of mature chickens. Thus, the most popular type of meat at Sacher Park is actually a bluff, or, in Israeli terms, a *combina,*[12] as it is the meat of old chickens disguised as that of young chickens. *Pargiot* is emblematic of the Israeli tendency to cut corners and shortchange, which in modern Hebrew is fondly termed *letachmen,* a word that implies cheating, but with a clever twist.

The widespread ingestion of processed meats (kebabs, hamburgers, and sausages, usually mass-produced, made of inferior meat, and diluted with water, flour, and vegetable protein), the relatively limited amounts of beef, and the fact that many opt to grill imitation products (such as "chicken steak"), raise doubts about the symbolic power embedded in the meat eaten at Sacher Park. If, as the anthropological literature suggests, the thick and bleeding steak represents masculinity, potency, and power, then chicken wings, industrial hamburgers, and particularly spring-chicken skewers symbolize weakness and vulnerability, or possibly an ambivalent sense of power and weakness.


## GETTING A GOOD SPOT: THE
## ORGANIZATION OF SPACE

While grilling meat is the professed purpose of Independence Day barbecues, another salient characteristic of the Sacher Park event is the spatial organization and particularly the constant struggle over getting a "good spot." As in Ben Shemen Forest, Tel Aviv's Charles Clore Park, and the Angels Forest near Kiryat Gat, thousands upon thousands of Israelis congregate in the fairly limited area of Sacher Park, making for a congested human mass shrouded in smoke, sweat, gasoline fumes, the scent of charred meat, and the loud sounds of music and heated conversations.

It is important to note that despite common perceptions, many of the parks in Israel are virtually deserted on Independence Day, as people tend to congregate in very particular places (mainly those mentioned above). On Independence Day 2006, a radio newscast reported that Ben Shemen Forest was completely full by noontime, while the nearby Britannia Park was empty. Celebrators were therefore instructed by the police to drive to the latter. That afternoon, while driving past Britannia Park, I noticed that it was still fairly empty while the roads to Ben Shemen Forest were heavily congested. Time and again, I observed that celebrators actually preferred locations that were known to be crowded on Independence Day.

At first, I thought that these gatherings were chaotic and lacked any organizing principles, but I gradually realized that they were more than just crowded human masses. In fact, the gatherings at Sacher Park were organized according to internal rules that were clearly familiar to regular participants and immediately imposed on newcomers. These rules were related to the organization of space and to its division among the participants, who were primarily looking for a "good spot," which was an object of desire, admiration, envy, and controversy, because occupying such a spot connoted seniority, experience, diligence, organizational skills, and, above all, power.

A good barbecue spot at Sacher Park is defined by several parameters, first and foremost being shade. Independence Day is celebrated in late April or early May—a fairly hot season—and shade is scarce at Sacher Park. Located along a wide boulevard that serves as the main traffic artery into Jerusalem, the park is divided into two elongated lawns surrounded by thin strips of trees. The areas around the trees at the edges of the lawns offer the ideal combination of shade and grass. The northern area, closest to the main access route and the parking areas, is considered best, mainly because the celebrators do not have to carry their equipment over a long distance.

Another parameter, extremely important in the Middle East, is access to water. The park has a limited number of water fountains, which the celebrators use for drinking, cooking, and washing dishes. The areas near the fountains are therefore the most sought after. A "good spot" is therefore a shaded area on the lawn that is close to a parking space and to a water source.

Some of the celebrators, mainly regulars with large families who require considerable space for their equipment, arrive early in the morning or even on Independence Day Eve, right after Memorial Day celebrations, in order to *litfos makom* (grab a spot). Grabbing a spot is done by fencing off or otherwise demarcating the desirable space. Those who arrive on Independence Day Eve use thick ropes or tarpaulin sheets that they tie to trees or to metal poles they plant in the grass. This preliminary fencing creates a dilemma, since light or ambiguous barriers such as ropes may be ignored or removed, but massive barriers may be vandalized or even stolen.

Though only a few celebrators reserve a spot the night before, many regular participants send an advance guard early in the morning on Independence Day. A sixty-seven-year-old I spoke to told me: "The objective is to come early . . . to grab a spot. I arrive early with my truck. We are fifty people from my side of the family alone—daughters and grandchildren. We come every year and get a spot there. . . . But this year, someone came at night and reserved it—we let them be." Another family came at 5 a.m.: "Our dad, may he rest in peace, used to come early, and now we come [early]." They found a spot in the shade close to the road and built a large pavilion with a metal frame. Once the structure was built, they marked their territory with adhesive tape and went home to rest, "leaving a guard behind."

As early as 6 a.m. on Independence Day, many of the preferable areas are marked off with ropes, plastic sheets, or colorful tape. Those with large amounts of equipment unload it from their vehicles and use chairs and other items to mark their territory. In 2007, one of these spaces was marked with thin ropes on which blown-up garbage bags were hung, while another area was marked with white and blue balloons (the colors of the national flag). Two spaces were marked with strings of small Israel flags. One was the huge camp of the International Evangelical Church, whose members are always among the most visible groups on Independence Day.

One of the interviewees, walking with her husband and son among the celebrators and observing these makeshift barriers, commented: "I'm a landscape architect, . . . and it is clear that demarcation is very important here." This being the case, the discourse around grabbing a spot is very central, and I overheard remarks such as: "These people came last night to grab a spot"; "Run quickly and grab a spot over there"; "Well done, Naor!" (to a child who ran ahead and grabbed a spot by standing in the shade of a tree, turning his own

7. *Meat, Masculinity, and the Frontier*

body into a demarcating element); "We have a big family, we need a lot of space"; and, *"Punct* [spot on], isn't it?" (a proud husband showing his wife a shaded spot on the grass, very close to the place where he parked his car illegally on the pavement). When I asked one of the celebrators why a territory has to be marked in advance, he replied: "That's the way Israelis are: they go to the beach, plant four stakes—and now this is ours and all trespassers beware."

The struggle for space naturally leads to friction and conflict. In the morning, people still try to keep some distance between spots, and whoever approaches too closely might be greeted with remarks such as, "There's plenty of room to spare! Why are you sitting right on our heads [*al harosh shelanu*]?" But later in the day, as it gets hotter, the park becomes more crowded, and the shade shrinks, people demand access to shade and start to crowd under the trees. Those who have demarcated their territories with light or heavy fencing are protected against such incursions, but those who have used chairs or bags often have to make concessions. Here are some illustrative quotes: "Your son invaded [*palash*] a territory that is not ours" (said a woman to her relative); "You can't just stand next to the car and say, 'This is our place'"; "They saved this spot for us"; and of course the ubiquitous, "We were here first."

In 2008, I witnessed an argument between an Ethiopian Jew,[13] who had used a rope to mark a space among the trees and then drove home to bring his family members, and men from three families who arrived later and divided the very same lot between themselves, ignoring the rope. When "the Ethiopian," as he was referred to by the other men, returned with his family, he claimed: "This area is mine because I put up a rope this morning." The encroachers denied that the area had been demarcated. The Ethiopian pointed at the rope, still hanging between the trees, but the response was: "Where were you all morning? Did you drive all the way to Tel Aviv to bring your family?" From where I was standing, I could hear the three men, who hadn't known each other previously, coordinating their versions of the story to refute the Ethiopian's claim. One of them approached him with language that combined familiarity ("Come here, bro") with a threat ("Come here and I'll kick your ass," while smiling and hugging him tightly) and offered him an adjacent sunny space. While his family members began looking for another spot, the Ethiopian man kept insisting: "We will go, but don't say I wasn't here first."

Beyond grabbing a spot, the other distinct characteristic of space management at the park had to do with equipment. While some celebrators settled for a small portable grill, a picnic cooler, and a blanket, many brought impressive amounts of gear. The grill itself could be large, heavy, and sophisticated. Some celebrators used massive high-tech, gas-operated devices with metal covers and surfaces for meat, spices, and forks. Someone told me: "You just wait and see the show we're going to put up here. This year, we bought a gas grill especially [for the Independence Day barbecue]." Gas camping stoves were also very common, particularly for making coffee.

In addition to the cooking and storage equipment, which included grills, picnic coolers, cardboard boxes, and plastic bags, many of the celebrators brought tables and chairs; some of them were foldable, but others were garden furniture items. Others put up light tents, mainly for children to play in, as well as mattresses, sleeping bags, and mats. Many retailers offer Independence Day packages that include, for example, a tent, mattresses, and sleeping bags or a folding table and chairs. Many of the celebrators had brand new equipment of this type. Such items were usually cheap and low quality, and they tended to break on first use. In addition, many would bring playthings such as balls, Frisbees, backgammon boards, *nargila* (hookahs), mobile audio and video players, and musical instruments, such as goblet drums and guitars.

Some encampments boasted pavilions with extensive equipment. In 2009, at what was consistently the largest camp I saw during the period of research, built yearly around one of the fountains (thus obtaining sole possession of a public source of water), I observed dozens of chairs, several tables of various sizes, two large grills, a gas stove, vegetable crates, picnic coolers, four sofas, and a large TV operated by a portable generator.

Scholars of the Israeli backpacking phenomenon[14] point to the extreme importance of equipment in the discourse and practice of young travelers. Yotam Jacobson (1997), Daria Maoz (1999), and Chaim Noy (2003) repeatedly emphasize the salience and importance of *tziud* ([traveling] gear), including backpacks, cameras, sleeping bags, mattresses, portable gas stoves, and a large variety of other practical paraphernalia, from "fixing kits" to drug implements.

The centrality of these items in Israeli society is derived from the direct relationship between mandatory military service and the so-called Great Trip, which is traditionally taken after completing military service. The two spheres influence each other: the military obsession with equipment and preparedness shapes backpackers' discourse and gear, while high-end backpacker equipment is coveted by many soldiers for military use. Israeli backpacker stores cater to soldiers and increasingly blur the two spheres (one of the largest retailers of camping gear is even called Ricochet). As already mentioned, many of the items used on Independence Day are cheap versions of backpacking or military gear, and the use of these products suggests the influence of military and backpacker patterns on Israeli daily practices.

## ALONE TOGETHER

Evidently, Independence Day celebrations at Sacher Park are not as chaotic as they seem and in fact follow clear cultural rules. At this point, I would like to suggest that one of the main principles that arranges and governs these events is that of being *levad beyahad*, or "alone together," a term suggested by Rina Shapira and David Navon (1991) in their analysis of the huge popularity of cafés in Israel. They suggest that the popularity of cafés stems from the Israeli tendency to prefer being alone together to simply being alone. They attribute this preference to the blurring of boundaries between private and public space, which helps individuals deal with the social and structural superiority of the collective in Israel. The café, they argue, enables Israelis to be together with other Israelis while maintaining a bubble of privacy.

This bubble is transparent, penetrable, and elastic, enabling café patrons to engage or disengage with the public at will, depending on the situation and context. As an example of this dynamic, the authors describe the moment when the siren goes off to commemorate the fallen on Memorial Day, when the boundaries of the private bubbles of the patrons, and the bubble containing the café itself, burst and those present at the café join the national space for a predetermined period of time—as long as the siren sounds (Shapira and Navon 1991, 114).

Sacher Park Independence Day barbecues accommodate a similar dynamic. Many celebrators reported that the event was a place of togetherness (*beyahad*), where "all the people of Israel" celebrate. In 2006, for example, two sisters told me that they had originally wanted to spend the day with their extended families at Ein Hemed (a popular park near Jerusalem) because they wanted to be "alone and quiet. . . . But the brothers wanted to come here, like all the rest of the people of Israel [*a'm Israel*]." Members of a family from Jerusalem's Ramot neighborhood, whose house borders a large wood, said they preferred Sacher Park because "where we live, by Ramot Forest, it's isolated." Many newcomers (primarily immigrants from Ethiopia, France, and the United States) told me that they came to Sacher Park to be "together with everyone" and to "connect with the people of Israel."

The crowding at Sacher Park has a significant explanation: on the most collective day of the Israeli calendar, the celebrators wanted to experience collective Israeliness. However, as in the Tel Aviv café studied by Shapira and Navon, the relationship between individuals and the collective at Sacher Park was complex and dynamic and not just a simple desire to experience the shared holiday together. First, the participants clearly challenged the park's designation as a collective and public space by carving and dividing it among themselves. One of the interviewees remarked: "They come for togetherness but immediately put up a fence." Second, the tension at Sacher Park is not only between the individual and the collective (as it is in the café) but also between families. The dominant social unit at the park was the extended family, with nuclear families second, and relatively few peer groups. Thus, unlike the Tel Aviv café patrons described by Shapira and Navon, extended families (not individuals) crowded into Sacher Park to be alone together while competing over temporary territories.

The desire to be alone together on Independence Day was one of the main reasons people came to Sacher Park, but it was also a key source of tension. This tension was managed by rules of conduct that generally prevented overt conflict. Nevertheless, every year I witnessed incidents of verbal and physical violence relating to "good spot" issues, which arose when territorial claims conflicted with the delicate balance between being alone and being together.

## TOWER AND STOCKADE

While the principle of being alone together organized the relations between those celebrating Independence Day at Sacher Park, it is the Tower-and-Stockade (*Homa u'Migdal*) script that organized their handling of space. Before I turn to explaining the term "Tower and Stockade," I will briefly discuss the handling of space by the white settlers who colonized the United States and the other modern colonial and immigrant nation-states discussed earlier as "barbecue nations": Brazil, Argentina, Uruguay, Australia, New Zealand, and South Africa.

A main characteristic of these countries was their sparse frontiers (Kimmerling 1989): vast border zones perceived as no-man's-lands and thinly populated by indigenous populations. To colonize these enormous territories, white European colonial settlers claimed ownership over huge stretches of land by fencing them in as herding grounds for their cattle. These men were essentially lone rangers, each driving his cattle into the empty wilderness, away from the other men, to claim his own territory. The essential tool and emblematic symbol of these settlers was the firearm, used to defend themselves from forces of nature (predators) and culture ("Indians" and other natives, as well as fellow colonizers competing over the same land and resources). The right to self-defense later became the basis for the controversial Second Amendment to the United States Constitution, and the rifle over the fireplace, in its various forms, remains a symbol of armed individualism, land ownership, and masculinity. These constitutive concepts were weaved into national day barbecues in these societies.

In prestate Israel (when the area was under Ottoman and British rule), Zionist Jewish settlers operated in a very different reality, that of a dense frontier (Kimmerling 1989): a tiny area with limited arable land and few water sources, densely populated and intensely farmed, where the indigenous population outnumbered the new settlers. Here, Kimmerling (1989) explains, spatial conditions shaped a form of colonization that was very different from that devised for the sparse frontiers of the New World: well-organized groups of settlers used money and/or force to claim small territories ("grab spots") and form enclaves. Due to the low quality of these lands and the serious security threats, lone rangers would not have survived (the few that did try were often killed and subsequently mythologized, as in the case of Giorah Zeid) and were thus replaced by collective and communal forms of settlement such as the kibbutz and *kvutza* (communal settlement, literally "group"), which proved more effective in managing the limited resources and handling security threats.

The resistance of the indigenous Palestinians to Jewish colonization meant that special security arrangements were required. Gradually, a militarized colonization pattern evolved, which involved spotting available land and then quickly settling and fortifying it. During the Arab revolt of 1936–9, this form reached its ultimate refinement with prefabricated houses and fortifications transported in the dead of night, set up within hours by volunteers mobilized for that purpose, and settled immediately. This form of settlement was termed Tower and Stockade after its most visible features: a watchtower and a defensive fence, essential for the survival of these enclaves.

Although only a few dozen communities were built during the Tower and Stockade period of 1936–9, this script continued to be the practical and symbolic model for Zionist settlements after the establishment of the State of Israel (Shenhar and Katriel 1992) and is representative of the logic and practice of Zionist colonization since the late nineteenth century. This script culminated in the Jewish settlement of the territories occupied in the 1967 war, in which similar organizational, material, and ideological strategies were employed, although the state played a complex and paradoxical role as both sponsor and enemy.

One of the paradoxes inherent to the Tower-and-Stockade script lies in the constant tension between the Zionist ambition of rectifying the Jewish diasporic condition by settling and farming Palestine (Liebman and

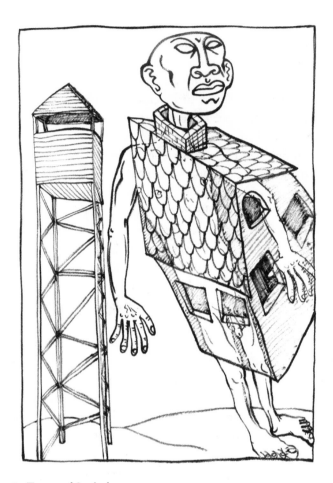

8. *Tower and Stockade*

Don-Yehia 1983, 4) and the light construction used to actually build the different forms of settlements: Early Zionist communities used tents; Tower-and-Stockade kibbutzim used prefabricated wooden structures; tents and tin shacks were used to house the mass migration of the early 1950s; settlers in the occupied territories in the West Bank—particularly in locations not sanctioned by the state—use caravans and other mobile structures that can be rebuilt quickly if demolished. During the 1990s, state authorities readopted the light construction approach to house the massive wave of immigrants from the former Soviet Union, and it was used again in 2005 to temporarily house Jewish settlers evacuated from the Gaza Strip back to Israel. Recently, Tower-and-Stockade methods have been used by *no'ar hagva'ot,* the unruly "hilltop youth," who challenge both the authority of the state and that of the established settlers' leadership and terrorize the Palestinians. By and large, the paradox lies in the tension between the Zionist ideology, which seeks stability and grounding as countermeasures to the diasporic experience, and its enactment in patently unstable structures.

My data on the spatial practices at Sacher Park indicates that "spot grabbing" follows the logic of the Tower-and-Stockade system: Israelis arrive to the park early, sometimes in the dead of the night; identify free space; quickly move into the space and fill it with portable equipment; fence the space off to claim it; and, finally, express a will to fight for their newly acquired territory while denying counterclaims to what is essentially public space.

I do not argue that this is a conscious process with overt or declared symbolic meanings. In fact, the term Tower and Stockade was never mentioned by any of the participants I spoke to at Sacher Park Independence Day barbecues. I do argue, however, that the celebrators follow a cultural script formulated during more than a century of Jewish colonization of Israel, which Israelis are continually exposed to as practitioners (pioneers or settlers) or as media and culture consumers. Grabbing a good spot at Sacher Park is not a conscious enactment of the Zionist myth but rather a self-evident practice organized in familiar, taken-for-granted, and nonreflexive cultural molds. The participants do not state, and, as far as I can tell, do not think that they are reenacting the Tower-and-Stockade operations of the 1930s but see themselves simply as grabbing a spot according to the Israeli custom. Nevertheless, their spatial practices are clearly representative of this formative Zionist pattern.

## MEAT, POWER, AND AMBIVALENCE

While the literature stresses the liaison between meat, masculinity, and power, the variety of meats consumed in Sacher Park, and particularly the huge popularity of spring chicken, raises questions about the cultural meanings of Israeli barbecues and exposes a sense of weakness and vulnerability. Similar claims have been made by Yael Zerubavel (1994) in her work on the Masada myth and by Jackie Feldman (2008) in a study of the trips of Israeli high school students to Auschwitz. Both analyze the cultural processes that structure feelings of weakness and vulnerability among Israeli Jews in recent decades. Both show how the constructed experience is not one of absolute weakness but rather of ambivalence, with power and potency interwoven with vulnerability and feebleness. This ambivalence is perfectly symbolized by the spring chicken skewers: ingesting meat connotes power and control, but this particular type of meat—succulent, "feminine," and vulnerable— is limited in its potential to charge eaters with strength. Sacher Park barbecues are not celebrations of power but rather ambivalent events in which potency and power are inseparably mixed with feebleness and victimization.

In the discussion of space, I emphasized two Israeli organizing principles that arrange the negotiation of space at Sacher Park: the desire to be alone together and the Tower-and-Stockade strategy. The first is about relation-ships among Israeli Jews, exposing the tension between the desire to be a part of the collective in the most important national moment of the year and the constant efforts of the participants to demarcate boundaries between them-selves and others. The second reflects the relationship between Jews and Arabs in the shared space they occupy and serves to explain the practice of spot grabbing. Oddly enough, although the celebrators at Sacher Park are almost exclusively Jewish, they follow the Tower-and-Stockade script of claiming territory in a land densely populated by the Palestinian Arabs. Spatial conduct in the park sheds light on inherent tensions between Jews and Arabs, particularly on the contradiction between the Jewish Israeli and Palestinian parallel claims for total ownership of the land. It also exposes the constant tension between the desire for stability and the practice of transi-ence in Israeli society.

The huge popularity of the Independence Day barbecues at Sacher Park derives precisely from the complex and polysemic nature of such events. Meat grilling en masse enables the celebrators to identify with a variety of cultural ideas and points to complex manifestations of power and hierarchy. At the same time, the event facilitates the expression of tensions between the indi-vidual and the collective and between different Jewish ethnic and socioeco-nomic groups. It emphasizes the centrality of the family as the most signifi-cant social unit and as an alternative to other collectives that used to be very central in Jewish Israeli society. The struggle for space between Jews and Palestinians is also reenacted on a day that celebrates Israel's victory over the Palestinians. As such, these apparently trivial barbecues encompass many of the most pressing issues and dilemmas of contemporary Israel.

Prior to Independence Day 2010, a friend who lives in a rural community informed me that someone (he did not know who) had placed an outdoor installation on a traffic island at the entrance to the community. The anonymous artist had nailed a small, synthetic-grass carpet to the asphalt, set a barbecue on it, and stuck a small flag, of the type commonly hung on car windows in the days leading up to Independence Day, among the coals. Near the flag, there was a sign saying "Occupied!"

This installation clearly interrelates with many of the ideas elaborated in this chapter, primarily the relations between Israel's Independence Day, grilled meat, spatial organization, and spot grabbing. It also touches on the key Zionist ethos of "blooming the wilderness"—the attempt to acculturate space by implanting Western European elements, such as grass, into the oriental landscape (Feige 2009)—as well as the Israeli dream of a private lawn in a densely populated country. The resolute claiming of this tiny space is an elegant illustration of Shapira and Navon's (1991) argument that the boundaries between private and public in Israel are blurred and that the state's claim over its own citizens produces a counterclaim, with many Israelis perceiving of public space as their own. This is how a public traffic island can become a private barbecue site.

The installation emphasizes the struggle for space characteristic not only of the celebrations at Sacher Park but also of a variety of public events in Israel. A kibbutz member who attended an event at which I presented my research on Independence Day barbecues approached me and pointed out that my description of grabbing a good spot at Sacher Park and the way it was occupied was "a precise description of what happens at our swimming pool on weekends." Thus, though Sacher Park barbecues are not representative, due to the socioeconomic status, ethnic origin, and religious affiliation of many of the participants, the celebrators at the park behave similarly to bathers at a kibbutz pool—their almost complete opposites in Israel's socioeconomic structure. This supports my claim that the social mechanisms and organizing principles described in this chapter are far from exceptional and can be observed in many other public arenas.

The artwork is also quite cynical. Grilling meat on a traffic island is a familiar local grotesque symbolic of the sweaty, loud, and exploitative redneck Israeli who does not recognize other people's rights to the public space he appropriates. The flag is a mocking reference to a part of the Israeli

9. *Occupied*

founding myth: the heroic act of hoisting the flag over occupied landmarks, such as over the Wailing Wall in the Old City of Jerusalem in 1967. Finally, the composition as a whole seems like a miniature model of settlements built in recent years (on both sides of the Green Line, Israel's border with its Arab neighbors until the 1967 war), with their cubical houses, synthetic lawns, security fences, and yellow electric gates—all of which shout "Occupied!" but at the same time communicate a sense of insecurity and transience.

Importantly, this installation was located at the entrance to a community whose cultural and socioeconomic characteristics are closer to the abovementioned kibbutz than to the celebrations at Sacher Park (which were described as "oriental, conservative, and of low socioeconomic status"). Nevertheless, the artist clearly assumed that the inhabitants would identify the cultural codes embedded in the installation and probably directed his or her social critique at them (otherwise there would have been very little point in placing the installation at the entrance to this particular community).

Thus, just like at *al ha'esh* events at Sacher Park, the installation is not only about the explicit links between grilled meat, national independence, masculinity, territory, and power but also about the significant yet implicit ambivalence concerning power in contemporary Israel.

THREE

———

*Why We Like Italian Food*

JOURNALISTS GIL GUTKIN AND SHIRI MAYMON wrote in 2015: "If aliens visited Israel, they would be positive that pizza is our national food. There is no neighborhood in Israel without at least a single pizzeria, and usually more."[1] In November 2015, the Jerusalem section of the entertainment guide Achbar Ha'Ir[2] listed 39 restaurants under the heading "Italian" and 17 more under "Pizza," coming to 56 food venues specializing in Italian food. In comparison, there were only 13 restaurants under the heading "Asian," and this included Chinese, Thai, Japanese, and Pan-Asian restaurants. The only category of ethnic food that came close to Italian was Mizrahi (see chapter 2), with 39 entries. These, however, included Iraqi Jewish, Moroccan Jewish, and Yemeni Jewish restaurants as well as Lebanese and Palestinian food venues. *Achbar Ha'Ir*'s Tel Aviv list reported 118 Italian restaurants and 50 pizza parlors (totaling 168), 58 Asian food venues, and 112 places serving Mizrahi food including falafel and hummus stands. Despite the major demographic, socioeconomic, and cultural differences between Israel's two largest and most important cities, Italian food dominates the culinary scene in both.

The telephone directory Dapei Zahav (Yellow Pages)[3] presented a larger number of food venues, but the ratios were similar: there were 1735 Italian restaurants and pizza parlors listed nationwide in November 2015 but only 492 "Asian Restaurants" (including Chinese, Thai, Japanese, and Pan-Asian venues). Once again, the only other category of ethnic cuisine featuring a comparable number of food venues was *mizrahiot* (Mizrahi), with 422 restaurants and 811 venues serving falafel, hummus, and shawarma, numbering 1233 food venues in total.[4]

The dominance of Italian food in Israel is further evidenced by the numerous ice cream parlors serving Italian gelato and the ubiquitous espresso bars serving Italian-style coffee. Moreover, menus at Israel's most popular culinary establishments, *batei kafe* (coffeehouses, or cafés)—of which there are almost 2,000 nationwide according to Dapei Zahav—routinely feature a substantial number of Italian dishes, such as pasta, pizza, mozzarella salad, and the like. And although I couldn't locate authoritative quantitative data regarding domestic preparation and consumption of Italian food in Israel, during my more than fifteen years of food-oriented ethnographic research, I couldn't help but notice how pasta, pizza, and, more recently, espresso machines have become extremely popular in Israeli domestic kitchens. So why is Italian food so popular in Israel?

When I began inquiring about this overwhelming preference for Italian food, the most common explanation was that Italian food is tasty. I received responses such as "For me, Italian food is simply the tastiest" or "Israelis love Italian food because it is tastier than any other food." While these statements clearly expressed the interlocutors' personal feelings about Italian food, one of the main contributions of the anthropology of food is the understanding that taste is culturally constructed (Bourdieu 1984; Mennell 1991; Lupton 1996). In Mary Douglas's (1978, 59) words: "Nutritionists know that the palate is trained, that taste and smell are subject to cultural control." The fact that Israelis like Italian food because they find it tasty does not explain its popularity. Therefore, the question should be why do Israelis find Italian food so tasty?

Most of the data presented in this chapter was collected during 2011 and 2012 in anticipation of a conference titled "Italian Food: Fact and Fiction" that took place in Perugia, Italy, in 2012. I conducted seven in-depth interviews with owners, chefs, and managers of restaurants specializing in Italian food in Israel. I conducted five additional in-depth interviews with owners and managers of pizzerias. Some of these food venues were located in Tel Aviv and Jerusalem, while others were in smaller towns. The interviews always included questions regarding the culinary biography of the interviewees and their own relationship with Italian food as well as their take on the popularity of Italian food in Israel. The interviews lasted one to two hours and were recorded in writing.

I made a point of ordering food and having a meal in each of these food venues, either right after the interview or on another occasion. These meals helped me expand the abstractions and relatively thin descriptions I collected during the interviews with lived culinary experience, giving the food a change to "speak for itself" and allowing me to make comparisons between what the chefs had in mind, the dishes they produced, and the ways in which these dishes were consumed and understood by their clients. I collected further data from numerous conversations I had in different contexts regarding the popularity of Italian food in Israel.

This study of Italian food in Israel may seem to be the least ethnographic of the research projects that make up *Food and Power* in the sense that much of the data is verbal and textual rather than material and embodied. Yet though the participant observation I carried out is limited in time and scope, it made a significant contribution to my understanding of the popularity of Italian food in Israel, mainly because it exposed the discrepancies between the intentions, ideologies, and insights chefs conveyed during interviews and the actual preparation, presentation, and consumption of their food, which often embedded other ideas. Most importantly, it was intriguing and insightful to realize that customers at these restaurants had their own interpretations of the food and context, which further added to my understanding of the complexity of the phenomena.

## ITALIAN FOOD IN ISRAEL

Like most so-called ethnic cuisines (Van den Berghe 1984), Italian food emigrated from Italy along with Italian immigrants looking for a better future. Italian restaurants were first established in Italian migration centers in the New World and Australia, such as New York, Chicago, Buenos Aires, and Sydney (Gabaccia and Pilcher 2011; Poe 2001; Schlüter 2000; James 2004). Like other ethnic restaurants opened by first generation immigrants, these venues catered mostly to fellow immigrants "from the old country" who wanted to eat the food they had eaten at home at prices they could afford (that is, cheap), hang out with their compatriots, speak their language, and soothe their homesickness, if only for a while.

Though restaurateurs and clients initially wanted to replicate the dishes, tastes, and aromas they were used to back home, the food was gradually modified for various reasons. First, there was the problem of specific ingredients, many of which were unavailable and had to be replaced by similar, but not identical, local products. Cooking techniques also changed due to necessity or comfort (e.g., wood-fired pizza ovens were replaced with electric ones) as well as sanitary regulations. Further changes were made to accommodate the palates and eating manners of non-Italian clients, both other European settlers and members of other ethnic groups who arrived later in the New World and wanted to consume Italian food but on their own terms.

In what Ivan Light and Edna Bonacich (1991) describe as characteristic of immigrant entrepreneurship, members of other ethnic groups started cooking and serving Italian food, too. Lawrence Lovell-Troy (1990), for example, shows that Greek immigrants in Chicago relied on their Mediterranean ethnicity as an asset that enhanced their success in the pizza business. One of my interviewees, an Israeli who owned a pizza parlor in Chicago, told me, "Pizzas in Chicago were an Israeli business," a phenomenon defined by Light and Bonacich (1998) as an "enclave economy," where members of certain ethnicities specialize in specific market niches that are not necessarily related to their ethnicity but where specific contexts, accumulated experience, and expanding social networks facilitate economic success.

Through these various processes, Italian food became an essential and extremely common and popular component of American cuisine (Mintz 1996) and, to a lesser extent, of Argentinian and Australian cuisines. Pizza is now just as much (and perhaps more) an icon of New York as it is of Rome or Naples.

The arrival of Italian food in Israel was different. The number of Italians (Jewish and non-Jewish) who have migrated to Israel over the years is relatively small, and the Italian Jewish community in the country has remained tiny, with an estimated three thousand members and a total of ten thousand descendants in 2012.[5] These migrants, most of whom arrived after the Holocaust, in the early years of Israel's independence, did not establish Italian restaurants, perhaps because they were not involved in catering in Italy to begin with and probably because they had enough economic, cultural, and symbolic capital to find more lucrative jobs.[6] In any case, Italian food did not arrive in Israel with Italian immigrants as it did in other parts of the world and as other ethnic cuisines have arrived in Israel up until recently.[7]

Food journalist Ronit Vered writes that the first pizzeria in Israel was established in Tel Aviv in 1957 by food entrepreneur Alex Schor, who was "the first to open a modern, designer fast food venue with a flashy neon sign. The highlight was Italian New York pizza, and crowds flocked and waited patiently for the blazing triangles" (Vered 2012, 71). Netanela Calo, in her master's thesis on Italian food in Israel, writes:

> Italian culinary patterns penetrated the Israeli food field through the modification of the American-Italian culinary repertoire. American culinary

patterns were first legitimized and adopted in Israel through contact agents [who] mediated between the Israeli taste preferences and demands and American culinary patterns. Imported American patterns and products were adopted and modified to suit Israeli taste and market demands. Only later did other contact agents approach Italian sources directly and import culinary products, patterns, and images straight from Italy. (2005, 12)

The Anashim Israel website, on its extensive page on Italian food in Israel,[8] concurs that Italian restaurants became popular in Israel during the late 1960s mainly as a consequence of the increasing influence of American popular culture after the 1967 war. The site quotes food journalist Ruth Heffer, who in 1972 stated of the newly opened Broadway Pizza: "It is hard to say that the pizzas here are similar to those eaten in Italy: they have the same taste and aroma of the pizzas made by Italians for Americans in the United States." Nathan Dunevich (2012, 354–356), in his review of Tel Aviv's culinary history, writes how during the early 1970s, a few pizzerias with the name Pizza Domino sprung up. The first was opened by Eitan Zehavi, who "borrowed" the name from the American franchise some twenty years prior to its official arrival in Israel. The other pizzerias, jealous of Zehavi's success, simply used the same name.

Some of my interviewees, especially pizzeria owners, explained their own involvement with Italian food as a consequence of their experiences in America: they left Israel for the United States for different, mainly economic, reasons and somehow became involved in the pizza business there, often as employees in pizzerias owned by other Israelis, in line with Light and Bonacich's (1998) "enclave economy" theory mentioned earlier. On returning to Israel, they set up pizzerias that were as similar as possible in structure and content to those they were familiar with in America.

Dapei Zahav's website comes in handy again, as it shows that a remarkable number of Israeli pizzerias have American names, such as New York Pizza, Chicago Pizza, Pizza Time, Big Pizza, or simply USA Pizza or American Pizza. In fact, such names are second only to Italian names, like Rimini or Sirocco, though the latter are also typical of Italian food venues in America and may thus be replicating the American model as well. It is important to note that the largest pizza franchises in Israel, Domino's and Pizza Hut, are American (and note that Domino is presumably an Italian name, while "hut" has American connotations).

A second wave of Italian food, including more traditional sit-down restaurants as well as stores offering an array of imported products such as pasta, cheese, and tomato paste, arrived in Israel during the late 1980s. Oren, the chef-owner of Trattoria, a small Italian restaurant located in a rural area in southern Israel, recounted how Italian food lost much of its popularity in Israel during the 1980s "but made a comeback, now in much better quality." This new and improved Italian food, however, was quite different from its predecessor. The main champions of the cuisine were now Israelis who had lived in Italy (mainly as students), experienced Italian food, and, according to their own testimonies, fallen in love with it. When they returned to Israel, they set up Italian restaurants and other food-oriented businesses. While the food writer and gourmand Dr. Eli Landau (who studied medicine in Italy) was probably the most influential spokesman of this trend, the classic proponent is Rafi Adar, the owner of Tel Aviv's Pronto.[9]

Adar, a filmmaker who studied cinematography in Rome, opened Pronto in 1988 to fulfill his dream of "set[ting] up a little corner of Italy" where he would serve Italian, and specifically Roman, food. This restaurant is reputed by Israeli connoisseurs, food critics, and foodies as well as Italian tourists to serve the best Italian food in the country. Food journalist Hila Alpert wrote on the jacket of Adar's cookbook *Pronto: Ochel, Tarbut, Ahava* (Pronto: Food, culture, love): "For twenty years, Pronto has featured life according to Rome: wine, food, and music are all cooked into a Roman scene as it broils in Rafi Adar's head" (Adar 2010). Yet David Frankel, Pronto's acclaimed chef,[10] told me in an interview in 2012 that he was changing the menu because his mission as a chef was to "re-educate the Israeli palate and expose the clients to real Italian food and not to touristy-Italian food that comes from America," insinuating that Pronto had been importing American Italian food and American Italian culinary trends and innovations.

The fact that Italian food originally arrived from the United States is important for two reasons. First, American things are popular in Israel (see chapter 2), and they denote modernity, sophistication, and cosmopolitanism. Just as important, however, is the fact that Italian food was imported from the United States and, to a lesser extent, Italy mainly by Israelis and not by Italian cultural agents. This means that Italian food had no local history or canon in Israel and has thus been highly susceptible to modification and adaptation. Rafi Grosglik and Uri Ram (2013) make a similar argument regarding Chinese food in Israel. Imported during the 1970s via America by Israelis and completely unfamiliar and foreign at the time, Chinese food was modified at will according to local demands and constraints, making for a unique Israeli version.

Indeed, it was made clear by the chefs I interviewed that Italian food had been heavily modified in Israel. Frankel explained, "We adopted the ingredients and dishes suitable for the Israeli taste." Davide, the only Italian Jewish restaurateur I was able to locate, who had immigrated to Israel in the early 2000s from Italy and set up an Italian restaurant in a Jerusalem suburb, was blunter: "The food here has nothing to do with the food in Italy, except for the terms 'pasta' and 'pizza.' My daughters ask me, 'What is the relationship between Italian food and what you serve here?'"

## MODIFYING ITALIAN FOOD

My interviewees depicted various ways of modifying and adapting (American) Italian food to the preferences of their Israeli clientele. First and foremost, Italian ingredients were replaced, at least up until the 1990s, by products made in Israel, which were of different, and arguably inferior, taste: fresh and canned Italian tomatoes and tomato paste were substituted with local paste made from Israeli tomatoes, which, according to my interviewees, are not as sweet as Italian tomatoes; mozzarella and other Italian cheeses were initially unavailable and were replaced by local cheeses and cheese substitutes; fresh pasta was replaced by industrially produced products that were not made of durum wheat; and relatively expensive olive oil was substituted with cheap margarine and vegetable oil.

It should be noted that such modifications, the outcome of necessity rather than preference (as better ingredients were unavailable or prohibitively expensive), have not been used in upscale venues since the 1990s. It is much easier to find high-quality imported ingredients from Italy in Israel nowadays, and the substantial rise in the standard of living and the emergence of an upper-middle class have led to many Israelis having enough money to pay for these expensive products. When it comes to restaurants and pizzerias in the periphery (spatial and/or socioeconomic), however, the use of cheaper, inferior local products was still very common in 2015.

It is important to note that Israeli foodstuffs such as olive oil, artisanal cheeses, vegetables, and wines have become "good enough," to say the least, in recent years, with some considered world class and having achieved international recognition. Wood-fired brick ovens are increasingly common at higher-end Italian restaurants, further facilitating the preparation of high-quality Italian food. And when it comes to cooking criteria, despite complaints by chefs that Israelis still prefer overcooked pasta, al dente has gradually become the standard in both high-end venues and many home kitchens. Let me turn now to the cultural adaptations, which have less to do with availability of Italian ingredients and cooking techniques and more to do with Israeli social arrangements and demands.

## KASHRUT AND DAIRY DISHES

The most noticeable adaptation of Italian food to the Israeli culinary sphere has been its reworking to meet kashrut dietary laws. In their report on the Jewishness of Israelis, Charles Liebman and Elihu Katz (1997, 11) pointed out that, at the time of their study, about two-thirds of Israeli Jews reported eating kosher. As kosher food is so ubiquitous in Israel (most food products sold in Israel are kosher; purchasing kosher food is therefore the default), the authors suggest that a better indicator for observance would be the separation of meat and dairy utensils, which can only result from informed decision making and active praxis. Such separation was reported by 50 percent of Israeli Jews. Furthermore, 40 percent of the respondents reported strict observance of Halachic[11] kashrut rules, indicating that they opted for kosher food actively and reflexively.

Twelve years later, Guy Ben-Porat and Yariv Feniger (2009) reported that 70 percent of Israeli Jews ate kosher at home, while 50 percent stated that they eat kosher in all circumstances. To understand the implications of such an overwhelming preference for kosher food, think of a society where some 50 percent of the diners are vegetarian or vegan and imagine how this would shape the local culinary sphere. Ben-Porat and Feniger's findings suggest that although substantial secularization processes are clearly evident in Israel, so is religious intensification, with kashrut remaining an extremely important aspect of the Israeli food sphere.

In a survey carried out in 2006 by an Israeli tour operator in an attempt to map the culinary preferences of Israelis when traveling abroad, over 50 percent of respondents said that they preferred kosher food. Interestingly, 40 percent of those who identified as secular in the survey said they preferred kosher food while abroad. In line with Ben-Porat and Feniger's (2009) find-ings about the intensification of religious observance in Israel, most of those who defined themselves as observant in the survey were youngsters aged fifteen to twenty-four, 55 percent of whom stated that they would strictly observe kashrut when traveling abroad.[12] Self-reporting bias notwithstanding, these numbers are powerful indicators of kashrut's importance in Israel among both observant and non-observant Jews.

Over the years, food entrepreneurs and chefs repeatedly told me that kashrut is an extremely important aspect of the professional Israeli culinary sphere. A prominent chef went as far as to say: "The first decision to be made when opening a new restaurant is whether it will be kosher or not. It is more important than deciding whether you want to serve Chinese or French food or if you would like to do it in Tel Aviv or Jerusalem. Location, customers, working hours, prices, and dishes are just an outcome of the decision on kashrut."

It is important to keep in mind that the scope and actual practices of kashrut in Israel (and elsewhere) are hardly defined or agreed on. Food journalist Hagit Evron points out in an article dedicated to the culinary preferences in the Israeli periphery (defined in the article as "everywhere beyond Tel Aviv and Herzliya"—that is, most of the country) that kashrut is an extremely important factor.[13] However, she quotes chef Leon Alkalai saying that kashrut does not necessarily entail rigid Orthodox Halachic rules: "Pork is the main taboo, followed by the mixing of meat and milk, while seafood comes only at the end. In Eilat, for example, people [he was referring to Israeli tourists] eat seafood but avoid pork, while in Haifa, pork is eaten because the Yekes [Jews of German origin, many of whom live in Haifa] will not give up their bacon [*schinken*]." In the same article, entrepreneur Guy Peretz explained that a successful restaurant in Beer-Sheva that he was working with operated on Saturdays (which prevented it from getting an official kashrut certificate) but served only kosher meat and offered parve (prepared without meat or milk) desserts.

Kashrut in Israel is therefore more flexible, self-defined, and context dependent than what might be deducted from the statistical data presented by Liebman and Katz (1997) or Ben-Porat and Feniger (2009), which was formulated by applying rigid categories and binaries that do not allow for the communication of nuanced and delicate kashrut patterns. Just like the various definitions and flexible kashrut patterns common among American Jews (see also Deutsch and Saks 2008, 49–50), kashrut in Israel means different things to different people, with a substantial measure of flexibility even among subgroups that define themselves as strictly Orthodox or strictly Halachic[14].

Considering the importance of kashrut in Israel, it is of little wonder that Italian food was modified to follow kashrut guidelines. As suggested by Alkalai, pork is the main taboo and is not served in most Italian restaurants in Israel even though it is a staple of authentic Italian cuisine. The separation of meat and milk is the second most important kashrut consideration, but mixing meat and dairy is a prominent feature of Italian food. Pepperoni pizza and Bolognese sauce with Parmesan, extremely popular Italian and American Italian dishes, can never be served in a kosher restaurant or a kosher home kitchen and thus are rare in most Italian restaurants in Israel. The most common way of making food kosher in Israel is removing meat from the dishes and kitchen and opting for *halavi* (dairy) versions.

Meat, however, is almost universally the most prestigious and sought-after food around the world (Fiddes 1991; Beardsworth and Keil 1996; Adams 1990). The separation of meat and milk in much of the Israeli private and commercial culinary sphere means that ritual, celebratory, and high-end meals are usually meat based and do not include dairy products. Dairy dishes, on the contrary, are generally considered ordinary and mundane. This observation holds true also for the daily food cycle: lunch, which is the main meal in Israel, is meat based, while breakfast and dinner, considered the minor meals, are dairy based or vegetarian. Sabbath dinner, the most important ritual and social meal of the week for most Israeli Jews, is the exception: though eaten on Friday evening, it is meat based, stressing its ritual importance and celebratory nature.

In practice, most Italian restaurants in Israel offer a dairy-only menu, in line with the cultural norms and market demands, even if they are not kosher, or they opt for serving the Israeli version of "kosher-style" food—that is, they use kosher ingredients and cooking methods but lack official rabbinical certification. When I inquired about the decision made by many restaurateurs to avoid meat in their Italian restaurants in Israel, it was suggested that dairy-based Italian food "works" and is "good enough." Oren, whose website reads "Kosher—no certificate," explained: "If you serve French food, you have to mix meat and milk. As a consequence, French restaurants in Israel often fail: they are either nonkosher and can't survive economically or they use dairy substitutes that make for unpalatable dishes. But with Italian food, the dairy dishes are very tasty, and Israelis love cheese."

Israeli Italian restaurants serve mainly dairy dishes, but they are exceptional in the Israeli culinary arena in that the dairy-based food they prepare is considered celebratory, suitable for special occasions and worthy of high prices. When Israelis want to opt for a meat-free meal due to health, ethics, or the time of day, Italian restaurants are often the only option.

So why are Italian restaurants considered fancy despite the lack of meat? I spoke to the chef-owner of an Italian restaurant about the popularity of Italian food in Israel, and I asked him why Israelis prefer Italian food over Mizrahi food (a point developed later in this chapter). He responded with a rhetorical question: "Would you propose [marriage] in a Mizrahi restaurant?" He was pointing to the wider cultural context in which Italian food is embedded. Italy is one of the ultimate romantic destinations in the West (A. Douglas, Mills, and Kavanaugh 2007). It is a place with a glorious past and a celebrated present, the birthplace of modern Western arts and sciences, and the location of sophisticated and refined beauty and, of course, wonderful food (see also Baloglu and Mangaloglu 2001). These attributes make for a very positive and lucrative perception of Italy and, consequently, its food, even a meatless version of it.

## FAMILY-FRIENDLINESS

Another attribute of Italian restaurants that makes them popular in Israel is their image as family-friendly. This is related, at least in part, to their *halavi* orientation, as Israeli children are fond of pasta and pizza and seem to prefer them over meat (for a study revealing a similar preference among American kids, see Skinner et al. 2002). Yet my data suggests that the tendency of Italian restaurants to be family-friendly is shaped by the importance and centrality of families and children in Israel. This would mean that we are dealing with another sociological attribute that has less to do with food preferences and more to do with social setting.

The idea that Italian restaurants in Israel are considered family-friendly was first conveyed to me in negative terms. A non-Jewish Italian-restaurant owner told me during our conversation that Israelis have a distorted view of Italian restaurants, thinking that they are great places for families and kids:

> I have no idea why they think that they can bring their children to my restaurant. . . . Maybe they have seen images of the Italian mama and the children running around the table in some American movie or television show and think that this is how Italian restaurants are. Israeli kids behave in ways that would be unacceptable in a restaurant in Italy. Over there, when a child is taken by his parents to a restaurant, he behaves accordingly and feels that he has been offered a wonderful treat. But Israeli kids run around, scream, throw food on the floor, and do not behave nicely. To be honest, when someone calls and asks to book a table for a family event that involves kids, I respond that the place is full and refuse the booking.

A father of five, I was taken aback by this blunt statement, partly because I had to admit to myself that I often take my kids out to eat, that my kids sometimes misbehave in restaurants, and that I am often lenient when this happens. I was also surprised because I assumed that children are well-liked and welcome everywhere in Israel. This, however, was my own cultural bias shaped by the Israeli perception of children and my long-term engagement with Vietnamese culture, which, despite prevailing age and gender hierarchies, is very children-friendly. It also made me realize that when it comes to eating out, the most common choices for my family and for many of our relatives and friends are falafel and pizza.

It is tempting to explain the popularity of Italian food among families in economic terms: a family with three kids will spend 50–70 shekels (US$13-17) for a family pizza or five falafel wraps, served in both cases with soft drinks, making these the cheapest family meals available in any culinary establishment in Israel. I did touch on the Israeli preoccupation with getting a good value for their money in the first chapter, and I return to it in the following section, but the comment mentioned above made me realize that Italian restaurants in Israel are considered particularly family-friendly and their affordable prices certainly contribute to their appeal.

This is especially true of the pizzerias where I conducted fieldwork, which do much of their business with families. Pizzas are ideal family meals because they have built-in commensality—they are meant to be shared. Also, the informal setting and etiquette allow and even encourage eating with the hands, which makes pizza appropriate and enjoyable for children. Moreover, pizza and other Italian dishes in Israel are baked, which makes them appear healthier than most other fast foods, which are often fried.

Falafel wraps, in contrast to pizzas, are almost impossible to share. The falafel chickpea balls are always deep-fried and somewhat greasy, and falafel stands are often criticized for their use of cheap ingredients and poor standards of cleanliness. Finally, Israeli falafel stands, even those that have tables and chairs, are not places for lingering and sharing food. Rather, they are no-frills places where people order, get their food quickly, and either consume it within a few minutes on the premises or take it to go. The large, sturdy tables at most Israeli pizzerias, on the other hand, allow for and even enhance family meals. The twenty minutes or so of waiting while the pizza is baking impose lingering, hanging out, and playing, practices which many pizzerias in Israel accommodate. Journalist Maya Avidan, in an article titled "The Best Pizzas in the Country," comments on Iceberg-Volcano Pizza, located in Fountain Square at the port of Tel Aviv: "Unrelated to the really excellent pizza served here, this place offers 'three for the price of one'—a meal for the whole family, good ice cream, and a child-friendly space, especially during the summer—when they can jump into the fountain."[15]

Italian restaurants in Israel and elsewhere often celebrate the notions of home cooking and a cozy atmosphere. The red-and-white checkered table-cloths, the rattan chairs, the partially melted candles in worn-out chianti bottles, the dim lights, and the references to the "Italian mama" in different textual and symbolic contexts (such as the restaurant's name, the menu, the pictures on the walls, etc.) convey not only the rustic setting of an Italian village but also that of the Italian home, with the alluded warmth, aroma of garlic and freshly baked bread, and the tightly knit extended family, conveyed so often in films and television series (for a discussion of similar notions of coziness in Italian restaurants in the United States, see Girardelli 2004).

Demographers Yoav Lavee and Ruth Katz (2003) argue that Israel is a family-oriented society: marriage in Israel is almost universal, and the 2.6 fertility rate is higher than in most developed countries, including the United States (2.07), Ireland (1.9), and Italy (1.2). "The family in Israel," they point out, "continues to be strong, central, and more stable than in most industrialized countries" (194). When it comes to children and their place in Israeli society, they elaborate:

> Israel is a "child-oriented" society. Married couples are expected to have children, and a childless couple is not considered a family. Nearly 60% of Israelis believe that childless people have an "empty life," and more than 80% believe that "the greatest joy in life is to follow children's growing up." ... On average, Israelis desire more children (3.5) and have more children (2.7) than people in other industrialized countries. *Children are highly valued not only by their parents,* who usually give the needs of their young top priority, *but also by society as a whole.* The welfare of children is considered a collective responsibility.... Children in Israel remain a central focus of concern for their parents for a longer period of time than in most industrialized countries.... Three years after completing military service, two-thirds of these young adults are still living at home and are economically dependent on their parents. (203–205; emphasis mine)

A recent update, published by Israel's Central Bureau of Statistics (CBS), titled "Selected Data for the International Child Day 2015,"[16] reaffirms the centrality of the family and of children. It found that, in 2015, 33 percent of Israelis were children (under the age of seventeen); Israeli families had, on average, 2.4 children under the age of seventeen (making the actual number of children per family higher, as many families have children who are older than seventeen but still live at home and belong to the same socioeconomic unit); and 92 percent of children live with two parents. Though trends predicted by Lavee and Katz (2003), such as rising marriage age, rising divorce rates, and decreasing numbers of children per family among groups that had relatively many children (e.g., Ultra-Orthodox Jews and Muslim Arabs), were confirmed by the CBS report, Israel remains the most family-oriented member of the OECD.[17] The CBS report also shows that families with children spend twice as much on "education, culture, and entertainment," which includes eating out, than families without children, suggesting that Israeli families and children are important clients of the restaurant industry.

The statistical data addresses families with children under the age of seventeen, but as Lavee and Katz (2003) argue, Israeli children remain kids many years after they complete high school. While completing their military service, most Israeli youth continue living with their parents, and most of my students at Beer-Sheva's Ben-Gurion University go home to their parents' houses almost weekly even though they are in their midtwenties and rent their own accommodations. These visits involve parental laundry and catering services, something that is clearly observable on Thursdays, when students come to class with huge backpacks full of dirty clothes and empty food containers, ready to go home for the weekend.

The fact that Israelis remain "kids" throughout their twenties and thirties was crystalized by the singer-songwriter Ehud Banai in his popular song "Maharinah" (Hurry up), better known as "Ha'Yeled Ben Shloshim" (The kid is thirty [years old]). The song describes a thirty-year-old man who is feverish and goes to his parents' house to be taken care of, a familiar and intimate scene for many Israelis. It continues: "Yes, he is thirty but still does not know what he will do when he finishes the army [service]."[18] The pun rests in the fact that even though Israeli men serve for about three years in the army, starting when they are eighteen, the protagonist, at thirty, is still uncertain about his first steps as an adult (in Israel, one is considered an adult after military service). This highlights the prolonged (if not endless) Israeli childhood and the ongoing importance and centrality of Israeli children in their parents' life.

Strong extended family ties, regular communication, and frequent meetings on religious and civil holidays and to celebrate lifecycle events, which always involve and are often centered on shared meals, are very much the norm among Israeli Jewish families. Yochanan Peres and Ruth Katz (1981) gave several explanations for what they call "the stability and centrality" of the family in modern Israel, including Judaism, social cohesion, and state-policies, and despite the many years that have passed since the publication of their article, these explanations remain relevant and are supported by recent statistical data, such as by the 2015 CBS report.

All in all, the family as a social institution and children as a social category are extremely important in Israel. It is of little wonder, then, that the image of Italian restaurants as family-friendly strikes the right chord in Israel, further contributing to the appeal and popularity of these restaurants.


## SIZE MATTERS HERE TOO

One of the main modifications to Italian food in Israel was a sharp increase in portion size, mainly of the pasta and antipasti dishes. A more implicit notion is that of value for money: Israeli Jews I spoke to expressed a clear preference for moderately priced large portions, while quality seemed to play a lesser role in their evaluations of the restaurants and the food.

This view was repeatedly reaffirmed in my interviews. When I asked Oren about portion sizes, he responded: "I had to go up to 150 grams of pasta. My wife said that I had to consider my clients." He also explained that his appetizers and antipasti were actually full portions served on large plates, a practice I observed in other Italian restaurants.

At Pronto, widely considered to be the most authentic Italian restaurant in the country, chef David Frankel suggested that the process of augmentation was ongoing: "In the new menu, I went down from 250 to 300 grams of pasta to 120, but people complained and I had to re-enlarge some portions." The restaurant manager told me later that the customers' reactions to the decreased portions were so bad that they realized that while it was possible to change some of the items on the menu and introduce new dishes such as risotto, when it came to size, portions had to remain large. "Actually," he added, "we had to further increase [the sizes]."

Davide, the Italian restaurateur, also disclosed, "In Italy, the standard is 80 to 100 grams of pasta, . . . [and] 100 is a lot. Here, I serve 300 grams." He later added that his best-selling dish was a portion of mixed grill, featuring "800 grams of meat served with potatoes, rice, and salad." He concluded that, for his Israeli customers, "The more there is—the better it is."

10. *Three Hundred Grams of Pasta per Person*

The demand, however, is not merely for large portions but also for moderate prices. The waitress in a packed Italian restaurant in Jaffa's gentrifying *shuk hapishpeshim* (flea market) area commented: "Don't you know why Italian food is popular? Israelis like cheap food, and Italian food is cheap even though the portions are large." In a similar vein, the chef at another restaurant pointed out: "The clients are *kamtzanim* [cheap]. They don't order a three-course meal. They want to order only one dish and get a lot for a small price. Italian food is perfect for that—you simply add pasta [to a dish]. I tried to serve grouper [an expensive wild-caught fish] kebabs for 90 shekels [US$22], but no one ordered the dish. I added pasta, and the dish became a hit. The clients felt that [once a substantial amount of pasta had been thrown into the bargain] they had cracked the system." Similarly, Davide explained: "In Italy, the meal consists of several courses: antipasti, pasta, secondi—which is the main course, [it's] meat or fish served with side dishes—salad, cheese, desserts, and coffee. In Israel, the meal is composed of an appetizer and a pasta dish. Sometimes, they ask for pasta with mushrooms and cream, and the meal is over." The elaborate and expensive main courses are rarely ordered, and customers are served large portions of cheaper pasta.

In chapter 1, I addressed the Israeli tendency to demand enlarged (and simplified) foreign dishes. I also suggested that this tendency stems from Jewish histories of insecurity, persecution, and hunger. I further argued that the preference for large portions of relatively inferior quality is shaped by the Israeli reluctance to be a "sucker," which translates into the customers' demands for big portions at moderate prices as well as into the restaurateurs' response of serving large portions of mediocre foods made with average ingredients. As my interviewees suggested, Italian food readily lends itself to such modifications, and Israeli customers do not merely embrace it in this form but are obviously very fond of it.

### MEDITERRANEAN FOOD, MEDITERRANEAN CHARACTER

While kashrut, family-friendliness, and supersized portions were suggested somewhat indirectly in my interviews and conversations to explain the Israeli penchant for Italian food, a more straightforward explanation had to do with geography and spatial orientation. Chefs and diners repeatedly argued that Israelis like Italian food because the similar weather and ecological conditions in the two countries make for similar ingredients, cooking styles, and taste preferences. They also argued that the similar ecology has resulted in social, cultural, and psychological affinities between Italians and Israelis, often described by my interviewees as *yam-tichoniut* (Mediterranean-ness).

Paulo, an Italian chef-owner of an Italian restaurant, explained: "It's easy to make good Italian food here. You can find fresh ingredients of high quality year round." Pronto's chef Frankel argued, "Italian food in Israel is very specific. We adopted the ingredients and dishes suitable for the Israeli taste, mainly the Mediterranean and Sicilian food. The ingredients are similar, *but also the temperament*. It's a geographical thing" (emphasis mine). Oren, whose parents came to Israel from Morocco during the 1950s, expanded the culinary-geographical scope: "I approach Italian food from the North African direction. Sicilian food was influenced by Moroccan cooking. They [Sicilians] know what couscous is!"

As Frankel's quote indicates, the interviewees didn't limit the comparison of Israel and Italy to the ecology, weather, and products, which conjure up the concept of terroir. They also argued that the national character and habitus (as defined by Bourdieu) of Italians, especially southern Italians, and Israelis were similar. The manager of a trendy restaurant in Jerusalem explained: "First and foremost, it is the proximity, the similarity between Israel and some parts of southern Italy, the Mediterranean influence, the ingredients, the olive oil. It is also about simplicity. *We, the Mediterranean people,* prefer simple and immediate food. French food is too complex. *We are* hyperactive, and *we* don't want to spend ten hours cooking" (emphasis mine).

In an interview for an article titled "Why We Like Italian Food the Best," Ronen Arditi, owner of the Tel Aviv restaurant Belini, explained to food critic Rina Goldstein that Italian cuisine matches perfectly with the conditions in Israel: "Italian food is suitable for the Israeli market because high-quality ingredients can be obtained in Israel—for instance, tomatoes, olive oil, and herbs such as arugula, thyme, oregano, and basil, which are successfully cultivated here." He added: "Italian food suits the Israeli beat: [it's] fast. The fact that one doesn't need to spend hours eating, as is common with French cuisine, makes it *appropriate for the Israeli mentality*" (emphasis mine).[19]

In the same article, Yoram Yerzin, owner of Café Italia in Tel Aviv, argued that simplicity constitutes the cultural common ground between Italians and Israelis, while Yona Sasson of Jerusalem's Topolino told Goldstein that "shared mentality" explains the popularity of Italian food in Israel. Similar insinuations regarding the affinity of Italian and Israeli character and temperament were made in many of the interviews and conversations I had.

Although Italy and Israel are Mediterranean in the technical sense, as they are both located on the Mediterranean Sea, Italy is a part of southern Europe, while Israel is an Asian country located some 2500 kilometers away, within the Arab Muslim Middle East. Furthermore, some 50 percent of Israeli Jews are of Middle Eastern or North African origin. So, wouldn't it be more reasonable to expect that Israelis would prefer a more local cuisine, one that evolved within a common terroir and similar cultural framework? To be more explicit: Wouldn't it make more sense for Israelis to prefer Middle Eastern, and for that matter Palestinian, cuisine?

The answer is, of course, complex. Middle Eastern cuisine is extremely popular across Jewish ethnicities and socioeconomic classes. However, as demonstrated in the previous chapters, many Israeli Jews consider iconic

Palestinian dishes such as hummus, tahini, tabbouleh, and baba ghanoush to be Israeli Jewish (Ranta and Mendel 2014). In fact, falafel is considered by many to be Israel's national dish, as can be discerned in a ubiquitous tourist postcard featuring a serving of falafel decorated with a tiny Israeli flag (Raviv 2003). Many Israeli Jews like Palestinian dishes very much, but they do not recognize them as Palestinian (Mendel and Ranta 2016).

Though many Israeli Jews are reluctant to acknowledge Palestinian food as such, the fact is that these dishes are mainly served at either Mizrahi or so-called Arab (that is, Palestinian) food venues. Dafna Hirsch (2011), in her analysis of the meanings attributed to hummus in Israel, quotes Israeli Jews who argue that hummus is best when "made by Arabs" and are willing to drive deep into the Israeli-Palestinian periphery in search of good hummus. It is also significant that Mizrahi and Palestinian food and food venues are relatively cheap and are usually associated with low prestige and social status. Israeli Jews like the food served in these venues and often consume it, yet they consider these restaurants unsophisticated. One of my interviewees, the owner of an Italian restaurant, pointed out, for example, that no one he knows would consider "celebrating a birthday party at a *hummussia* [hummus place] or taking his girlfriend for a romantic meal at a *shipudia* [grilled-meat place], like they do at my restaurant." Thus, although Israeli Jews like Mizrahi, Arab, and Palestinian food very much, they consider it ordinary and mundane.

At this point, the meaning of *yam-tichoniut* is revealed: Italian food allows Israeli Jews to construct an alternative spatial *and cultural* imagination of Israel, one that is associated with the Southern European-Mediterranean region rather than the Arab Middle East. When Israelis say that they like Italian food because it is Mediterranean just like they are and when they argue that Israelis and Italians share not only ecology and terroir but also mentality and temperament, they imagine themselves somewhere along the coasts of southern Italy. Italian food allows for the great escape of Israeli Jews from the Middle East, where they live and where many feel trapped, to where they imagine they would fit much better: a small Italian village, where the weather, landscape, plants, and aromas are just like in Israel, but where the neighbors are "just like us"—that is, European rather than Arab.

Italy's appeal lies also in the fact that for most Israeli Jews, the country is not connected with the Diaspora. Unlike Eastern or Central Europe, where most Ashkenazi Jews originate, Italy is not associated with the Holocaust. And despite Italy's colonial past, as far as Israeli Jews are concerned, it is not

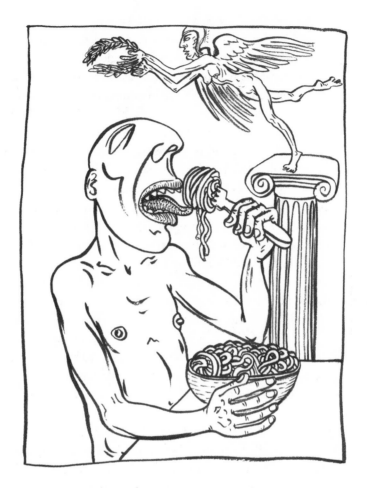

11. *Imagining Southern Italy*

related to North Africa or the Middle East, the regions where most Mizrahi Jews originate and with which they have a complex love-hate relationship (A. Levy 2015).

Yet, at the same time, as a Mediterranean nation, Italy does not stand for the iconic West, that of northwestern Europe and North America, where the largest Jewish diasporas and largest Israeli Jewish immigrant communities are now located. These parts of the world are perceived in contemporary Israel as *sir habasar* (the meat caldron)—a derogatory term used to describe biblical Egypt during slavery: a rich and comfortable place where Jews lack national identity as well as personal human dignity and freedom. The cold weather in northwestern Europe and North America is another recurrent theme in Israeli discourse, an important ecological factor that alienates Israeli Jews even after decades of living in these regions.

Italy seems to have the best of everything as far as Israeli Jews are concerned: the weather, ecology, and terroir are similar to those in Israel; there is hardly a diasporic context; and, most importantly, Italy is not in the Middle East, an area that many if not most Israeli Jews loathe.

Former Prime Minister Ehud Barak described Israel on several occasions as "a villa in the jungle" (Bar Yosef 2013), making a distinction between modern, rational, and prosperous Israel and its savage, chaotic, and dangerous Arab neighbors, whose irrational tendencies and behavior threaten Israel's existence and culture and are the reasons for the turmoil in the region. While the explicit conclusion of these statements was that Israel needed to be powerful so that it could defend itself from the violent chaos surrounding it, the underlying feeling is of the uneasiness sensed by many Israeli Jews when it comes to the Middle East. Despite the outcries these statements provoked, I have heard Israeli Jews using them time and again, usually with a sense of despair or recognition of a harsh but unavoidable reality. Indeed, in February of 2016, Prime Minister Benjamin Netanyahu elaborated his plan for defending Israel from the violence ensuing in its Middle Eastern neighbors: "We'll surround Israel with fences to defend ourselves against wild beasts."[20]

But Barak's and Netnayahu's metaphors are more complex. They actually depicted Israel as the classic image of the colonial bungalow in India or the Congo with the rest of the Middle East as the jungle, the frightening yet seductive background. Their metaphors also capture the tension built into the colonial situation between the desire to maintain the colony and the longing for (an imagined) home back in "civilization," where there are no jungles and no wild beasts and everyone presumably lives in villas in blissful tranquility.

These notions of the "villa in the jungle" and the "wild beasts" underlie much of the popularity of Italian food in Israel. Italian restaurants are imagined villa-style spaces that allow Israelis to leave, even if just for a couple of hours (and only in their imagination), the jungle and its wild beasts and to pretend that they are in Europe surrounded by other villas. At the same time, these restaurants maintain the Mediterranean features that Israeli Jews do like: the weather, vegetation, and produce that are similar to those in Israel, the land of milk and honey. The neighbors, however, are different. They are Italian, "just like us," and not Arab.[21]

Italian restaurants that cater to a sophisticated and affluent Israeli upper-middle class prepare supposedly authentic Italian fare and offer their clients a short respite from the dusty, sweaty Middle East. These culinary venues are located mainly in the area that stretches between central Tel Aviv and Herzliya as well as in other affluent and gentrifying enclaves throughout the country. Pizzerias in the Israeli periphery, however, take this iconic Italian dish in a different direction, adjusting it to other tastes and preferences and charging it with different meanings.

A few words are due here about the definition of the Israeli periphery and its relation to the Israeli center. An obvious designation would be spatial: Tel Aviv is clearly the economic, cultural, and gastronomic center of the country, and thus the farther away a location is from Tel Aviv, the more peripheral it is considered to be. A more nuanced definition perceives of the area between central Tel Aviv and Herzliya, along with elite enclaves in other predominantly urban areas, as "the center," with the rest of the country, including much of Tel Aviv and Jerusalem, as the periphery.

In his critique of the term "periphery." in the Israeli context, Shlomo Svirsky writes: "I don't like the term 'periphery.' I prefer the explicit expressions that hide behind it: Arabs, Mizrahi Jews, unrecognized [Bedouin] villages, low-tech industries, etc."[22] Indeed, the Israeli periphery is not a clearly demarcated area nor is it homogenous. Socioeconomic and cultural considerations define Palestinian, Israeli,[23] and Haredi (Ultra-Orthodox) neighborhoods as well as urban concentrations of African asylum seekers and Ethiopian Jews, some of which are located in the heart of Tel Aviv and Jerusalem, as the hard-core Israeli periphery.[24]

The dismissive term *Israel hashniya* (second Israel—implying that there is a first, or primary, Israel) addresses what is understood by most Israeli Jews as "the periphery." This social segment is practically defined by its population, which is made up almost exclusively of North African and Middle Eastern or Mizrahi Jews who immigrated to Israel in the 1950s. They were first settled in what came to be known as "mixed towns": former Palestinian towns such as Jaffa, Lydda, and Ramla, where Jewish immigrants were given some of the "deserted property" of the Palestinians who fled the Israeli forces or were deported by them. Others were given apartments in urban housing developments that were built in a rush with few resources, and these quickly became hubs of poverty and neglect. A policy of populating the nation's vulnerable frontiers relegated some of these immigrants to "development towns" and moshavim in the literal geographic margins, far from the center. These peripheral, essentially completely Mizrahi neighborhoods, towns, and settlements rate lower than average on all socioeconomic parameters, including employment opportunities, income, access to education and medical care, cultural resources, and leisure opportunities.

It is important to note that I am not suggesting a distinction between "low" and "high" culture (Bourdieu 1984), terms that I find arrogant and misleading in general and particularly in the Israeli context. Rather, I am arguing that cultural resources of any sort are hard to find in the periphery in comparison to the center and that access to these scarce resources is further limited by socioeconomic and material constraints.

When it comes to food, the Israeli periphery is very much a "culinary desert": a space with limited access to reasonably priced nutritious foods (Wrigley 2002) and culturally satisfying dining options (Neal 2006). Let me clarify again that this is not a highbrow observation about the lack of gourmet restaurants in these areas but rather an empirical observation: a constant complaint of my neighbors (I live in a peripheral, rural settlement in southern Israel) is the lack of "good places to eat"—that is, places serving food my mostly Mizrahi neighbors consider culturally satisfying and economically accessible.

Pizzerias, however, are ubiquitous in the Israeli periphery, even though pizza is not customarily associated with Mizrahi cuisine, and they are notoriously cheap. In Beer-Sheva, an iconic Israeli peripheral town that is often referred to as the "Capital of the Desert," it is possible to buy a "family pizza" for 42 shekels (less than US$11) and a "family deal" that includes a family pizza, two extra toppings, and a soft drink for 50 shekels (US$13). Such prices, common throughout the Israeli periphery, are equivalent to those of four or five falafel wraps (which are also cheaper in the periphery, although not as cheap as pizza), making a pizza the cheapest meal option for a family dining out. Price is an extremely important factor in the Israeli periphery, where the estimated average family income is substantially lower than in the Israeli center.[25]

The cheap price of periphery pizzas is partially the result of lower wages, profit margins, and real estate and rental prices, but, no less importantly, it is due to the use of low-quality ingredients and cooking techniques. Periphery pizzas usually consist of thick pastry made from the simplest refined-flour dough, processed canned pizza sauce, and cheese substitutes made from milk proteins mixed with vegetable fat. In a 2013 Hadshot Arutz 2

12. *The Orientalization of Israeli Pizza*

(Channel 2 News) report,[26] a salesperson for Israel's largest producer of processed cheese asserted that he supplied eight hundred pizzerias and that "they all mix" (mozzarella with cheese substitutes), suggesting that this is very much the norm (even though pizza parlors and restaurants in the center state clearly on their menus that they use only cheese and no substitutes, a point also made by food critics).

Some of my interviewees were very clear about their use of cheap ingredients and specifically cheese substitutes. They mentioned price as the main reason but also insisted that the taste of these products was "just as good."

One of them told me that he had tried using pure (that is, processed, shredded, frozen) mozzarella but said that the cheese would melt and drip off the pizza, upsetting his customers and inflicting burns, while the cheese substitute was more stable and easier to handle.

The preference for cheap ingredients and substitutes among periphery customers has been shaped by socialization and by what Bourdieu (snobbishly but accurately) termed "taste of necessity" (1984; see also Gvion 2006a, 2006b): through the process of socialization, people with lower socioeconomic status develop a preference for the cheap ingredients and unrefined cooking styles to which they are exposed at home and when eating out because of their economic and cultural marginality. My children, for instance, insist that the pizza served at our moshav pizzeria is "the best in the world" despite its use of cheese substitutes, canned tomato sauce, and simple pastry, and they tend to dismiss quality and gourmet pizzas.

Although cheap ingredients were imposed on periphery pizzerias due to socioeconomic demands and constraints, the pizzas were also modified through the process of *mizruah* (literally "orientalization"), which added to pizza the tastes and aromas relegated in Israel to Mizrahi cuisine. In the Israeli periphery, I found that "traditional" pizza toppings were usually limited in number, whereas industrially processed and cheap ingredients such as canned corn, mushrooms, green and black olives, and tuna were common. Fresh mushrooms, tomatoes, peppers, basil, Kalamata olives, and feta cheese were rare and often cost extra. In terms of seasoning, sesame, cumin, and harissa, to which I turn shortly, were components of the orientalization of pizza in the Mizrahi periphery.

Aziza Khazzoom (2003), in her analysis of what she terms "the great chain of orientalism" in Israel, describes how the mainly Ashkenazi Jews that founded Israel worked hard to remove the oriental stigma attributed to Jews of the Diaspora by trying to develop a Western nation-state. As a consequence, anything perceived of as Eastern or oriental was rejected by the pioneering elite. The influx of North African and Middle Eastern Jewish immigrants in the 1950s, as well as the substantial number of Palestinians who became citizens of the new state, threatened the processes of "self-improvement" and Westernization. As a consequence, and despite the huge cultural and socioeconomic heterogeneity among the Jewish immigrants and Palestinians, these individuals were grouped into the categories of Arabs and Mizrahi Jews.

These newly invented categories were arranged into a "chain of orientalism," with Ashkenazi (that is, Eastern and Central European) Jews located at the "western" end, which implies modernity, sophistication, and civilization, while Arabs, and to a lesser extent North African and Middle Eastern Jews, were relegated to the "oriental" end (Said 1978). Khazzoom (2003) shows how this chain became the framework for social stratification in Israel, with newly arrived immigrants slotted into categories and assigned to relative locations according to their assumed proximity or distance from the desired Western standard.

Mizrahi cuisine, just like Mizrahi ethnicity, is therefore a modern Israeli invention, the outcome of a process whereby the varied Jewish cuisines of many cultural regions in North Africa and the Middle East (and to a lesser extent Asia Minor and the Balkans) were stripped of their uniqueness and complexity and simplified into a limited set of emblematic dishes, cooking techniques, spices, aromas, and tastes. Most importantly, Mizrahi cuisine is defined in Israel as *harif* (spicy), a quality that became its distinguishing characteristic, even though many dishes and some entire Middle Eastern and North African cuisines (such as Iraqi, Kurdish, and Iranian cuisines) are not spicy. For many Mizrahi and non-Mizrahi Israelis, Mizrahi cuisine is also red in color, a quality related to its spiciness and extensive use of peppers and tomatoes. A perfect example for this essentializing process can be observed in the dish *dag mizrahi* (oriental fish) discussed in chapter 4, which is essentially spicy and red.

A somewhat broader definition of Mizrahi cuisine includes all the oriental stereotypes, such as an extravagance of colors, aromas, and tastes as well as lavishness, excess, and conspicuous consumption. These are contrasted with the rational, moderate, pale, frugal Western/European/Ashkenazi cuisine, which was defined until recently as "Jewish cuisine," implying that all other cuisines in Israel were not really Jewish. In a quote that clearly demonstrates the Ashkenazi ambivalence toward Mizrahi cuisine, Sara Netanyahu, the wife of Benjamin Netanyahu, Israel's prime minister, accused one of her Mizrahi employees of serving her large quantities of tasty food that made her gain weight: "We are Europeans. We are refined. We don't eat as much as you Moroccans. . . . You are fattening us up, and then when we are photographed abroad, we look fat."[27]

While North African and Middle Eastern Jews do not yield to these narrow definitions in their own kitchens and prepare a huge variety of dishes employing different ingredients and cooking styles, pizzas, which were never an organic component of North African and Middle Eastern cuisines, easily yield to the orientalizing processes. Although I have observed numerous subtle processes of orientalization, three culinary products were salient: sesame, harissa, and cumin.

When we first visited our village pizza parlor, we were surprised to find the crust sprinkled with sesame, something that we had never experienced before in Israel or elsewhere. Within a few months, however, I realized that this was a common practice at pizzerias in the Negev (southern Israel).

Sesame is widely used in Asian cuisines and is very popular in Israel. The most common form in which sesame is consumed in Israel is tahini paste, from which both tahini dip (the paste mixed with lemon, water, and spices) and hummus dip are made. Tahini is also the base of halva, a popular Middle Eastern sweet. While sesame paste is ubiquitous, sesame is most observable when sprinkled over pastries such as *bourekas* (*börek* in Turkish) and sesame rings. Sesame rings (*ka'ak* in Arabic) are Jerusalem icons, and they can be purchased warm from Palestinian vendors in and around the Old City, to be eaten dipped in *za'atar* (a mix of wild oregano, thyme, sesame, and salt, za'atar is a Palestinian staple and symbol of Palestinian perseverance and connection to the land; see Mendel and Ranta 2016). Sesame is also sprinkled on another Jerusalem classic, *abadi* salted cookies. These pastries are all clearly identified in Israel as oriental, Mizrahi, and Arab, and sesame is therefore a marker of oriental cuisine. Sprinkling pizza crusts with sesame thus makes them Mizrahi.

Another ubiquitous "oriental" feature of periphery pizzerias is harissa, a spicy Tunisian paste popular throughout North Africa, made from roasted red peppers, hot chili peppers, garlic paste, coriander seed, and caraway mixed with vegetable or olive oil. Israeli pizzerias routinely offer their customers a large array of sauces, including Thousand Island dressing, garlic dill, sweet chili, hot garlic, and pizza sauce. These are industrially produced sauces prepacked in individual vacuum-sealed sachets, handfuls of which are added casually to carry-out pizza boxes or offered to eat-in customers. Periphery pizzerias serve these sauces too, in addition to harissa.

Harissa, however, is never offered in industrial sachets but rather in a large saucer placed on the counter, suggesting that it is not an industrial product (even though harissa is commercially produced in Israel and I have no doubt that some of the harissa offered in these pizza parlors is industrial). The proprietors often refer to the harissa, encourage customers to try it, and boast that it was homemade or at least produced from a secret recipe by someone they know.

A commercial article about a pizzeria in Eilat (a beach resort in southern Israel with many hotels that can also be defined as a predominantly Mizrahi peripheral development town) reads:

Sophie [the proprietor] obtained the recipe of her harissa, the best I have ever had—no exaggeration, from her late mother-in-law, Fortuna, who brought it directly from Tunisia, her country of origin. "My mother, may she rest in peace, loved harissa. Wherever she went, she carried a small saucer of harissa along," remembers Marco [Sophie's spouse and Fortuna's son]. "No wonder she knew the secret of peppers and was a harissa expert. She wouldn't eat anything without some of her private harissa."[28]

While sesame may be dismissed as decorative, something that one of my interviewees actually suggested, harissa is clearly "ethnic," North African, and as such, Mizrahi.

Finally, in quite a few periphery pizza parlors I visited, along with the standard oregano and ground chili, ground cumin was offered as a seasoning. Cumin is one of the oldest Middle Eastern spices, and it is also widely used in North Africa and India, where it is an important component of curry dishes (for a deconstruction of curry, see Narayan 1995). Cumin is therefore "oriental" in the broad, derogatory sense as much as it is Mizrahi. Cumin's distinctive and powerful aroma makes it a domineering spice that easily over-shadows other tastes and smells. Just like cilantro (*kusbara* in Hebrew), it evokes a strong, dichotomous response among Israelis: it is a must for many but a disturbing and even intolerable presence for others. In most cases, the dividing line is ethnic: cumin was never a part of Ashkenazi cuisine but it is central in Middle Eastern and North African cooking, making it one of the clearest markers of Mizrahi food.

A pizza prepared in the Israeli periphery with coarse pastry, canned pizza sauce, and cheese substitutes, sprinkled with sesame, garnished with harissa, and powdered with cumin is a Mizrahi dish, one that does not offer respite from the Middle East, as some Italian restaurants in the Israeli center might; on the contrary, it celebrates Middle Eastern and Mizrahi identity. This culinary declaration, however, remains part of an internal, peripheral Mizrahi discourse, which is hardly acknowledged by the Israeli center.


## THE MEANINGS OF ITALIAN FOOD IN ISRAEL

In their insightful article "New York Jews and Chinese Food: The Social Construction of an Ethnic Pattern," Gaye Tuchman and Harry Gene Levine tackle the following culinary puzzle: Why is Chinese food so central in the culinary praxis and local identity of New York Jews? First, they argue, New

York Jews "construed Chinese restaurants as cosmopolitan, urbane and sophisticated" (Tuchman and Levine 1993, 385). Therefore, starting in the 1930s, eating Chinese food was a way that recent Jewish immigrants from Eastern Europe could distinguish themselves as modern and savvy rather than "greenhorn or hick" (385). Second, Chinese food was not kosher, yet Chinese cooking techniques (mincing, shredding, wrapping, etc.) transformed the ingredients to such an extent that the *treyf* ("nonkosher" in Yiddish; *trefa* in Hebrew) ingredients virtually disappeared, making the food "safe *treyf*" (388–392). Finally, the facts that the Chinese were located socially below the Jews and that Chinese restaurants were cheap "made Jews feel safe and comfortable in Chinese restaurants" (386).

Italian restaurants play an important part in Tuchman and Levine's analysis. The authors point out that within the socioeconomic context of the 1930s, the only other ethnic cuisine approachable spatially[29] and economically to New York City Jews was Italian. While Italian restaurants, too, were affordable and could stand for modern, urban sophistication, these venues made Jews uncomfortable for several reasons: the restaurants displayed Christian images and served visibly nonkosher food (chunks of pork, dishes that had both meat and dairy products, red wine); Jews and Italians had a long history of strained relations deeply enmeshed in anti-Semitism; and the Italians were southern Europeans and therefore held higher social status than Eastern European Jews. New York Jews opted for Chinese rather than Italian food precisely because it was so distant culturally and socially, making it "a flexible, open-ended symbol, a kind of blank screen on which they have projected a series of themes relating to their identity as modern Jews and as New Yorkers" (383).

The case of Italian food in Israel is similar in many ways, though Italian restaurants in Israel fulfill a role similar to that played by Chinese restaurants in New York. My interviewees suggested that Israeli Jews like Italian food because it comfortably handles kashrut issues with its emphasis on nonmeat and diary dishes. Italian cuisine is also perceived as facilitating consumption of large quantities of moderately priced food, hence dealing effectively with the Israeli obsession with hunger and with the deeply ingrained fear of being a sucker. Furthermore, Italian restaurants in Israel are deemed family-friendly, an essential factor in a nation where the family is such a strong and important institution. Finally, Italian food, redefined as Mediterranean food, allows Israeli Jews to imagine themselves as belonging to the Mediterranean region— that is, to southern Europe rather than the Middle East, where many of them feel trapped. However, pizzas in the Israeli periphery are garnished with sesame, harissa, and cumin, celebrating an emerging Middle Eastern identity among Mizrahi Jews.

These processes of interpretation, just like the various meanings attributed to Chinese food by New York Jews, are possible precisely because Italian food has very little to do with Jewish food. Thus, just like Chinese food in New York, Italian food, imported to Israel via America by Israelis, was disconnected from its cultural roots and meanings, making it a white canvas on which Israeli Jews draw imaginary portraits of themselves.

# FOUR

# The McDonaldization of the Kibbutz Dining Room

> Since the beginning of kibbutz life, eating together has been a uniting element.... Whatever changes the kibbutz will experience, it is only reasonable to assume that the dining room will remain the symbol of kibbutz "togetherness" and the heart of hearts of any settlement that remains a kibbutz.
>
> STANLEY MARON 1997, 22

> Many [kibbutz] dining rooms were turned into full-payment cafeterias, often operated by outside contractors and their staff.... Once the dining room is completely or partly shut down, the family receives additional funding for its home economy budget.
>
> ELIEZER BEN RAFAEL 1996, 128

THIS CHAPTER DEALS WITH YET another emblematic Israeli culinary institution: the kibbutz dining room. Kibbutz members have always made up only a tiny fraction of Israeli society (6.5 percent of the population at the peak in 1948, 2.2 percent in 2005,[1] and 2 percent, about 165,000 members, in 2015[2]), but they were perceived for many years by many Israelis as the spearhead of Zionism and the jewel in Israel's crown. Despite their socioeconomic decline and the mounting critique of their privileged access to resources and abusive treatment of other social classes (Mizrahi Jews, Palestinians, and, as of recently, migrant workers), kibbutzim remain unique Israeli creations, inspiring and resilient utopias whose social, cultural, and economic achievements[3] are acknowledged in Israel and abroad.

The *hadar ha'ochel* (dining room) has always been the spatial and social heart of kibbutz communal life. Ideological and socioeconomic adjustments and transformations were decided on in the *asefa klalit* (general assembly), which was traditionally held in the dining room, while informal discussions, debates, and negotiations took place in the intimate context of daily communal meals. The 2009 secretariat report of Kibbutz Yotveta states: "The dining room is the pulsing heart of the kibbutz, the central institute where our 'togetherness' is expressed daily" (Garfunkel 2010, 74).

As the dining room was a pillar of kibbutz communal life and ideology, it is little wonder that it was often the direct target of criticism and renovation plans meant to adjust the room, and the kibbutzim themselves, to changing times, circumstances, and ideologies. This chapter is focused on the major changes that kibbutz dining rooms underwent over the years, including the shift from table service to self-service in the 1980s and the switch to privatization in the 1990s and early 2000s. These shifts, the outcome of increasing liberal and neoliberal trends in Israeli society, have much in common with what sociologist George Ritzer (1983) termed "McDonaldization," a process in which irrational systems are reformed for efficiency, predictability, calculability, the introduction of non-human technology, and control over uncertainty. Ritzer went on to argue that McDonaldization, sometimes described as globalization or Americanization, is a deterministic, unilateral process that will inevitably result in a standardized, uniform, flat, irrationally rational, and disenchanted social world, one reminiscent of Max Weber's bureaucratic "iron cage."

Ritzer's theory instigated a great deal of academic research that expanded and modified the McDonaldization thesis (e.g., Ritzer 1998; Alfino, Caputo, and Wynyard 1998; Smart 1999; Ram 2012). Anthropologists, probably because of their attention and sensitivity to cultural differences and daily practices, have been struggling with the universal uniformity and conformism instigated by the McDonaldization thesis (Watson 1997; Matejowsky 2008). In this chapter, I show how the McDonaldization of the kibbutz dining room resulted in the reemergence of premodern social categories at kibbutz socialist ideology had tried to get rid of and that the standardized McDonaldization flow was supposed to eliminate. This chapter is therefore both an extension and a critique of the McDonaldization theory.

## LUNCH AT KIBBUTZ DAROM

In May 2006, I had an appointment with Jacob, the community manager of Kibbutz Darom[4] in southern Israel. I had just landed a job at Ben-Gurion University in Beer-Sheva, and my wife and I had decided to move to the vicinity of the university. As I had nice memories of kibbutz life from my military service in the Nahal[5] some twenty years earlier, I suggested that we explore the option of moving to a kibbutz.

Jacob and I had a pleasant conversation that mainly concerned the privatiza-tion process the kibbutz was going through. We also discussed Jacob's title. Originally, the position he held was termed *mazkir* (secretary), the socialist idiom for a head of a political or administrative unit. While there has always been a treasurer and a *merakez meshek* (farming and economy coordinator) in charge of the economic affairs of the kibbutz, they were subordinate to the *mazkir*, who was clearly the kibbutz leader and main authority. Jacob, however, was titled *menahel kehila* (community manager), an oxymoron representing the impossible coalescence of neocommunal and neoliberal agendas in contempo-rary kibbutzim. He explained that economic affairs were now handled by independent professional managers, either qualified kibbutz members or hired executives, who reported to the board of management and not to the *asefa klalit* (general meeting), the main venue of the kibbutz direct democracy in the past.

It was noontime, and Jacob had invited me to have lunch in the kibbutz dining room, so we climbed the stairs from the *mazkirut* (secretariat, which had retained its old name; some traditions are die-hard) to the dining room. Stepping into the dining hall itself, I was engulfed by nostalgia. Everything was so familiar: the large hall with its surrounding windows; the 360-degree view of trees, small houses, fields, and azure sky; the stainless-steel buffets; the humming of the large dishwashing machine (after the meal, the diners placed their own dishes onto trays on the dishwasher conveyer belt); the groups of men in shabby blue working clothes and muddy boots occupying some of the larger tables; the school kids eating together in another corner; the white-collar kibbutz members sharing smaller tables; and the aroma, not of mom's cooking but of a large and busy, no-frills kitchen. The few young men and women, who looked somehow European, reminded me of the vol-unteers on my old kibbutz, but they were speaking Russian not Danish.

We approached the food-serving area, picked up trays and cutlery, and joined the line by the buffets. The first featured four trays of main dishes: roasted chicken thighs, meatballs in gravy, turkey in red sauce, and, to my pleasant surprise, whole fish grilled with garlic, rosemary, and lemon. I was thinking that the variety and quality of food had improved substantially since my kibbutz days. Then I noticed that there was a small sign with two sets of numbers by each tray. When I asked Jacob about this, he explained that the dining room was now privatized and that diners had to pay for what they ate. "This," he pointed out, "was a very important step toward efficiency and saving, as the members now think twice before filling up their plates, making sure to take just enough."

13. *Kibbutz Lunch: To Each According to His Needs*

When I asked why there were two sets of prices for each dish, Jacob added, "The lower price is for kibbutz members, whose food is subsidized. The full price is for the others." He went on to explain that "the others" were mostly employees at the kibbutz's factories along with some hired professional workers and *socharim* (renters)—people who rented a house on the kibbutz and purchased some of its services (mainly education for their children) but were not kibbutz members.

We chose our main courses, which were portioned by a dining room worker, and moved on to the side dishes and salad bar, where we helped ourselves to a choice of steamed rice, baked potatoes, or boiled vegetables and a variety of fresh vegetables. There were two sets of prices for each of these items as well. The subsidized meal seemed quite cheap, but I calculated the full-priced meal to be roughly twice as expensive (about 30–35 shekels, or US$8–9), which was fairly pricy when compared to similar meals in other institutional dining rooms and canteens.

I followed Jacob and joined the line for the cashier, yet another innovation as far as I was concerned. When we reached it, the elderly female cashier nodded toward us and asked Jacob, "Are they your guests?" Jacob responded agitatedly, "Yes, they are the secretariat's guests." "The secretariat does not have a dining room account," she responded. Jacob asked us to wait and went to discuss the matter with some of the diners. He returned, visibly relieved, and told the cashier, "Just put it on the culture committee's account; they'll manage it." The food itself was mediocre at best, just as I remembered it from my kibbutz days, similar in taste and quality to the fare in most commercial mass dining rooms in Israel.

While we were eating, Jacob returned to our conversation about the privatization of the kibbutz and recounted how he once proposed that the renters not pay full price in the dining room: "Let the renters pay the subsidized price, I said at the meeting, let us make them feel at home. . . . After all, we want them to stay!" When I asked about the reaction to his proposal, Jacob said that it had been declined.

I found this lunch both disturbing and intriguing. I realized that the kibbutz dining room, which I remembered fondly as a warm space of community and camaraderie, had changed dramatically. I also realized that I was facing a new and exciting research field that combined my interests in food, postsocialism, and social change.

The lunch touched on the main issues I will discuss in this chapter, which focuses on the ideological fundamentals of the kibbutz movement: the tensions between the collective and the individual in contemporary Israeli kibbutzim, and kibbutz power structures as they are manifested in the kibbutz dining room. I explore each of these issues in the context of two drastic changes made to kibbutz dining rooms over the years: the shift from table service to self-service and the privatization of the kibbutz culinary system. I present each of these changes as a major ideological shift, explore the power struggles that surrounded them, and discuss their consequences.

I argue that the most important competitor for kibbutz members' loyalty and commitment is not the individual or individualistic tendencies[6] but rather primordial social institutions such as extended family and ethnic groups as well as newly reestablished socioeconomic classes and allegiances. This chapter therefore suggests that neoliberal processes of dining room privatization, reminiscent of what George Ritzer (1983) described in his "McDonaldization" thesis, may result in unexpected twists and allow for the reestablishment of traditional social entities and/or the establishment of new ones.

## SHARING FOOD: COMMENSALITY,
## COMPETITION, AND COERCION

Kibbutz dining rooms were established as hubs of commensality and food sharing. Breaking bread and eating together have long been recognized by social scientists as exceptionally important venues of group consolidation and solidarity (Sobal and Nelson 2003). In his article "The Sociology of the Meal," Georg Simmel suggests that communal eating was among the earliest human steps toward social integration: "We know of very primitive peoples that they do not eat at set times, but rather anarchically—eating individually whenever each person gets hungry. The shared nature of the meal, however, brings about temporal regularity, for only at a predetermined time can a group of people assemble together" (2000, 130). Audrey Richards (1939) notes that the need to obtain food and process it fosters and even compels social cooperation, an observation that has been repeatedly reaffirmed in other contexts (Thiel 1994; Hawkes, O'Connell, and Blurton Jones 2001a, 2001b).

Food sharing, however, is not only about inclusion. It also works to demarcate group boundaries and define exclusion. Mary Douglas (1975) pointed out that while drinks are for strangers, meals are for family members and close friends. Leonore Davidoff elaborated that "who partakes of the meal, when and where, helps to create the boundaries of the household, of friendship patterns, of kinship gradations. . . . These eating patterns vary between and help to define the boundaries of classes, ethnic, religious, age, and sexual groups" (1995, 76).

While the daily meal eaten at home is the clearest expression of the family (Charles and Kerr 1988; Murcott 1997), family boundaries are routinely expanded during feasts, ritual meals, festivals, and other occasions to include larger social circles, such as the extended family, the community, or the clan.[7] Taking part in such events and sharing the food serves as a token of membership in the social group.

Communal meals are social arenas where norms and hierarchies are enacted and reaffirmed. A classic example is Richards's observation that among the Bemba of Congo, "the preparation of porridge . . . is the woman's most usual way of expressing the correct kinship sentiment toward her different male relatives" (1939, 127). The elevated status of men in patriarchal societies is expressed by their privileged access to food, and especially to meat (Herzfeld 1985; Fiddes 1991; Adams 1990), while in societies or social echelons that adhere to other systems (matriarchal, bilateral, egalitarian, child-oriented, etc.), other forms of food sharing and distribution arrange the meals.

Shared meals are also arenas for social competition and conflict (Bove et al. 2003), where alternatives are suggested, negotiated, enacted, and, at times, rejected. Richards (1939) recounts how, in instances when a Bemba woman would dish out porridge in a sequence that somehow contested her husband's vision of the social order, he would react swiftly and forcefully. In my own work on Vietnamese foodways, I highlight similar occurrences and show how time and again, the social order is not only enacted but also subverted, negotiated, and challenged during the meal (Avieli 2005a, 2007).

Finally, spaces of communal eating, and dining rooms in particular, can work as spheres of coercion (Moore 1999). Food sharing expresses intimacy and mutual obligation, but dining rooms are also social arenas where eating is managed, limited, and, at times, denied. Regulating the food intake of others or preventing them from eating altogether is the utmost form of coercion (Counihan 1998). In this context, I argue that while much of the literature conceives of the kibbutz as a social utopia (Spiro 1963, 2004; Blasi 1978; Gavron 2000) or social dream (Bettelheim 1969; Lieblich 2001), Erwin Goffman's (1968) concept of "total institutions," and specifically of "open total institutions," are disturbingly appropriate for thinking about some aspects of kibbutz life, particularly kibbutz dining rooms.

According to Goffman, "total institutions" are social settings where individuals sleep, play, and work in the same place, with the same coparticipants, under a single authority, and in adherence to a single rational plan (Davies 1989). Goffman defined a more nuanced subcategory that he termed "open total institutions," where individuals are free to join or leave and where all positions in the hierarchy are (theoretically) open to everyone.

These definitions apply to the kibbutz, a social organization where members live, work, and spend their free time and where an overarching ideology arranges most aspects of public and private life. Kibbutz members are free to leave the kibbutz at will (though social sanctions abound), and the principle of rotation means that all positions are potentially open to every member.

Goffman points out that one of the main mechanisms that facilitates managing inmates in total institutions is "the stripping of self-identity," which involves loss of personal possessions, intrusions on privacy, and submission to demeaning practices (Clark and Bowling 1990). Goffman observes that dining rooms in total institutions are the main venues for such stripping of self-identity, as inmates have no control over the choice, quality, and quantity of food; are allotted limited portions; are denied knives and forks; and must ask for their most minute needs (e.g., a drink or permission to go to the restroom). Inmates are often required to eat all their food, and if they decline, they may be force-fed.

If kibbutzim are open total institutions of sorts, their dining rooms are important spheres of social control, ideological indoctrination, and potential coercion. Kibbutz dining rooms are obviously very different from those at prisons or nursing homes, mainly because members eat there voluntarily and may come and go as they like. However, some of the attributes of total institutions' dining rooms, in a diluted and mild form, can be observed in kibbutz dining rooms, mainly those concerning free choice and autonomy. In fact, surveillance and oppression were mentioned repeatedly in my interviewees' recollection of their dining room experiences, highlighting the coercive nature of these institutions despite the fact that attending them is voluntary.

## RESEARCHING KIBBUTZ DINING ROOMS

The data presented in this article was collected between 2006 and 2009 in three kibbutzim in different stages of privatization (a process I will explain later in this chapter): a fully privatized kibbutz, a kibbutz going through the painful process of privatization, and a kibbutz that has maintained its communal characteristics. Many of the interviews and a substantial part of the fieldwork were conducted at Kibbutz Dagan, where I lived with my family for two years, from 2006 to 2008, and where we experienced kibbutz life at its worst moments: the year preceding *hafrata* (privatization) and the year that followed this radical change. I experienced kibbutz life from a renter's perspective, which is essentially one of the lowest-ranking and weakest social positions in what is meant to be an intimate, utopian, and egalitarian society.

While living at Kibbutz Dagan, we ate in the dining room quite often. We regularly had our Sabbath evening meals there and occasionally also our weekday lunches. We also participated in some of the festive meals (Sukkot, Chanukah, and Shavuot). I had dozens of informal conversations with kibbutz members and other dining room patrons regarding their eating experiences and held several semistructured interviews with kibbutz members that worked or used to work in the dining room. I also had dozens of informal conversations with members of other kibbutzim and had meals in various kibbutz dining rooms whenever I had the chance.

To make sure that my reading of the kibbutz dining room dynamics was not biased by the state of affairs in Kibbutz Dagan during privatization and by my complex status as a renter, I worked with a research assistant, Ortal Buhnik, who conducted participant observation and interviews in two other kibbutzim in 2008 and 2009: the fully privatized Kibbutz Hanoter and the fully communal Kibbutz Tipa. All three of these kibbutzim were established in the 1940s and were relatively well-off during the research period, so the state of culinary affairs was shaped not by economic constrains but rather by informed choices made by dining room operators and patrons.

Ortal made trips to Hanoter and Tipa roughly once a fortnight at different times of the day, and these included participant observation, informal conversations, and semistructured interviews with various diners and dining room functionaries. The data was transcribed during these trips or immediately after their conclusion, and some of the interviews were taped and transcribed.

## "THE KIBBUTZ"

A review of the vast sociological, historical, economic, and psychological academic literature on the kibbutz movement and its recent socioeconomic crisis is a major project and should be done by those more qualified than me (see also Ben Rafael 1997; Gavron 2000; Lanir 2004; Palgi and Reinharz 2014; and Spiro 2004). I therefore limit myself to three sociological observations I made based on the academic literature while carrying out fieldwork, which are essential for understanding the arguments I make in this chapter.

First, "the kibbutz" as such does not exist. My interviewees repeatedly pointed out that "each kibbutz is different" and said things like, "In our kibbutz, we do things this way." Interviewees also tended to point out that "things were different" in other kibbutzim. In such instances, the comparison was often accompanied by an observation regarding the essence of the difference. For instance, a hitchhiker from a neighboring kibbutz said about Kibbutz Dagan, where I was living: "Well, they have exactly the same food every Sabbath eve because they are *Yekes*" (German Jews, who are notorious for being particular, orderly, and strict; see Zimmerman and Hotam 2005).

I found the fact that each kibbutz is different to be especially true when exploring meal compositions, specific dishes, and seasoning styles in each kibbutz. While eating procedures were very similar in the three dining rooms

I studied as well as in dozens of other kibbutz dining rooms in which I dined over the years, the dishes themselves varied substantially, as both choice and taste had to do with the ethnic composition of each kibbutz, its ideological position,[8] historical events that left a culinary legacy, and specific people running the dining room or kitchen.

In his analysis of structure and content in commercial culinary establishments in Israel, Uri Ram (2004) suggests that the meal structures in these establishments are often global, yet the food served tends to be local or modified according to local tastes. In kibbutz dining rooms, however, differences in structure and content are created within the tension that exists between communal ideology and the demands made by local subgroups on each kibbutz.

The second observation is that the kibbutz movement has been situated since its beginning within an irreconcilable tension between radical revolutionary innovation and extreme conservative rigidity (Punch 1974, 315). In other words, kibbutz members have always been torn between the demand for strict ideological commitment and adherence to norms and the fact that their ideology is all about radical social change (Fast 2000; Talmon 1972; Aviezer et al. 1994). The kibbutz project was revolutionary, but maintaining the revolution called for extreme conformity to the newly established rules. The staunch resistance to change and the reluctance, established early in the movement's history, of many kibbutz members to rethink or reform social arrangements, such as communal child-rearing (Gavron 2000) and equal salaries (Rosner 2000), express the unyieldingly rigid aspect of kibbutz life. A common complaint among younger interviewees (under the age of fifty) concerned the difficulties they faced when suggesting changes or deviating from norms or standard procedures. The term they often used was *kashe* (hard or difficult), as in, "It is so hard [*kashe*] to change anything here," or, "People here are so difficult [*kashim*]."

This inherent tension leads to my third observation: the most common expectation among my interviewees was that the social experiment of the kibbutz would imminently fail and cease to exist. As early as 1926, economist Franz Oppenheimer predicted the "immediate, inevitable demise" of kibbutzim (quoted in Rosner 2000, 1), while Eliezer Ben Rafael wrote that "seventy five years after the first kibbutz was established, it seemed that all efforts have failed to create communities based on sharing and equality" (1997, 1). On the one-hundredth anniversary of the kibbutz movement, Daniel Gavron (2001, 1) lamented, "The dream that begun ... with the establishment of the first kibbutz . . . is disintegrating, . . . with less then half of the 120,000 [kibbutzim] members believing that the kibbutz has a future."

While the arguments regarding its collapse are decisive and authoritative, the kibbutz is still alive and kicking, and, as of recently, it has been experiencing yet another period of revival (Hammershlag 2008; Shani 2009; G. Adar 2009; Palgi and Reinharz 2014). In fact, in each of the three kibbutzim I studied, plans had been made for future development, which took the future of the communities for granted (though there were explicit concerns about what this future would look like). I therefore think that instead of conceptualizing this looming notion of the end of kibbutz as a doomsday prophecy, it might be more fruitful to think about it as one of the kibbutz's essential constants, an outcome of the inherent tension between the revolutionary edge of kibbutz life and the conformity demanded of its members.

These observations—that each kibbutz is different, that kibbutzim are structured around the tension between revolutionary innovation and conservative conformity, and that any change is perceived as the end of the kibbutz—serve as the sociological context for the findings and arguments presented in this chapter. Although I point to common characteristics and processes in the three kibbutzim I studied (which may be applicable to other kibbutzim), my arguments should not be generalized and expanded without modification as, indeed, each kibbutz is different.

## THE FIRST DINING ROOM CRISIS: THE SWITCH FROM TABLE FILLING TO SELF-SERVICE

The dining room has always been the physical and symbolic heart of the kibbutz. Located right at the center of the kibbutz grounds, usually between the living and working zones (Chyutin 1979; Halfin 2016), it was clearly the main hub of collective life. Most kibbutz members frequented the dining room for their three main meals and usually for one or more minor food events (e.g., morning coffee, four o'clock tea, nighttime snack). As the central kibbutz edifice, it was the venue for the weekly *asefa klalit,* for the celebration of festivals and rituals, and for any activity that required the community to assemble. The dining room was where communal life materialized most frequently and concretely and where communal ideology was endorsed publically. Simon (fifty-six, Kibbutz Tipa) pointed out: "The dining room *is* the kibbutz, *is* the ideology. . . . You come to the dining room and see the manager sitting with the worker. We are all equal, all engaged. Here there is really no impression [*roshem*]—there is kibbutz."

In the early years of the kibbutz movement, the dining rooms were modest structures, but they soon became the focal points of architectural attention and were planned with the goals of maintaining and expressing the success of this utopian revolution.[9] Most existing kibbutz dining rooms, called *hadar ha'ochel*, were built during the 1960s and '70s, when many kibbutzim were prospering socially and economically. They are therefore large and imposing concrete, modernist buildings with the dining space itself located on the upper floor, with large windows overlooking the kibbutz, and most other important social venues (secretariat, treasury, main billboard, members' club, canteen, mailboxes, infirmary, etc.) are located on the first floor or in adjacent buildings.[10]

These new dining rooms were not only large, comfortable, and luxurious (most were air-conditioned and equipped with water coolers, soda fountains, and other amenities) but also planned so as to facilitate a new mode of dining: *hagasha atzmit* (self-service). The diners would line up, pick up trays and utensils, dish out their own food from a buffet, and then choose their seats. This mode of eating was very different from the previous culinary arrangement, termed *miluy shulhanot* (literally "table filling"), in which each arriving member would take a seat at the table that was being filled up and food would be served only once the table was fully occupied. Self-service allowed diners to choose their food and their company; table filling facilitated neither.

The original system of table filling was a clear enactment of the kibbutz movement's anti-bourgeois ideology of extreme egalitarianism and asceticism: all members were equal and food was meant to give them the necessary energy to work. There was no place or prerequisite for personal choice when it came to food or companionship. Alternatively, as some of my interviewees pointed out, table filling could be read as an expression of the feeling among many members that the kibbutz was not an *alternative to* family, as is often argued (Spiro 1954; Talmon 1972) but rather an *alternative family*, whose members were all siblings and therefore happy to take a seat next to and eat with anyone present. Both understandings of the table-filling system can be discerned in Rachel's (seventy-three, Kibbutz Tipa) recollection of the dining room at her kibbutz in the 1950s, when table-filling was still practiced: "We would come up to the dining room, and one wouldn't have to think, 'Who should I sit with?' You would just take a seat wherever there was one available. We were served some bread, jam, cheese, and a pot of tea. We would eat, and then we would all go to work."

This eating arrangement is remembered fondly by many kibbutz members. Muki Tzur's book *All the Beginnings: 1937–1987,* published to celebrate Kibbutz Ein Gev's fiftieth anniversary, recounts how "in the previous system, in which dining room staff served the food and demanded that members would fill up the tables, members would dine with different members in every meal. With self-service, breakfast is almost a 'permanent seats' affair, based on country of origin, work units and age, lunch is a job thing and dinner is by families" (Tzur 1987, 52).

Nostalgia notwithstanding, most of my interviewees were critical of the traditional system. For instance, the tables were set up for eight people,[11] and food was served to a table by *toranim* (shift workers; all kibbutz members took turns working shifts serving food and dishwashing) only once it was fully occupied. This meant that the diners had to wait, sometimes for quite a while. Yohanan (sixty-eight, Kibbutz Tipa) commented: "What I found most disturbing was that a table of seven had to wait for the eighth diner to start eating."

Since food was served to whole tables rather than to individuals, members had to be considerate, patient, generous, and careful not to consume more than their share. This, however, was not easy in the early years, when kibbutzim were rather poor, food was meager and unwholesome, and members did demanding manual labor. Hanna (seventy-four, Kibbutz Mishmar) recalled: "At first, there wasn't much of a budget. You would come up hungry for lunch, but the rest [of the members at your table] would eat faster than you and get much of the food. It brought the beast out of the human. . . . Shameful [*busha*]."

Obviously, there was also an issue of preferred company, as Rivka (fifty-four, Kibbutz Dagan) pointed out: "What happens when a particular member does not want to eat with someone? Or when I arrive with two friends and there is only one seat available?" Under such circumstances, the tensions surrounding the need to wait for the table to fill up and to share food with whomever was sitting at one's table were further exacerbated.

The shift to self-service was described by most of my interlocutors as a necessary and welcome alternative to the inefficient table-filling system and a practical solution to the increasingly complex demands of growing kibbutzim. Yael (sixty-two, Kibbutz Mishmar) said: "The kibbutz was getting bigger. We couldn't eat all at once—it was problematic, and we had to find a solution. Self-service was a good solution because meal times were extended, people were more flexible with their meal times, and members did not come all at once to eat."

Arye (sixty-seven, Kibbutz Yafit) told me that lining up in the old dining room, especially on Sabbath eves, became extremely irritating: "You had to wait for your seat, then wait for the 'train' of trolleys, get your soup, then wait again for the main courses and the dessert, and, once you left, the table had to be cleared, cleaned, and set again, along with a white Sabbath tablecloth. People would have to line up outside and wait for very long time, and in the winter it was really miserable." Self-service was devised to overcome such inconveniencies, as timing became more flexible and diners did not depend so much on the schedules of the other members.

Some interviewees even described self-service as a strategy of saving the kibbutz. Shaul (sixty-four, Kibbutz Dagan) told me: "I insisted on self-service! Right, it is not very ideological, but with ideology we lose the young people. Life changes! It is not what it used to be for my father and grandfather. We had to move on to the next millennium with our kibbutz style."

This restructuring of the dining system was not accepted without resistance. Some kibbutz members, such as Dov (seventy-six, Kibbutz Mishmar), pointed out that they grasped this supposedly practical change as a major ideological threat: "I knew that this was the beginning of the end. Everyone said, 'It is only for the good! There will be more choice! People will be satisfied!' ... But since the legitimization of self-service, whereby members sit wherever they like, there is no more 'us.' In my days, one wouldn't even drink a cup of tea alone—the members gave you everything." Yael added: "I knew that this was the end. It started with drinking tea in one's room[12] and ended in a meal where one is like a guest: you pick up your food, sit, eat, and leave. You don't care about other members. It was the end of ideology."

Jacob (seventy-one, Kibbutz Dagan) explained: "When a kibbutz member chooses where and with whom to eat, the kibbutz loses its privileged status as above everything else." Argaman (fifty-two, Kibbutz Tipa) asserted: "The buffet crushed us. Supposedly, it was just an easier way to eat, but it was against the values for which my father built the kibbutz." Shani (forty-six, Kibbutz Mishmar) also mentioned her father: "I remember my father fighting unfalteringly [beheruf nefesh] against self-service, arguing that today it is a kettle, tomorrow a gas stove, and by next week there will be no dining room."

Indeed, self-service stresses different social ideas and ideals then those governing table-filling meals, requires different abilities, and fundamentally alters the diners' relationships with one another (Wildt 2001). First, while table service renders diners passive and static, self-service requires diners to actively pursue their food. It therefore demands initiative, motivation,

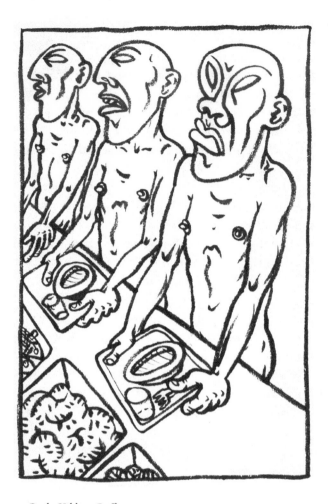

14. *By the Kibbutz Buffet*

and dynamism. Second, self-service allows for a wider range of dishes than table service because it is more efficient, involves less food waste, requires less manpower, and is technically more flexible (as it only requires additional food trays at the buffet). The system is therefore more tolerant of personal preferences and enhances choice. Finally, diners are not obliged to be considerate of one another: the food is served in large pans that are constantly refilled,[13] and there is no sense of sharing food at the table.

The shift from table filling to self-service was not only about efficiency and practicality but also about ideology. Specifically, it was about the legitimization of individualistic wishes, tendencies, and choices. The self-service system acknowledges that kibbutz members have personal culinary and social preferences and that these are legitimate. It is important to note that this legitimization occurred within the central, most public communal kibbutz institution: the dining room.

## THE SECOND DINING ROOM CRISIS: PRIVATIZATION

By the mid-1980s, the kibbutz movement was struck by a major crisis, the sources of which were political, economic, and social (Ben Rafael 1997; Lanir 2004; Lapidot, Appelbaum, and Yehudai 2006). The Labor Party, the movement's main supporter, lost much of its political hegemony in 1980s and had to share power with economically liberal and politically conservative parties. The shift in political power exposed the deep resentment many Israelis—mainly Mizrahi Jews in the periphery, who lived next to kibbutzim and were often employed by them but lived under very different socioeconomic circumstances—harbored against the predominantly Ashkenazi kibbutz movement, with its privileged status and discriminating policies (Fogiel-Bijaui and Egozi 1985). This was exacerbated by an unstable economy and misguided economic decisions made in many kibbutzim and fanned by Likud electoral campaigns.

The wider context for these changes was the demise of socialism in Israel, the adoption of neoliberal ideology and practices at the national and personal levels, and the country's gradual shift from "melting pot" and "conscripted society" ideologies toward multiculturalism, individualism, and capitalism. The kibbutz ideology and way of life lost much of its appeal, and the ever-increasing number of "kibbutz leavers" was no longer counterbalanced by enthusiastic young recruits. By the early 1990s, it was clear that a radical change was needed. Once again, this crisis period was perceived as "the end of the kibbutz": it was obvious that the kibbutz in its present form would not survive for long, yet a radical change would challenge its fundamental ideology and might alter it to the point of extinction.

The main solution to the kibbutz crisis was *hafrata* (privatization; Helman 1994; Rosner 2000; Sosis and Ruffle 2003; Fogiel-Bijaui 2007; Halfin 2016). The first step in this process was that most of the communal budgets (education, health, and culture as well as "personal maintenance," which included food, clothing, and car use) were divided among the members, who could now make their own economic decisions.[14] The next stage was usually a move toward a differential salary.[15] By the end of 2010, of a total 264 kibbutzim in Israel, 193 (73 percent) were *mithadshim* (privatized; literally "renovating"), 62 (24 percent) remained *shitufi'ym* (communal), and 9 (3 percent) had devised a "combined model" (Getz 2011).

It should come as no surprise that the dining room was identified once again as an important component of the crisis. In many kibbutzim, the dining room was the first institution to be privatized, and this often was deemed the most urgent step in the attempt to overcome the crisis. Quite a few interviewees pointed out that a communal, fully functioning dining room is the most salient feature that distinguishes communal kibbutzim from those that are in the process of becoming privatized or are already privatized. Privatization of the dining room meant, first and foremost, that members who had gotten their food for free now had to pay for whatever they ate.

While my research focused on a communal kibbutz, a privatized kibbutz, and a kibbutz undergoing the process of becoming privatized, the critiques made by interviewees from the three kibbutzim regarding their dining rooms were quite similar. First, they depicted the dining rooms as wasteful. Danni, Kibbutz Dagan's former *econom* (dining room manager; note that the title reflects the notion that the person entrusted with feeding the community is considered its economic authority), told me that diners would fill up their plates with huge amounts of food and then end up throwing much of it away: "When we had to share our food with the other diners, members would see if someone took food in excess and would criticize him for that. They would often joke about it, but it wasn't really joking. Also, each table had a limited amount of food, so there was very little left over. But with self-service, people would load their plates and then simply throw good food into the garbage."

From my own experience living on a kibbutz in the 1980s, long before privatization, I vividly remember that dog owners would place boxes with their dogs' names on them by the garbage bins so that members could throw in their leftover meat. My *gar'in* (military peer group) members, who mostly came from lower-middle-class families, were disturbed by the amount of perfectly good meat that was given to the dogs and often commented negatively on what they perceived as an unacceptably wasteful practice. Privatization was meant to put an end to such wasteful practices, a goal that was apparently achieved. An article by Michal Navon (2001) quotes a kibbutz functionary who reported a 75 percent decrease in garbage output in privatized dining rooms. This is very much in line with my own observations in privatized dining rooms: kibbutz members were very careful to take only what they intended to consume, and leftovers were routinely packed up and taken home.

More important than waste, however, were issues of choice and quality. While self-restraint and frugality had been idealized during the early years of the kibbutz movement, by the 1980s and '90s, members wanted to enjoy the fruits of their economic success (Palgi and Reinharz 2014). They were also influenced by the increasing importance of consumption in Israeli society, specifically by the new attention being paid to the nutritional and cultural qualities of food (Kleinberg 2005; Gvion 2005). Yet the large, communal kibbutz dining rooms, which often fed thousands of people daily, were managed and operated by people with limited culinary backgrounds and gastronomic abilities, whose palates had been developed in institutional food venues, and while they produced food that was rationally planned, edible, and possibly nutritious, it was hardly tasty or exciting.

Despite the arguments made repeatedly in this book—that taste is culturally constructed and that people develop a taste for what they have to eat, "a taste of necessity" (see chapter 3)—my interviewees complained bitterly about the food in the communal dining rooms of the 1980s and '90s. This was very much in line with their criticism of dining rooms in other Israeli total and quasi-total institutions, such as military and academic institutions, hospital cafeterias, and factories. The food, I was told, was greasy, under- or overseasoned, under- or overcooked, industrialized, tasteless, characterless, monotonous, and generally unappetizing. Nurit (fifty-four, Kibbutz Hermesh) recounted that, in the 1980s, "The new *econom* decided to add Chinese food to the menu. Every Tuesday we had stir-fried vegetables with chicken. But he had no idea how to cook it. He used cheap soy sauce and overcooked the vegetables, and, as the dish was kept warm throughout the meal, it became soggy and disgusting." Oded (forty-five, Kibbutz Hermesh), who spent a few years in Singapore as a kid, complained about the food during the 1980s: "There are so many ways to cook great rice, so why was the rice *always* undercooked and tasteless?"

Another problem created by the self-service buffet system was the ease with which kibbutz members could take food home. This was termed the "plastic-box phenomenon" (after the type of container members would use to take food home). Under the old system, all food had to be eaten in the dining room, but the introduction of self-service allowed members to take large amounts of food home and dine there with their family members, further eroding the communal lifestyle. The following exchange, which took place at Kibbutz Tipa during a dinner in 2009, exposed the tension surrounding this phenomenon. A member named Nehama approached Dan, a fellow member. "Is everything ok?" she asked. "You are taking food to your room again! Is Miriam [Dan's wife] okay?" Dan explained that everything was fine but that "things were a bit busy with the kids," so he was taking some food home. When he left, Nehama said angrily, "This is the third time this week he is taking food home, oblivious of everyone, thinking that this is a restaurant."

Privatization legitimized the plastic-box phenomenon, as members paid for all food they ate, whether they consumed it in the dining room or at home, but at the still-communal Kibbutz Tipa, the practice was seen as problematic and considered a breach of proper conduct. Michael, the manager of Tipa's catering system, explained: "The kibbutz is not what it used to be. Even though we have no privatization and we are communal, members were coming into the kitchen and taking boxfuls of food home. We had to stop it. We locked the refrigerators. Otherwise, the kibbutz would have gone bankrupt. Members were merciless [*hasrei rahamim*] and took food with no consideration of what would be left for the others."

Despite the criticism of the communal system, the suggestion of privatizing the dining room sparked a debate that was much more intense than that preceding the shift from table filling to self-service. While some members thought of it as an urgent and even inevitable move, others felt that it would lead to the end of kibbutz.

David (fifty-eight, Kibbutz Mishmar), for example, felt that there was no other choice but privatization: "There was a time when no one came to the dining room anymore, only the old people. Everyone thought that the kibbutz was over, but privatization resuscitated the kibbutz and gave it a few extra years. Now the kids come home from school and have lunch in the dining room. There is a feeling that there is choice and that everyone can find a place in the dining room. We even reintroduced Sabbath meals."

Yet other members of the same kibbutz felt very differently. Becky (seventy-three) said: "Before, we had a limited choice of food, but the dining room was meaningful for the members. Today, we have a lot of choice, but the dining room seems nonexistent for the members." Ruha (sixty-eight) added bitterly: "It is all over. There is no togetherness. Everyone is on his own." Joe (who gave his age as "almost eighty") went as far as to say: "When it was decided to privatize the dining room, I felt as if one of my limbs had been amputated. That's it! What else is left?"

While Tipa's dining room remained fully communal, the dining rooms at Dagan and Mishmar went through a process of privatization that included a gradual move toward full economic independence and commercialization. The dining room budget at each of these kibbutzim was divided among the members and the food was priced. The kibbutzim subsidized the price for members, but outsiders had to pay the full price (and most likely even extra, resulting in some profit for the kibbutz). The dining rooms were taken over by kibbutz members with previous catering experience, who tried to run them as profitable businesses. The food was diversified, and there were attempts to improve quality and taste. This, however, failed in both kibbutzim, as there was no change of kitchen personnel. As there was less and less demand for food, it was decided that the dining rooms would stop serving weekday dinners and cancel Saturday operations altogether, and, in Dagan, breakfast service was also eliminated, leaving only weekday lunches.

There were debates regarding the partial closure of the dining room. Avi (forty-five, Kibbutz Mishmar) said: "I knew that this was the beginning of the end. Everyone said, 'It's only dinner,' but I liked dinners the best. During breakfast and lunch I was anxious to return to work, but during dinner you would meet friends, talk, enjoy. Since we legitimized having dinners at home, ... there is no more 'us.'" I attended the last breakfast served at Kibbutz Dagan. The feeling was very much that of a kibbutz veteran's funeral, with just a few elderly members attending and a strong sense that it was "the end of an era."

Once it became clear that kibbutz members were unable to successfully operate the dining rooms of Dagan and Mishmar, the work was contracted to nonresident, professional caterers. In both cases, this decision resulted in the improvement and diversification of the food, but there were also price hikes, which caused a lot of resentment because many members had no experience with managing their personal budget and didn't know how to deal with unstable and volatile prices. Zeev, who was in his seventies, (Kibbutz Mishmar) commented: "I would rather eat a set menu at a restaurant than eat in the dining room, where prices rise every day. We joke that, as promised, there is a daily surprise in the dining room."

However, the privatized Mishmar dining room featured an ice cream machine, an espresso machine, and a sophisticated kitchen that produced a variety of dishes prepared by a professional chef that, according to some interviewees, were tasty and appealing. Leah (seventy-six) explained: "The children wanted [sophisticated gourmet food], and times have changed. If this makes them come here, it's ok. We didn't lose anything, we only gained." In fact, Mishmar's privatized dining room was visited by outsiders, some of whom ate there on regular basis.[16] Other interviewees, however, complained that the change was only about appearance, arguing that the taste and quality of the food remained inferior.

At Dagan, according to Bat Sheva (fifty-seven), the nonresident chef "took it as a personal quest to save the dining room. So he decided to serve dinner once a week, but he serves very special things, like pizza and moussaka. Believe it or not, the dining room is packed. People missed dining room dinners. My daughter is crazy about it. She says that it is so comfortable with the kids."

Tipa members, however, staunchly resisted privatization and considered their dining room to be the main proof of their ideological commitment. Nachum (sixty-two) stated: "The fact that we are still here, eating together, verifies that the dream is alive. The kibbutz is [still] above everything." For Nachum, and for other members of both communal and privatized kibbutzim, a collective dining room is still the most important authentication of the kibbutz and its unique way of life. Iris (forty-one), who rents a house in Kibbutz Beit Yehuda, told me, "There is no dining room; they closed it down. And I know that this means that this is not a kibbutz anymore and not even a community."

## THE REEMERGENCE OF FAMILY, ETHNICITY, AND CLASS

Kibbutz scholars seem unanimous in their contention that the kibbutz crisis is very much a consequence of the shift from collective ideology to individualistic tendencies (Leviatan and Rozner 2002; Ruffle and Sosis 2006). In their book *Crisis in the Israeli Kibbutz,* Uri Leviatan, Hugh Quarter, and Jack Oliver state: "The Israeli kibbutz is experiencing major changes. . . . The underlying debate is about what values should govern kibbutz functioning: Collective and altruistic values are clashing with individualistic and egocentric values in determining policies and directions for the future of the kibbutz society" (1998, vii). Sylvie Fogiel-Bijaui (2007, 103) adds that in the context of neoliberalism, the contemporary kibbutz emphasizes meritocracy, defined as a combination of individualism, capability, ambition, competition, and hierarchy, all of which are individualistic qualities.

The term "individualism" is highly contested, but the scholars quoted above seem to take it for granted in choosing not define it. Both academics and kibbutz members seem to perceive of any group formation that does not include all kibbutz members as individualistic. This, however, challenges Ulrich Beck and Elisabeth Beck-Gernsheim's (2005, xxi) definition of the "self-sufficient individual" as lacking any sense of mutual obligation toward other members of society. It also contradicts the vast sociological literature that explores the tensions between the individual and the family, the village, the ethnic group, and any other social collective for that matter.

My findings suggest that the collective ideology of the kibbutz was not challenged merely by individualistic values or selfish inclinations but also by other collectives, which competed over members' loyalty and commitment, including the family, ethnic groups, and new socioeconomic classes that have evolved within the processes of kibbutz privatization, or McDonaldization.

## The Family

Melford Spiro (1963) and Yonina Talmon (1972) recognized well before the kibbutz crisis of the 1980s and '90s that the family was a main competitor for members' allegiance (Halfin 2016). In the kibbutz dining rooms I studied in the late 2000s, it was clear that this battle was over and that the nuclear and extended family had overwhelmingly prevailed.

In her seminal research on the family in the kibbutz, Talmon pointed out that the family and family meals were recognized as threats to kibbutz communal ideology that needed to be tackled: "The inherent tension between the collective and the family . . . led to far-reaching limitations on the functions of the family. . . . Among the many devices used to prevent the consolidation of the family as a distinct and independent unit [was the fact that] . . . all meals were taken in the common dining hall" (1972, 6). She added that the children ate their meals in "children houses" and that members' rooms had no cooking facilities (beyond a kettle), so family meals could not exist as such.

But with the institutionalization of kibbutzim, the family gradually reemerged along with the urge for family meals. Talmon (1972, 82) detailed how, even during the table-filling period, dinner (as opposed to lunch and breakfast) became a family affair within the dining room, a custom which self-service further facilitated (see also Tzur 1987, 52). Once *lina meshutefet* (the practice of all the children in a kibbutz sleeping together in one place) was abolished and parents took over the nurturing of their own children, family dinners, whether in the dining room or at home, became the norm.

The dining room at Dagan stopped serving breakfast during my research period, but the members of Tipa continued to have communal breakfasts. Most working members sat with their workmates, while older, retired members usually opted to sit with others of their age group. I was told that the elderly preferred the company of those members they had immigrated to Israel with because they had the same mother tongue and shared memories and history from the old country. Thus, age and ethnicity were important considerations during weekday breakfasts and lunches.

In the privatized dining rooms of Dagan and Mishmar, dinner service was offered only for the Sabbath meal, which was predominantly a family affair. In communal Tipa, most diners ate with their nuclear family members during the daily dinner service. Quite a few members ate at home with their families. Ravit, an *ironit* ("urbanite," a kibbutz term for city people that connotes contempt and jealousy) who had married a Tipa member, explained: "I don't eat my dinners here. I don't have a kibbutznik soul. I prefer eating at home with my kids; I find it uncomfortable taking them to the dining room."

At the three kibbutzim, the Sabbath meal was a celebration of the family and the *hamula* (an Arabic term often used in kibbutzim to refer to the extended family). The dining rooms were packed on these evenings, and there were often some lines at the peak dinner hour (around 7 p.m.). The diners sat at tables with multiple generations of extended family. Many of the younger diners were children and grandchildren who had moved off the kibbutz but returned to have the Sabbath meal with their parents and grandparents. Older kibbutz members often approached the visiting siblings of other members to see their young children, who had been born elsewhere.

Quite a few members filled large plastic containers with food to take home, where they had their Sabbath meal in the private company of their own family members. Others used dinner plates as serving trays, heaping them with food to be shared by their family members at the dining room table. As the privatized, self-service system and the cashier were designed to handle individual patrons, each with a single portion served in designated, standardized, and prepriced plates and bowls, the large takeaway containers or improvised serving trays often created friction and arguments regarding pricing, exposing the incongruence between the privatization processes, which was intended to accommodate individuals, and the actual preferences of many kibbutz members, who preferred eating as family units.

Eventually, the dining rooms I studied transformed to meet the demands of nuclear and extended kibbutz families and began accommodating family meals, eaten in the dining room or at home. While kibbutz scholarship tends to perceive family orientation as a form of individualism, what I saw in kibbutz dining rooms, both privatized and collective, was a celebration of the family, and for that matter the extended family, over all other social relations.

### Ethnicity

One of the main features of the kibbutz dining rooms I studied was the fact that the food was structurally and materially Ashkenazi. Structurally, daily lunches and all festive meals consisted of starters; soup; a main course featuring meat, cooked vegetables, and boiled or baked carbohydrates; dessert; and hot beverages. This meal composition clearly adheres to Douglas's (1972) and Murcott's (1982) models of British and Western meals, but it was introduced to Israel and to kibbutz dining rooms by their founders: Eastern European Ashkenazim.

The same was true for cooking modes, choice of dishes, and seasoning. Schnitzel, boiled or broiled chicken, and meat stews were very common, and they were most often served with boiled vegetables, baked or mashed potatoes, pasta, and steamed rice. The seasoning was mild, often resulting in bland food. One of the main features of Kibbutz Dagan's lunch was the pale color of the dishes, another consequence of mild seasoning.

Breakfast and dinner were similar, both featuring raw vegetables (for salads), bread, a few kinds of soft cheeses, boiled and fried eggs, butter, jam, coffee, and tea. During winter, breakfasts sometimes included semolina porridge, and dinners featured the occasional "warm dish," such as soup, pasta, or quiche (often made from leftover vegetables from lunch or potatoes). While large amounts of raw vegetables and salads for breakfast and dinner are characteristic of modern Israeli eating, the other components are essentially Ashkenazi.

15. *The Basic Structure of the (Western) Meal*

The Ashkenazi character of the food was most obvious during Sabbath meals, which featured Ashkenazi classics such as chicken soup with egg noodles, beef stew, and roast chicken, and during Jewish holidays, when gefilte fish, chopped liver, matzo balls, and *regel krusha* (chicken-leg jelly) were served.

Like the majority of Jews that immigrated to British Mandate Palestine, most kibbutz founders had emigrated from Eastern Europe and were of Ashkenazi descent. It is therefore hardly surprising that the ethnic origins of these immigrants as well as their humble socioeconomic backgrounds were reflected in kibbutz food: bread, hard-boiled eggs, meat and fish balls (small amounts of animal protein augmented by onion and stale bread), herring, porridge, boiled pearl barley, borscht, clear soups, *of mechubas* (boiled chicken, literally "laundered"), boiled potatoes, jam, and tea. The main "native" ingredients added to the menu were olives, halva, coffee, fruit (mainly bananas and oranges), raw vegetables (tomatoes, cucumbers, and peppers), and an array of milk products made in kibbutz dairies.

Israel's ethnic composition has changed substantially over the years, mainly during the 1950s, with the mass migration of Jews from Middle Eastern and North Africa, and in the 1990s, when roughly a million immigrants arrived from the former Soviet Union. The ethnic composition of the kibbutzim was also affected by these demographic changes, and they are not nearly as homogenous today as they were during the prestate period.

Sylvie Fogiel-Bijaui and Avi Egozi (1985) estimated some twenty-five years ago that roughly 9 percent of kibbutz members were Mizrahi. Israel's Central Bureau of Statistics estimated this to have risen to 12 percent in 2005, but it is unknown how many of the 37 percent of Israelis categorized as "born in Israel" were Mizrahi or of mixed ethnicity. While calculating the exact number of Mizrahi kibbutz members is tricky, it was clear to me while living on Kibbutz Dagan that the number of Mizrahi members was well beyond 10 percent and was in fact closer to 30–40 percent (including the second-generation Mizrahi who were born in Israel and the children of mixed Mizrahi-Ashkenazi marriages), a supposition that was confirmed by Dagan's telephone list, which included a significant number of Mizrahi surnames. Moreover, a substantial number of dining room customers were renters and kibbutz employees, many of whom came from neighboring development towns and moshavim, where a large percentage of the population is Mizrahi. Other Mizrahi customers in Dagan's dining room were visitors who were staying at the kibbutz guesthouse.

This significant number of Mizrahi diners, however, had only a minimal impact on the food composition and none on the meal structure, both of which remained essentially Ashkenazi. A kibbutz physician who had immigrated to Israel from Russia told me that he found the dining room food "really, really homemade" and specifically mentioned the soup, which he perceived as a mealtime must. He lamented that soup was not always available in other Israeli commercial dining rooms he knew but said that it was always on offer in Dagan's dining room.

The three kibbutz dining rooms I studied occasionally served falafel, hummus, and pita bread. As argued in earlier chapters, these are highly contested culinary artifacts in Israel, perceived by many as emblems of Israeli national identity and not as Middle Eastern, Arab, Palestinian, or Mizrahi foods. Kibbutz dining rooms occasionally served emblematic Mizrahi dishes such as couscous or *dag Mizrahi* ("oriental fish," a fish fillet cooked in red sauce; sometimes termed "Moroccan fish"). However, the spiciness of these dishes was significantly toned down, and, though colorful, they didn't feature the complex tastes and aromas of the original North African dishes.

Yafa (Kibbutz Mishmar), a Mizrahi interviewee (her parents had emigrated from Morocco) in her forties who had married a kibbutz-born Ashkenazi, explained: "They cook Moroccan food here. They even asked me once to teach them how to cook it, but it turned out that my cooking was too spicy. So they replaced the hot paprika with sweet paprika. They have even replaced the beans in my *hamin* [Mizrahi cholent] with pearl barley. In short, [it's only] Morocco in style." David (Kibbutz Tipa), who was in his fifties, rejected the assumption that kibbutz food was predominantly Ashkenazi and explained: "We have everything here: falafel, fish. . . . Truly, there is no ethnic discrimination. This kibbutz is the melting pot Ben-Gurion was talking about." However, when asked whether the food was spicy, he replied: "No. . . . Who would eat it? This is a kibbutz after all."

David's and Yafa's words expose the gap between the perception among many kibbutz members that their fare is multiethnic, pluralistic, and based on egalitarian ideology and the culinary reality shaped by "melting pot" ideology, which practically meant that Mizrahi Jews had to be recast into Ashkenazi molds. Mizrahi food in kibbutz dining rooms is more about looks than substance: the food looks colorful and spicy, but the taste remains bland. This is true of most institutional dining rooms in Israel, where meal structures and food seasonings are essentially Ashkenazi.

This is all the more interesting when considering the fact that most employees in Israel's catering industry, as well as in the kibbutz dining room I studied, are Mizrahi Jews, Palestinians, and, as of recently, migrant workers and refugees. Though they cook the food, their own culinary heritage is barely represented, and cooking remains restricted to hegemonic Ashkenazi standards.[17]

*Class*

Privatization set the ground for the restratification of the kibbutz. While kibbutzim, like all other social organizations, had their own power structures, hierarchies, elites, modes of social remuneration and punishment, silent majorities, and marginalized minorities, the basic economic equality meant that social prestige and positions of leadership and decision-making were the main positive reinforcements. While age and seniority (in terms of years of membership) defined members' entitlement to socioeconomic benefits such as larger homes, new appliances, paid vacations, and so on, the introduction of differential salaries based on members' professional qualifications, expertise, and skills, meant that within a few years, some kibbutz members, mainly those holding managerial positions in the kibbutz industries, became relatively affluent (A. Cohen 2010), while others, mainly those who had fewer skills or whose jobs got outsourced or canceled, became the new kibbutz poor. Though most kibbutzim going through the process of privatization devised mechanisms that were supposed to prevent substantial socioeconomic gaps, these procedures were undermined by the increasingly powerful members of the managerial elite.

While most well-off members at Dagan were careful not to flaunt their new wealth, which could cause anger, jealousy, and criticism, the newly impoverished members were clearly observable in the dining room, where they had taken over food-serving and dishwashing jobs to earn extra money. In communal kibbutzim, these tasks were performed by all members in *toranuyot* (rotation shifts). Managers of multimillion-dollar factories took their turns by the dishwasher just like everyone else, enacting the egalitarian principle. But privatization meant that these shifts, just like the nightly security watch, were either canceled or assigned a wage. As manual, nonprofessional jobs, they were priced according to Israeli minimum wage, which was roughly 21 shekels (US$6.50) per hour in the early 2000s. While the busy managers eagerly dropped their kitchen shifts, the new kibbutz poor discovered that this was an opportunity to generate extra income after working hours. In fact, some of the more desperate members even competed over these jobs, especially during weekends and night shifts, when pay increased by 50 to 100 percent. Thus, the new poor became very visible in the dining room—they were serving the food, cleaning the tables, and washing the dishes.

The economic distress of certain members also resulted in conflicts regarding meal prices and in the development of techniques to reduce these quarrels. Dafna (fifty-six), a Dagan member who had lost her kibbutz factory job and was essentially trying to survive, told me about a particular incident:

My daughter was on a diet, but one day there were French fries [a rare treat in kibbutz dining rooms], and she just wanted to have a bite. So she took a couple of fries. The cashier charged her for a full carbohydrate portion. The French fries were priced as a "special carbohydrate," so the cashier charged her twice the price of a full carbohydrate portion, maybe one shekel [20 cents]. I was furious.... I yelled at her so that everyone heard.... Where was her common sense?

Samuel (sixty-four, Kibbutz Dagan) explained how meal prices were calculated: "There are two bowl sizes. It was decided that a small bowl equals one portion and a large bowl equals two. But sometimes kids or guests don't know that and place a spoon of rice or salad in a large bowl. The cashier charges them for two portions even though they took less than one. But what can I do? It's embarrassing to tell your guests that they should only use small bowls." He also told me that some members would stuff the small bowls and even compress the food so as to get more of it: "If you take the small bowls and empty them into the large bowls, you'll see how they manage to squeeze two portions into a small bowl and pay for only one portion."

Misunderstandings and overpricing, however, were much more common when it came to serving members of the newest social echelon of the kibbutz: the renters. During the 2000s, many kibbutzim with dwindling populations rented out available dwellings, warehouses, farm structures, and services such as education, to outsiders to generate extra income. While some of the renters were members' children who wanted to live on the kibbutz to be near their parents but maintain economic and social independence, others were attracted to the peaceful green setting, reputedly good education, and high-standard facilities. A significant number of renters were from neighboring development towns and moshavim, and their relations with kibbutz members were already particularly strained due to many years of animosity, jealousy, and contempt. But no matter who they were, renters were all considered temporary outsiders, even if they had lived on the kibbutz as adults for many years (for a discussion of various tensions between renters and members, see Halfin 2016).

Discrimination against renters was institutionalized in the cost of food, for which renters were charged the same prices (in most cases, double what members paid) as occasional patrons stopping over for a single meal. While there were other modes of institutional discrimination against renters, they were concealed (usually in the contract renters signed with the kibbutz). The double-price system, however, was public and enacted in the dining room, the heart of the kibbutz and the main hub of communal egalitarianism. Commensality was clearly not meant to include renters.

Yet renters were further discriminated against by the nontransparent food pricing and by the cashiers, who routinely overcharged them. In the three kibbutzim I studied, there was no price list and no explanation of the pricing system. At a Shavuot meal I attended, one of renters told me, "When we finally reached the cheese buffet, there was hardly anything left. We had to make do with a few half cheese balls, torn cheese slices, miserable vegetables, and squashed buns. But the cashier charged us the full price, and we paid much more than the price of a couple of cheese sandwiches in a cafeteria."

At a Sabbath meal, one of my friends, who was tasked with dishing out the meat course, carefully laid two slices of beef, one on top of the other, on my plate and told me: "Make sure that she [the cashier] charges you only for one portion." At another meal, he used the ladle to scoop a bunch of chicken necks from the soup container and dished them into my bowl. When I discussed these events with another renter, she said: "Don't you know? The price of the meal depends on your relationship with the cashier." This was confirmed by other renters, who told me that their personal relationships with the dining room staff or cashiers resulted in discounted and/or enlarged meals.

It turned out, then, that the restratification of privatized kibbutzim found its most blatant expression in the dining room, the previous hub of commensality and egalitarianism. So did the family and the ethnic group, social categories that kibbutz ideology had sought to eliminate.

## MCDONALDIZED KIBBUTZ DINING ROOMS

The Socialist-Zionist kibbutz movement was devised as a modernizing self-improvement project intended to emancipate the Jews from their impossible diasporic condition and return them to history as *am ke'chol heamim* (a nation among nations): independent, productive, and self-sufficient. As a modernizing project, the kibbutz was very much a product of a McDonaldization process, as described by George Ritzer.

Ritzer applied Max Weber's theory of rationalization to the world around him, observing the consequences of an emphasis on "efficiency, predictability, calculability, substitution of non-human for human technology, and control over uncertainty" (1983, 100). McDonald's restaurants, in Ritzer's view, are the ultimate expressions of rationalization, hence the term McDonaldization.

Each of the five components of Ritzer's McDonaldization theory carries a specific meaning. The first is efficiency, or optimization—that is, getting the most and best rewards with the least amount of investment. The second is predictability, the ability to be predicted, which allows expectations to correspond closely to outcomes. Ritzer posits that mass-production techniques, especially the assembly line, are necessary for achieving predictability. In a rationalized society, then, production shifts away from artisanal craft and toward systematized manufacture.

Third among the components is calculability, the ability to measure and compare by quantity. The fourth is quality, which is especially tricky and time-consuming to gauge. So, rather than risk efficiency, a McDonaldized system will develop "a series of quantifiable measures that it takes as surrogates for quality" (103). However, because humans are unpredictable and quality can vary between products produced by imperfect hands, rational systems seek to replace human action with nonhuman technology. Machines are built to be more efficient, more predictable, and therefore more calculable than humans. By combining these four factors, rational systems produce control over uncertainty, especially the uncertainty of human beings.

Ritzer concludes his seminal article with a discussion of the "irrationality of rationalization." In line with Weber's warnings that modern bureaucracy would make for an "iron cage" in a disenchanted world stripped of magic, fascination, and delight, Ritzer argues that McDonaldized systems tend to dehumanize people and create bleak and uninteresting realities. McDonald's is the perfect example of this process of disenchantment: the giant food franchise has practically given up on taste as a feature of the food it offers.

Ritzer and many others have criticized, expanded, and fine-tuned the McDonaldization thesis. In an article that I find particularly relevant to the examination of kibbutz dining rooms, Ritzer and Todd Stillman (2001) analyze the evolution of the modern American ballpark as an example of how the rise of rationality ultimately detracted from the purpose of rationalization. They show that dehumanized parks were disenchanted and therefore less enjoyable. As a consequence, they became less profitable, defying the rationality of the process. Ritzer and Stillman argue that postmodern ballparks have therefore attempted to conceal their dehumanizing aspects by simulating the nostalgia and magical allure of yesteryear without sacrificing their reforms, which have followed all five components of McDonaldization. These hybrid systems, featuring rationalized irrationality, seek to combat the blandness of perfection.

McDonaldization processes were clearly at play in the kibbutz dining rooms I visited, but, just as in American ballparks, these processes, aimed at improving efficiency, calculability, and predictability, have resulted in paradoxical outcomes. Kibbutz dining rooms were devised as rational institutions aimed at providing regular meals for pioneering Zionists under conditions of limited economic means and manpower. They were also modernizing ideological tools intended at replacing the identification and loyalty felt by kibbutz members toward traditional primordial social entities, such as family, ethnic groups, and social classes, with a modern, egalitarian collective.

Both socialism and McDonaldization became blunter once kibbutz members started forming families and having children. While *lina meshutefet* was the most radical move against the family in the kibbutz, the communal dining room was just as important in undermining blood-based kinship. As many of the older kibbutzniks interviewed for this study argued, the kibbutz *was* the family, and nothing made this clearer than the table-filling system, in which members were expected to share their meal with any other kibbutz members.

The introduction of self-service was also the result of a long process of McDonaldization. Kibbutz members at self-service dining rooms were able to eat whenever they wished and with whomever they wished, eliminating long queues and saving precious work time. The buffet and dishwasher replaced much of the unpredictable human labor. These rational reforms increased efficiency and productivity, as less time and human labor were spent preparing the food and consuming it.

This process of modernization also had an ideological edge: it gave kibbutz members increased choice, autonomy, and flexibility. The buffet system allowed members to sit with whomever they wanted, control their own time, and choose from a wide range of culinary options with little, if any, consideration of other diners. These changes expressed and facilitated shifts in kibbutz ideology, mainly the diminishing importance of the collective, which had to yield to the desires and needs of other social players and institutions. While most of the literature positions the individual as the key player undermining the collective's authority and power, my findings suggest that the family was the main social body accumulating power at the dining room buffet.

The next step in the McDonaldization of the kibbutz dining room was its privatization. At this point, the McDonaldization process became even more obvious: standardizing portion sizes helped kibbutzim ration and price food, hence enhancing predictability and calculability; increasing economic efficiency not only saved money but also allowed for the diversification of the food and for more choice; and the installation of a cashier decreased waste and led to more control over consumption. Privatized kibbutz dining rooms were fully McDonaldized.

However, just like in American ballparks and other McDonaldized systems, increasing rationalization led to disenchantment. Unexpected price hikes and irregular food quality led many of my interlocutors to give up on the McDonaldized kibbutz dining rooms or, if they had no choice, to bitterly complain about them. And just like in American ballparks, professional caterers were expected to simultaneously cut down on expenses, diversify the food, and improve its quality. These attempts at "re-enchantment" were only partly successful, mainly because rationalized irrationality can't provide for the human touch necessary to create food that enchants eaters.

While these outcomes are predicted by the McDonaldization theory, the McDonaldization of kibbutz dining rooms led to some unexpected consequences. The very primordial social categories that both Socialist Zionism and the standardizing flow of McDonaldization were expected to eliminate reemerged. Privatized kibbutzim were restructured along class lines, with newly rich and newly poor kibbutzniks sharing the space they used to own collectively. While socioeconomic class was most obvious in the private realm of members' dwellings, the dining room became the sphere where lack of economic means was publically pronounced. It was where the poor had to limit their food intake, argue with the cashier about the ways in which their food was (over)priced, and take on dining room jobs and extra shifts that exposed them to the public gaze. Thus, the very exploitative social structure that socialism intended to eradicate found its most blunt expression in the McDonaldized dining room.

Ethnicity and gender, categories that socialist egalitarian ideology also aimed to eliminate, reemerged in the privatized dining room, too. The hegemonic Ashkenazi cuisine was challenged by Mizrahi and other paying clients, who demanded that their culinary preferences, shaped by their ethnic identities, as dynamic as these may be, be accommodated. And as women in the kibbutz were relegated to service and domestic jobs, it is of little wonder that many of the kibbutz poor who took on dining room shifts were women.

Most salient, however, was the blatant public victory of the family, and for that matter of the extended family, over all other kibbutz social components. Nowhere was this triumph more obvious than in the dining room, "the symbol of kibbutz 'togetherness' and the heart of hearts of . . . [the] kibbutz" (Maron 1997, 22). In a bizarre way, the McDonaldization of the kibbutz led to a social structure that most Israeli Jews erroneously attribute to traditional Arab *hamula,* or extended family: multigenerational, patriarchal, patrilocal, and very much endogamous.

FIVE

# Meat and Masculinity in
# a Military Prison

IN THIS CHAPTER, I TURN to what is probably the most complex, controversial, and problematic feature of contemporary Israel: the strained relations between Israeli Jews and the Palestinians living in the territories occupied by Israel in the 1967 war. I deal with one of the most disturbing questions regarding contemporary Israel: How is it that the citizens of a state established only recently by a people who have been persecuted for millennia and who were the ultimate victims of the twentieth century now take part in the long-term victimization of the Palestinians held under their military control? While this issue has been the subject of heated political, moral, and academic debate, I examine some minute and taken-for-granted aspects of the daily practices of the occupation, namely culinary features, to expose what I term "the logic of the occupation": the cognitive and emotional processes that allow Israeli Jews to reinterpret and redefine their relations with the Palestinians so as to maintain a sense of weakness and victimization that justifies their ongoing control over and abuse of this population.

Ethnographically, this chapter is engaged with the interaction between Jews and Palestinians in the most extreme form of Palestinian subjugation by Israeli Jews: a military prison for Palestinian detainees arrested for *averot bitahon* (security offences). Power was therefore observable in this context as in no other realm, institution, or social interaction in Israel. Yet despite the common-sense expectation that the armed Israeli Defense Force soldiers on a short *sherut miluim* (reserve service) assignment of guarding the military prison would feel empowered and in total control over the Palestinian prisoners, this chapter shows how they redefined themselves as the victims of the situation and of the detainees. The ethnographic data presented in this chapter was collected while I was on reserve duty. I elaborate

146

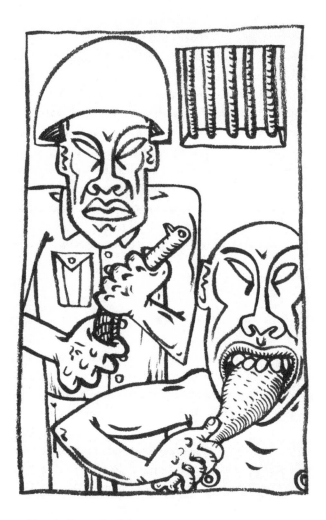

16. *They Are Eating Our Meat*

on this situation and discuss its ethical complications and dilemmas later in the chapter.

The fact that the guards cultivated a sense of weakness and victimization despite the undeniable power dynamics between themselves and their prisoners was facilitated by a culinary situation: the soldiers argued that their food, and specifically the quantity and quality of the meat they were allocated, was insufficient and inadequate for their mission. They further argued that members of the other two groups of men at the prison—the Palestinian prisoners and the military police (who managed the prison)—were fed more and better meat. As a consequence of this relative lack of meat, the reserve soldiers argued that they were at the bottom of the prison power structure and as such were the victims of the situation, the MPs, and the Palestinian detainees.

It is important to note that lack of meat became the pretext for a sense of weakness and victimization *in the context of the prison.* I do not argue that a practical or perceived lack of meat universally underlies the Israeli sense of victimization, which in turn justifies the military control of the Palestinians. Indeed, I have shown in my analysis of Independence Day barbecues (see chapter 2) that an abundance of meat may lead to ambivalence regarding the Israeli Jewish sense of power. Clearly, such power reversals take place in other cultural realms and contexts in Israel, specifically within the strained Israeli-Palestinian relations. The point I wish to make in this chapter is that in specific contexts, the culinary realm becomes a privileged arena for such power reversals.

## MEAT AND MASCULINITY IN COERCIVE SETTINGS

In chapter 2, I reviewed some of the literature that deals with meat and the important role it plays in the construction and maintenance of power and masculinity. While the nutritional contribution of meat to physical power is controversial to say the least, the ethnographic literature I cited is very clear in demonstrating meat's symbolic and social importance. Anthropologist Craig Stanford goes as far as to argue that the origins of patriarchal dominance are linked to meat acquisition, "especially through the cognitive capacities necessary for the strategic sharing of meat with fellow group members" (1999, 5). This chapter amplifies and complicates the potential symbolic and social meanings of meat (and lack of meat). In the Israeli military prison I studied, a perceived lack of meat was the cultural mechanism that instilled a sense of weakness and victimization in the Israeli Jewish guards, which in turn underlay their ill treatment of the Palestinian prisoners.

Hegemonic masculinity is a "narrow version of the idealized man, including qualities such as authority, rationality, physical strength, and/or an enthusiasm for sport" (Sumpter 2015, 105). This interpretation of masculinity hearkens back to the days of hunter-gatherers, when prowess in hunting, and the enjoyment of meat that a successful hunt allowed, led to increased chances of survival. Hunting, just like war, has always been a male-dominated activity, and militaries, with their imposed routines, have a substantial influence on the culinary habits of soldiers and society more broadly (Cwiertka 2002). Indeed, Katarzyna Cwiertka credits the early twentieth-century Japanese military with diffusing the consumption of meat, a nontraditional part of Japanese cuisine, into broader Japanese culture.

There is significant variety among coercive settings, yet the connection between meat and masculinity seems to remain constant. Militarized societies are not the only environments that coerce a similar version of hegemonic masculinity. Patrick McGann (2002, 86), for example, quotes former college and professional football players who remarked on the pressure to eat more, especially more meat, to "maintain or increase body size and strength." Carol Adams (1998, 66–68) concurs that football, meat, and masculinity are all intimately connected; the team ethos, especially at the professional level, is a coercive setting that requires eating "like a man." McGann (2002, 87–88) also remarks on the semiotic associations of the words "meat" and "fruit" in American idioms: one gets at the meat of the matter, but a fruit is a particularly effeminate gay man. Team sports push a hegemonic masculinity based in ferocity and aggressiveness, two values tied to the consumption of meat.

Studies have shown that gendered perceptions of meat, even in less militarized societies, such as the contemporary United States, begin at such a young age that boys in primary school are more likely to prefer red meat than their female classmates (Sumpter, 2015, 106, articulating the conclusions of Caine-Bish and Scheule 2009). Citing Jemal Nath's (2011) and Joseph Gelfer's (2013) research on homosocial outdoor male gatherings at the grill and men's ministries, Sumpter argues that "when consumption rates are high, the act of abstaining could automatically place a vegetarian male out of the social circle" (2015, 111). Wesley Buerkle (2009) argues that the emergence and popularization of metrosexuality, a subversive masculine identity, has led burger advertising to draw an increasingly close connection between meat consumption and traditional, heteronormative masculinity. While contrasting notions of masculinity do exist, they are often formed in protest to the still-hegemonic masculinity that emphasizes the connection between masculinity and meat.

The decision to consume meat or embrace a vegetarian lifestyle can be subversive regardless of which option is the cultural norm. Thus, in Indian society, which is rigidly dictated by varnas and castes, untouchables and Indian Christians consume meat, especially beef, to reject India's hegemonic masculinity, which is tied through Hinduism to vegetarianism (Staples 2008). In India, meat consumption increases the virility of the powerless; it is, to use a term of James C. Scott's, a "weapon of the weak." Vegetarianism in India is often tied to coercive Hindu nationalism, but Swami Vivekananda once prescribed "'beef, biceps, and Bhagvad-Gita' as the antidote to colonial accusations of Indian effeminacy" (Staples 2008, 43–44). The link between beef consumption and overcoming the limitations of social structures, regardless of whether those structures are caused by colonialism or nationalism, is proof of the semiotic significance of meat in coercive cultures. In a militarized society such as Israel (Kimmerling 1993a, 1993b), military cuisine, intended to enhance strength and valor in battle, is expected to highlight meat. Israel's militarized society, like Meiji Japan's, forces a connection between meat consumption and hegemonic masculinity. Real men are soldiers, and real soldiers eat meat. Strong soldiers are modern hunters: they protect, they fight, they kill, and they produce spoils. Just as masculinity among the hunters of yore was connected to providing meat, hegemonic masculinity among contemporary Israeli men is closely connected to consuming large amounts of meat. Lack of meat, which denies soldiers the ability to achieve hegemonic masculinity, thus constitutes a major social problem, as I learned during my tenure at Megiddo Prison.

### "A SERIOUS MEAT PROBLEM"

"We should eat something before we get there," said Captain Ami, the commander of Pluga Aleph (Platoon A). "Yes," said David, the regiment adjutant. "We should stop in one of the restaurants in the Waddi Ara [Ara Valley] and have some meat. The food at the prison is awful, and we have a serious meat problem."

It was July 2002, and we were driving through the Ara Valley, on an ancient route turned modern highway that links Israel's coast with its northern hinterland. The valley is dotted with Israeli Palestinian villages and towns (Palestinians living in areas that came under Israeli sovereignty after the 1948 war became Israeli citizens). Quite a few of these Palestinians make a living by capitalizing on their Arab Palestinian ethnicity in the only way considered acceptable by the Israeli Jewish majority: producing and selling "Arab food," similar to that served in Abu Gosh, the site of one of the battles of the Hummus Wars (see introduction). Beyond olive oil and *baladi* (literally "village," referring to the fact that this produce is home grown and supposedly of traditional varieties) fruits and vegetables, dozens of fast-food joints and restaurants along the highway serve a limited array of Palestinian dishes to Israeli Jewish clientele, including hummus, falafel, shawarma, tahini, tabbouleh, baba ghanoush, labane, and finely chopped "Arab salad," along with different kinds of meat grilled *al ha'esh* (over fire). In the aftermath of the Al-Aktza Intifada (also known as the Second Intifada), which began in September 2000 in the occupied territories but ignited large protests and violent clashes with the police in the Ara Valley and other Israeli Palestinian centers, many Israeli Jews, who perceived of these demonstrations as acts of treason, boycotted Israeli Palestinian restaurants, causing this area to sink into economic crisis.[1]

But here we were, four IDF officers (including myself, an anthropologist in the making), driving toward the military prison at Megiddo, located near the ancient site of Armageddon, where our battalion had already been positioned for a week. Despite the negative sentiments harbored by many Israeli Jews toward the Israeli Palestinians of the Ara Valley at the time, only two years after the uprising, we stopped at one of the shawarma stands and purchased pitas stuffed with warm, fatty meat, hummus, and vegetable salad, topped with tahini and fragrant *amba,* a tangy, Middle Eastern mango condiment whose pervasive smell lingers for days.

As soon as we arrived at the prison and met our reserve companions, I realized that there was a food problem, or rather a meat problem, evolving. The battalion commander told me that the soldiers kept complaining about the food, especially the quantity and quality of the meat. When I asked him if the food was really so bad and the amount so meager, he replied: "You know, this is the army, we all know how the food is here. It does not look very different from what I have experienced during previous tours of reserve duty." He added that the unusual extension of the tour of duty to thirty-two days from the routine twenty-four days (the result of the recent reoccupation of areas previously under the control of the Palestinian Authority, part of Operation Defense Shield, which was initiated to curb suicide bombings) put extra pressure on the soldiers. The chief of operations dismissively added: "Soldiers are soldiers, they will always complain. . . . If the food was okay, they would complain about something else."

However, as I continued to talk to the officers and soldiers, I realized that the issue of meat was more complicated. Each and every soldier and officer I talked to in the first days of *miluim* complained about the food, and specifically about the quality and quantity of the meat, but the intriguing aspect was that many of my military companions presented the situation in comparative terms. They argued that the Palestinians detained at the prison, as well as the Israeli MPs who managed the prison, were served more and better meat then they were. They also compared the food to what they were used to eating at home and claimed that they always had greater quantities of better meat as civilians. If we bear in mind the ample literature cited earlier that ties meat to masculinity and potency, by arguing that they had more and better meat as civilians, the soldiers were hinting that they felt more masculine and mighty as civilians than as soldiers.

Some of the officers pointed out that the food allocated was not appropriate for the mission. They said that they had gotten better food and more meat when they were assigned to more conventional military operations, such as patrolling the border or controlling the occupied territories. Both officers and soldiers made repeated trips to nearby towns to eat meat dishes, and purchasing meat to roast in the yard next to our quarters became an almost daily practice. It became clear to me that something unusual was going on and that it had to do with meat.

At the time, I was in the final stages of writing my PhD dissertation in anthropology, focused on food and social relations in a small town in central Vietnam. For years, I had been thinking about food as one of the most salient but least studied means of social interaction, so I couldn't resist my ethnographic urge and launched an ethnographic research project while doing my reserve duty.

### ETHNOGRAPHER IN ARMS

So what was I, a PhD candidate in anthropology, doing in a military prison for Palestinian detainees? While I can't address here the various social forces and dilemmas that influence Israeli soldiers when performing their military duties, as an anthropologist I feel that I have to explain my presence at a military prison. To do this, it is necessary to give some context regarding the military unit that was guarding the prison.

I grew up in a "leftist" house (that is, my family voted for the labor party, Ha'Avoda), and, like most Israelis, I was not opposed to serving in the IDF. Neither were my parents, siblings, or friends. In many ways, it was a class issue: membership in the privileged social echelon of Ashkenazi veterans was often paid for in the willingness to shed blood for the country.

So when I was eighteen, I joined the army and served in an infantry unit (to which one volunteers). I spent much of my service in the occupied territories, and, though I did harbor private concerns about my role as a soldier taking part in the occupation of the Palestinians, I did not protest or resist openly. Once I had concluded my almost four years of service, I was assigned to a reserve unit. I tried to avoid reserve duty as much as I could, often by being abroad during the appointed periods. However, I never refused to enlist. When circumstances forced me to enlist, I attempted to eliminate my cognitive dissonance by convincing myself that my presence at a checkpoint or in other realms of interaction with Palestinians would mean a more humane treatment for them than if a right-wing soldier were manning the post.

After the assassination of Prime Minister Yitzhak Rabin in 1995 and my personal realization that the peace process initiated by the Oslo Accords was undermined by Israeli politicians (from the right and the left), I realized that I was misleading myself by failing to stand up against what I found to be destructive to the Israeli cause, to Zionism, and to universal and Jewish ethics. I concluded that any participation in the occupation was politically and ethically wrong. I therefore decided to refuse further *miluim* orders. Coincidentally, as I was making this decision, my aging platoon was reassigned to the newly established Home Front Command (Pikud Ha'Oref).

One of the consequences of the 1990 Gulf War was the dismantling of the outdated Civil Defense Corps (Hagna Ezrahit, abbreviated to Haga), which had proved inadequate and ineffective in dealing with missile attacks on Israeli cities, and the establishing of the Home Front Command, headed by an active (rather than reserve) general and command. The Home Front Command reserve units were trained mainly in rescue and relief operations.

Increasing awareness of the necessity of effectively handling the needs of Israeli civilians under attack led the Home Front Command to create a new military profession: behavioral sciences officer (BSO). These officers would advise the military command on civilian matters and serve as liaison officers between the military and the Israeli civilian authorities and population. These new posts were to be manned by social scientists who were active reserve officers capable of combining their professional and military skills. As there were only a few active reserve officers trained as social scientists, the Home Front Command actively sought soldiers with the proper academic qualifications to train as BSOs.

So when I got my next reserve order, I asked for a personal interview with my battalion commander and told him that I was unwilling to participate in the military occupation of the Palestinian Territories. He informed me that the battalion in its new guise was now intended for domestic rescue operations and that he expected me to be willing to take part in that mission. He added that, as I was a PhD candidate in anthropology, he had the perfect job for me: a behavioral sciences officer.

Within the confines of my upbringing, social status, and self-perception, I was unable to reject this offer. I was actually relieved and pleased that my commander had addressed my moral reservations and offered me a military position that had nothing to do with the occupation. Instead of refusing further *miluim,* I accepted an invitation to a BSO course. Quite content with the way I had successfully managed my divorce from the occupation, I was surprised and angry when I received an order for *miluim* at Megiddo Prison a few months later. I immediately called my commander, who explained that "during wartime, we are assigned with the rescue of Israeli civilians, but our routine reserve mission includes securing Home Front military posts, such as the prison."

The data presented in this chapter was collected during this tour of *miluim* in 2002. Because the post of BSO was new and because there was no need for a civil liaison officer at the prison, I had a substantial measure of flexibility. My role was that of an organizational advisor, helping run the operation room that was tasked with managing manpower and assigning soldiers to their different duties. Unfortunately for me, this sterile definition of my duties turned out to be inaccurate, and I was often required to complete officer duties that involved direct contact with the Palestinian detainees.

Following this reserve tour, I told my commander that I would refuse to take part in future reserve duties that involved the occupation of the Palestinians. Although he noted the serious penalties that might result from such refusal, I told him that I was willing to bear the consequences. This, however, never happened. Following a couple of years abroad as a postdoc, I received an official letter thanking me for my military service and dismissing me from further military duties.

The first draft of this chapter was written in 2002, a few weeks after my reserve tour at Megiddo Prison. Upset and confused, I used writing to process my experience. I also felt that Israeli citizens, the vast majority of whom know very little about the daily practices in the IDF's engagement with the Palestinians, should know about the impossible situations forced on Israeli soldiers during *miluim.* Lastly, I wanted to publicize the destructive consequences of places such as Megiddo Prison, which was described by one of the battalion soldiers as "a university for terrorists under the auspices of the Israeli army." The present chapter, however, is more ambitious: my aim is to expose the logic of the Israeli occupation and the cultural mechanisms that translate this logic into practice.

The data presented in this chapter was collected during thirty-two days of reserve duty at Megiddo Prison during the summer of 2002. In the introduction to this book, I pointed out that I was reluctant to view my daily life as ethnographic participant observation, but in this case I made an informed decision to conduct participant observation while on *miluim*. I took field notes, documented daily practices, and conducted over forty interviews with officers and soldiers. The reserve soldiers turned out to be the most accessible interviewees I have ever encountered: they were extremely bored during their guard shifts and became increasingly upset during our tour of duty. My visits to their towers and watch-posts were always welcomed, and, as these conversations were within the parameters set for my job as a BSO, the soldiers happily shared their observations, insights, complaints, and feelings. Moreover, as an officer, I participated in the daily practices of the battalion and was able to collect data at daily staff meetings and consultations with the MPs, during meals, at the canteen, in the sleeping tents, and during the few hours when we were allowed to leave the prison, when soldiers escaped to nearby towns to look for meat.

## MEGIDDO MILITARY PRISON

The material and practical arrangements at the Megiddo military prison were typical of the Israeli tendency to devise ad hoc solutions to emerging problems that are actually the consequences of major, highly complex conundrums. These temporary solutions tend to become "permanently temporary" (*zmani'im beofen kavuah*). Once such temporary solutions become permanent, they require increasing investments of energy, resources, ingenuity, and skill for their maintenance. The high expenses involved in the maintenance of structures that were meant to be temporary further contribute to their consolidation as permanent.

Originally a British Tegart fort,[2] Megiddo Prison was overtaken by the Israeli army after the British withdrawal in 1948 and assigned as a military police station and prison.[3] I couldn't find an authoritative historiography of Megiddo Prison, but one of the soldiers I interviewed told me that his brother-in-law, who was assigned to guard Syrian POWs at Megiddo during the October War in 1973, said that the prison compound had been made up of mostly the same structures then as it was in 2002. Over time, the original British police station was expanded into a major Israeli military prison, but this apparently happened without anyone ever having made a formal decision to turn it into one. No effort was made to hide this fact; the prison's commander explicitly conveyed this message to us in his welcome speech when he pointed out that the prison structures were improvised (*meultarim*). He also admitted that securing the jail was not, in his opinion, a mission for IDF soldiers and pointed out that he would prefer that the civilian Israeli Prison Service to take charge of Megiddo.[4]

Thus, instead of a properly planned, equipped, and guarded detention center that would be easy to handle and control and where detainees would be imprisoned in reasonable or at least acceptable conditions, Megiddo Prison was a hodgepodge of makeshift pens, military tents, buildings, and improvised facilities, reinforced and buttressed with patches of fence, concrete, barbed wire, and iron bars. The fences and water, sewage, and electricity systems were constantly on the brink of collapse during our reserve tour, and there were repeated sewage spills that resulted in a foul odor and an extremely disturbing mosquito infestation.

The prison commander informed us that there were some 1,200 Palestinian detainees at the prison "in different stages of juridical processes, but none with blood on their hands" (a term used to denote prisoners convicted of killing Israeli Jews). He added that "none of the prisoners had been sentenced to more than five years," implying that the prisoners had not been convicted of heavy offences that would have carried longer sentences. The prisoners at Megiddo were held in three pens surrounded by barbed wire fences. They slept in American-surplus military tents, which are routinely used by IDF units in temporary positions. A few prisoners of higher profile were kept in cells inside the original Tegart fort.

The pens were very crowded, as were the tents. I counted over twenty beds in tents originally planned for a dozen soldiers. The tents were extremely hot and stuffy during the summer and miserably cold during the winter. They lacked insulation and mosquito nets, which are integral components of these tents when they are used by IDF soldiers but were absent at the prison. Most importantly, when IDF soldiers make use of such tents, they sleep in them for a few weeks at a time but are not confined to them day and night for years. Military tents are temporary shelters, but in the prison they were being used as permanent dwellings.

The prisoners maintained and cleaned their own showers and squat toilets, but the plumbing was falling apart and suffered from repeated clogging and spillage. The prisoners had built makeshift decks in the showers so they could walk above the murky puddles of sewage.

An unexpected and, as far as the reserves soldiers were concerned, disturbing aspect of Megiddo Prison was the "*shawish* [Arabic for 'sergeant'] system" that governed living arrangements. Under this system, prisoners ran their own daily affairs within the pens and were allowed a large degree of autonomy so long as order was maintained and the rules (which were never explained to us explicitly) were not violated. Each of the pens had a *shawish* and several deputies, elected by the prisoners as their representatives and acknowledged by the jail authorities. These functionaries were charged with managing daily affairs within the pens and interacting with prison authorities. The prisoners, under the leadership of the *shawish,* were formally responsible for cleaning and hygiene and for arranging classes, hobby clubs, physical exercise, religious activities, and social events. Another privilege was the ability to order their own provisions and cook their own food.[5] The prisoners operated their own pita bread bakery, which supplied them with fresh bread. Because baking was done during the late hours, nights at the prison smelled of wood oven-baked bread mixed with the sour stench of urine and open sewage.

Each of the three pens comprising the prison was controlled and managed by one of the main Palestinian political organizations: Fatah, Hamas, and Islamic Jihad. When a new prisoner arrived at Megiddo, he was assigned to a pen according to his organizational affiliation. If he didn't have any, he was instructed to choose one. Thus, Israeli military police officers jailed Palestinian detainees according to the prisoners' identification with what the Israeli state and army perceive as enemy organizations.

MPs, who worked in the prison full time and long term and thus had more experience with and knowledge about the prison's workings than many of the reserve soldiers, told me that the *shawish* were not necessarily the actual pen leaders. The *shawish* often served as a façade for prisoners who were higher in their respective organizations but preferred to remain behind the scenes. The prison commander commented that pen leaders kept in constant contact with their respective commands through concealed cellular phones and that they organized political and religious orientation classes as well as military training, some aspects of which, such as hand-to-hand combat, were observable from the watchtowers. It's not surprising, then, that a fellow soldier described the prison as a training ground for terrorists.

Why did the prison commander grant the Palestinian prisoners such autonomy and privileges? I quickly realized that the *shawish* system could be easily justified in organizational terms. Commanding a military prison is a default position for lieutenant colonels in the military police on the path of career advancement. The prison commander made clear that manning the prison was not a job for IDF soldiers, but he didn't explain why he had accepted the role of prison commander if he had felt that way. Also left out of his welcome speech was the fact that his own promotion required him to have a successful tenure commanding the prison—that is, he needed to make sure that the jail remained "quiet" and did not cause "noise" by attracting negative media attention.

The decisive quest for a "quiet" term was observable in the "instructions for opening fire" (hora'ot pticha be'esh), the essential mode of conduct expected from IDF soldiers in their respective missions. These instructions were specified by the prison commander on our arrival day and reiterated at all joint staff meetings with the MPs. The instructions were simple: we were never to open fire except in the case of a direct threat to our own lives or to those of other IDF soldiers. In the case of a prisoners' escape, we were instructed to call out to the runaways and demand that they stop, but, in contrast to the IDF's regular procedures, we were not allowed to open fire even if the prisoners refused to yield and continued to run. In the case of a large-scale prison break, the guards were instructed to remain in their towers, lock them, and use their guns only if the prisoners tried to break in. Otherwise, they were to let the prisoners run away. The rest of us were to regroup at our residence zone and prepare to protect ourselves, but we were to refrain from trying to stop the escapees and to avoid opening fire at all costs.

The dismayed soldiers challenged the prison commander and asked him to explain his orders because they were radically different from the regular IDF instructions, which call for commitment and engagement (d'vekut bamesimah veshe'ifa lemagah). The commander responded: "This is a sensitive place, and a violent event here might ignite the entire Middle East." He told the soldiers that he would rather have a few prisoners run away than have them injured or killed, which would inevitably result in another round of violence, the outcome of which could be far worse.

My understanding was that mass escape and soldiers injuring or killing large numbers of escaping prisoners would inevitably result in a mess, and as a consequence, the "quiet" tenure would become "noisy." To ensure stability and order, concessions were granted in an ongoing process of negotiation between the prison authorities and the prisoners, which had resulted in the shawish system.

According to the MPs, the *shawish* amassed substantial personal power vis-à-vis the prison authorities, their respective political organizations, and the other prisoners. They also had personal privileges, the most salient of which was the fact that they didn't live in military tents like the other prisoners but rather in makeshift huts that were better equipped, warmer, more comfortable, and carefully maintained and decorated.[6] In what was arguably the most bizarre rule in the unwritten agreement between the prisoners and the MPs, these huts were exempt from searches, and MPs were allowed to enter them only "by invitation." We observed from our watchtowers how unpermitted equipment, documents, and, most importantly, cell phones were quickly passed into the huts during our occasional search operations, where they remained out of the reach of MPs. The *shawish* were also invested in maintaining the system that privileged them politically and personally, so they tended to cooperate with the prison authorities because they wanted to protect their own concessions.

Maintaining stability in a prison that was built hastily some thirty years earlier, never planned properly, and in constant need of fixing and patching necessitated a large number of guards and security personnel. Though IDF military prisons are formally commanded and managed by the military police, the Home Front Command served as a subcontractor tasked with securing this prison. Thus, while the MPs handled the daily administration and maintenance of the prison, the armed reserve officers and soldiers of my battalion were tasked with guarding and securing jail activities and operations. We were expected to handle our own affairs, manage our manpower, operate the watchtowers, and supply armed escorts on demand, even for routine prison procedures. We also ran our own dining room with food provided by the MP kitchen. Finally, we were expected to perform our duties as instructed and solve our difficulties and problems by ourselves.

## MEATLESS AND POWERLESS

I was standing with one of the battalion soldiers in one of the watchtowers overlooking the kitchen in one of the pens. The Palestinian prisoners working in the kitchen below us were cutting meat with sword-like knives, which, while essential for preparing food for hundreds of prisoners, could be easily turned against the IDF soldiers. The knives were therefore brought into the pens every morning by the MPs and then carefully counted and collected every evening. One afternoon, as the battalion soldiers were about to enter the pens for the evening count, the *shawish,* who had had a dispute with the MPs during the day, instructed the cooks not to hand the knives back. This led to an immediate state of alert, and only after some forty or fifty minutes of tense negotiation were the knives returned and routine restored. The meat knives were therefore means of power, which both sides tried to harness, with the Palestinian prisoners sometimes having the upper hand.

The reserve soldiers, who secured the count between their guarding shifts, returned from their mission an hour later than expected, angry and upset. As the *miluim* period progressed, the heavy load of guard shifts and other missions took its toll, and the extra hour of work wasted precious sleeping time. They told me that the Palestinian prisoners had been "toying" (*sihaku*) with them again and that they were unable to restore order or retaliate.

Back in the tower, the soldier sniffed the air and said: "Can you smell the meat? It drives me crazy! As if they were in a hotel. They exercise, play volleyball, and then have the best food: spicy seasoning, fresh pita bread, and lots meat. And us, we get overcooked pasta, cottage cheese, and stale bread in plastic bags for dinner and one-eighth of a chicken or an industrial schnitzel for lunch."

The notion that the prisoners were having great food and a great time at the prison was expressed by many of the battalion soldiers. One of them angrily complained: "What goes on here is not right. These terrorists get everything and laugh in our faces. They curse us, they are cheeky to the MPs, they delay everything on purpose, and we have to wait hours in the sun for them to cooperate. But when they are sick, we have to take them to our hospitals. . . . I mean, look at their food! They have a lot of meat every day while we eat shit."

Quite a few soldiers and MPs went as far as arguing that the Palestinians were better off as prisoners than as free individuals. One of them of told me: "Their situation here is better than back in their villages,[7] where they have no work and nothing to eat. Here, they eat meat everyday, but over there, in the village, they can only dream of it." In a conversation about prisoners returning to their villages, one of the soldiers insisted, "When they are released from the prison, they often cry and even refuse to leave because they know that life back in the village is much harder."

In fact, some of the prisoners did shed tears when they were released from the prison. I observed several "release ceremonies" that included speeches, dances, and festive meals with lots of meat. It is hardly surprising that a man about to be released from prison would be emotional and shed tears of both joy and sadness: soon he would be reunited with his relatives and friends, but he would also be leaving behind comrades with whom he intimately shared his life for a significant period. Even though the soldiers considered the jailed Palestinians to be terrorists, I was still surprised that they could not imagine any reason why the prisoners might be overcome with emotions on their release other than that they must be sad about leaving the perfect lives they had at the prison. The reserve soldiers also insinuated that these Palestinians would voluntarily give up their own freedom for the "meat cauldron," despite the fact that they had been detained precisely because they rejected the "meat cauldron" of Israeli occupation and were willing to give up their freedom and even their own lives for ideological causes.

Meat, however, remained the biggest complaint of the soldiers and officers throughout our reserve tour. One morning, while securing a search of one of the pens, a platoon commander, wearing a bulletproof jacket and helmet and keeping his finger on the trigger of his M-16 as he watched over the cooks, pointed at the trays of roast chicken, winked at me, and whispered: "See, here is *our* lunch." The Palestinian cooks also used one of the IDF's most iconic rations: *luf*, a type of canned meatloaf that is an important component of the IDF's iron rations and a key item in army folklore and nostalgic story-telling.[8] One of the MPs explained that the army allocated a budget to the prisoners with which they ordered ingredients according to their own preferences from both military provisions (e.g., the *luf* cans) and the civilian market. The budget was further supplemented with money from the Palestinian Authority, allowing for the purchase of better products and more meat.

My *miluim* comrades, however, had a different interpretation of the situation. While discussing the assumed culinary privileges of the prisoners, one of the reserve soldiers commented: "The sons of bitches get money to buy meat from the *irgunim*." In contemporary Hebrew, *irgunim* (literally "the organizations") denotes Palestinian terror organizations. If the "organizations" had been the true sponsors of the meat, the prison's paradox would have been exacerbated. In that case, it would have been the enemy (and not the Palestinian Authority, Israel's supposed peace partner) that was providing the prisoners with better meat in larger quantities. As far as the reserve soldiers were concerned, the enemy was directly involved in enhancing the imprisoned terrorists' power and masculinity with extra meat. Without extra meat to match, the soldiers felt weak and disempowered.

Palestinian prisoners were not the only ones accused of appropriating the reserve soldiers' meat. Another commonly expressed notion held by the reserve soldiers was that the MPs, whose kitchen supplied the battalion's food, were embezzling the provisions, specifically the meat. "Did you have a chance to eat in their dining room?" I was asked by a soldier who had dined in the MP dining room. "For one, it is air-conditioned. And then, they have better food! They get all the chocolate Milki [a popular milk drink] and send us this odd vanilla Milki that no one ever buys at the supermarket. And then they get all the meat! They have real schnitzels at least twice a week, and you can always have an extra portion when you ask for it."

It is important to note that we were not suffering from a shortage of food. We had three meals per day, which included vegetables and fruits, dairy products, eggs, bread, and some kind of cooked starch. There were always some loaves of bread with some sort of spread as well as pots of tea and coffee. The food was plain, not very fresh, and served offhandedly. However, there was enough of it, and no one went hungry. The only thing lacking in quantity was meat, and this was the soldiers' main complaint. Some meat, usually defrosted, low-quality, processed hamburgers and schnitzels, was served daily for lunch and devoured by the soldiers, who complained bitterly about its low quality and small quantity.

The notion that the MPs were enjoying "our meat" brought sentiments to the verge of crisis during the second weekend we spent at the prison, in an incident that I termed the "meat mutiny." In Jewish tradition, Saturday is the day for meat, poultry, and fish. Consuming animal flesh is considered a must for a proper Sabbath meal among most Israeli Jews. Nonobservant Israeli Jews also consider the weekend a time for leisure and pleasure, often centered on conspicuous consumption of meat.

According to Halachic rules, cooking is not permitted on the Sabbath, so preparations for the Sabbath meal must be completed by Friday afternoon, and special arrangements must be made to ensure the availability of well-prepared, warm meals throughout the Sabbath. Since the IDF is kosher, military kitchens prepare Sabbath meals in advance, just like observant homes. However, while those who cook at home make major efforts to ensure that meals are tasty and sumptuous, IDF Sabbath food is notoriously inedible.

The main military Sabbath meal, served on Friday evening, is usually reasonable, as the food is made just a few hours prior. Saturday lunch is more complicated, as the main dish served in IDF kitchens is cholent, a meat, bean, and potato stew cooked overnight over low heat. Cholent is not an easy dish to prepare. A classic poverty meal, it is made from coarse ingredients that call for attentive use of spices and careful cooking; it requires expertise and attention that military cooks often lack. Furthermore, most members of the IDF logistics team go home for the Sabbath, so only those low in the hierarchy remain on duty during the weekend, and they are not the most capable nor are they eager to deal with preparing a complicated dish such as cholent.

On the first weekend we spent at the prison, industrial schnitzels were served with the cholent for Saturday lunch. The soldiers ignored the cholent and went for the schnitzels, but these had not been defrosted or even heated, because there was no heating device available that was appropriate to use on the Sabbath. The soldiers angrily rejected the semifrozen, soggy, reconstituted meat and left most of the food uneaten. But since they were still fresh from home, they didn't make too much of a fuss about it.

For the next Saturday lunch, we were served only cholent, which was scorched, unappetizing, and had no traces of meat in it. Shortly after lunch, some dozen soldiers approached the operations room. They were *shalv-bet-niks*, literally "second graders," recent immigrants from the former USSR who had already served in the Russian army and were now serving a shortened compulsory service of three months in the IDF. After a period of basic training, they had been sent to Megiddo and placed under our command to remedy our battalion's severe manpower shortage. They generally kept to themselves, were more low-key and obedient than the Israeli reserve soldiers, and did a lot of physical exercise.

One of them stepped forward to announce that they refused to continue guarding because "they didn't have the meat necessary to provide the energy to perform the duties." He added: "We exercise daily, and then we climb the towers and guard. We need meat! No meat, no towers!" They argued that the MPs embezzled the meat that was intended for our battalion and left us with only "small amounts of second-grade meat."

The reserve officers realized that this could turn into a serious predicament and decided to contain it. One of them led some of the soldiers to the MP dining room, where they inspected the food and found out that the MPs were eating the same meatless, scorched cholent for lunch. They entered the kitchen and discovered that the entire catering staff was off duty, having left behind an inexperienced and rather helpless cook's aid. Going over the documents in the kitchen, they found out that the provisions for the weekend included only 10 kilos of meat instead of the 100 kilos that should have been supplied for some 250 soldiers, resulting in a net amount of

17. *Searching the Pens during Lunch*

40 grams of meat per person. Though this amount could make for a tiny hamburger, the cook's aid on duty explained that the long cooking of the cholent had made the meat dissolve.

The reserve officers made the aid unlock the pantry, and they took several packs of *luf* cans. These cans would hardly have satisfied native Israeli soldiers, who would have rejected them disgustedly, but the recent arrivals from Russia, where preserved foods had been appreciated and perceived of as a sophisticated, modern form of food distribution, were pleased. Despite the fact that the MPs had been served the exact same meal as the reserve soldiers during this weekend, many of the soldiers mentioned the event time and again as a proof that the MPs were "stealing our meat."

Some of the soldiers blamed the battalion's dining room attendants for not handling the food properly and accused them of helping themselves to the common meat cauldron: "When you ask them for an extra portion of meat, they say that there are only just enough portions for everyone, but later you can see them nibbling a piece of chicken or a schnitzel, and eventually, they throw a lot of leftover meat into the garbage or feed it to the cats." These attendants were actually reserve soldiers from our battalion who had been exempted from full military duties for different reasons and instead charged with logistics. They didn't have to guard day and night and were not part of the minimal emergency quota, so they were therefore able to go home frequently while the rest of the soldiers worked much harder and were rarely allowed leaves. Although the attendants were clearly not the source of the meat problem, the reserve soldiers were willing to blame anyone and everyone for the situation.

The battalion commander offered a different perspective for understanding the meat problem. In a meeting with the Home Front Command general and his staff, he suggested that the definition of the mission was incongruent with its practical demands and that the lack of meat was a result of this:

> The menu and the food allocation are appropriate for a nonoperational unit [such as the MP unit at Megiddo Prison, which was the formal addressee of the food provisioning]. However, our regiment is assigned with a fully operational mission of manning guard posts twenty-four hours a day, thirty days a month, just like combat units patrolling the border. It is obvious that the catering arrangements, such as providing only three meals per day or having meatless Sundays, are intended for military bases where soldiers work nine-to-five and go home for the weekends and get extra meat. But we need a more comprehensive diet in order to keep up the energy of our soldiers. I suggest that the definition of the assignment be adjusted to its operational realities because we need a proper lunch with enough meat and an extra meat-oriented late-night meal for the night shifts seven days a week.

The commander was pointing out that according to IDF regulations, soldiers in operational units and activities are provided with more food, and specifically more meat, than nonoperational soldiers. He was arguing that the military bureaucracy failed in making a distinction between the nonoperational MPs at Megiddo Prison, who went home almost daily, and the reserve soldiers, who were part of a fully operational unit that was confined to the prison for security and alert (*konenut*) reasons. He expected that once the bureaucracy recognized the battalion soldiers as "real" soldiers charged with full operational missions, orders would be issued to feed them as proper soldiers are fed in the IDF—with more food, and especially with more meat.

The commander's observation regarding our erroneous classification as nine-to-five soldiers supplied with nine-to-five food was confirmed during the daily trips the reserves officers made to the military court in Salem, some 5 kilometers from the prison, but within the occupied territories, just over the Green Line (the de facto Israeli border up until the 1967 war). One of the lawyers I met at the court told me that the IDF located this military court in the occupied territories because the area was under martial law, which was stricter, allowing it to function with fewer restrictions than a civil court in Israel would and for more convictions to be made on less evidence than would be required by an Israeli civilian court.

A military police truck transported prisoners from Megiddo to the court in Salem daily, escorted by reserve soldiers and officers. The number of guards was determined by the number of prisoners, and, during the month we spent at Megiddo, most of the officers and soldiers in the battalion participated in these escort missions at least once.

The reserve officers charged with escorting prisoners to the military court raved about the food they had in Salem. One of them told me, "You should see the salad bar. It looks like the ones in a good Italian restaurant, with grilled zucchini and peppers seasoned with oil and vinegar. Then, there was chicken breast in sauce. I expected it to be dry and hard, but it was soft and tasted great. And there were only the two of us at a table for six, so we got the entire tray of meat to ourselves."

The point was that a nine-to-five military unit located only 5 kilometers away from the prison and assigned with the nonoperational, essentially secretarial duties of a military court was classified as a front-line unit due to its location in the occupied territories, whereas the Megiddo units were not. The military court in Salem was therefore supplied with a better catering staff, better food, and more meat. So when discussing the food at Salem, the officers and soldiers insinuated again that despite the operational missions they were charged with, they were not getting the appropriate provisions, specifically meat, while other military units, charged with nonoperational jobs, were getting larger quantities of tastier meat. This further contributed to their sense of powerlessness and to what I came to realize was their narrative of victimization.

## NARRATIVES OF VICTIMIZATION

As my circle of interlocutors widened and I became familiar with more aspects of prison life, I realized that the three very different groups of men confined to the jail—Palestinian prisoners, MPs, and reserves soldiers—as distinct and set apart as they were, shared a narrative of victimization. It turned out that, at Megiddo Prison, everyone perceived of themselves as the real victims.

An uninvolved onlooker would find it easy to understand why the Palestinian prisoners felt and expressed victimization. The Palestinian people perceive of themselves as victims of the Jews and of the State of Israel, recounting a blissful past in Palestine that was shattered by Zionism, which they perceive as a belated form of European colonialism. The Palestinians living in the territories occupied in 1967 live under martial law, and their desperate political and military attempts at gaining independence have been crushed time and again by the Israelis and their powerful security apparatus. In 2002, just prior to the events described in this chapter, they failed at yet another attempt at revolting, and many of the prisoners at Megiddo during my service had been detained during this uprising and its aftermath. These unsuccessful revolts led to the implementation of stricter security measures by Israel and a vicious cycle of violence, with the Palestinian casualties numbering roughly ten times the Israeli ones.

The Palestinians incarcerated at Megiddo had been taken away from their families, friends, jobs, and studies and subjected to what they perceived of as biased and incomprehensible judicial processes. They were imprisoned in pens under very harsh conditions, forced to live for years in overcrowded tents in a prison with dilapidated infrastructure. According to their narrative, the Palestinian prisoners had been arbitrarily deprived of their freedom without fair trials or a sense of when their freedom might be restored. Regardless of the validity of their claims, the Palestinian prisoners' assertions of victimization are easy to understand.

The narrative of the MPs, however, surprised me. The Israeli MPs saw their employment as proof of their own victimization. Indeed, among IDF soldiers, the military police is considered the most shameful appointment.

MPs are nicknamed *maniakim* (maniacs), and there exists a structural and ethical dissonance between them and the rest of the IDF. Because their mission is to police their own comrades instead of fighting the enemy, MPs are treated as a sort of enemy by the rest of the IDF soldiers, and military folklore abounds with stories recounting violent confrontations with MPs that always end with the latter's humiliation and defeat. In my interviews, the MPs at Megiddo blamed their victimization on a "the system"—that is, the military bureaucracy that had channeled them into the military police—as well as their own imperfect bodies, which had denied them combat postings.[9]

The narrative of my fellow reserve soldiers, however, perplexed me the most. These men, armed with automatic assault rifles and combat vests and assigned to man towers overlooking the pens and to guard prisoners for only a few weeks, told me that they felt bullied and victimized by the unarmed prisoners and, to a lesser extent, by the unarmed MPs. Also surprising was how thoroughly this sense of victimization penetrated the reserve unit: each and every soldier and officer I interviewed or talked to during that tour of *sherut miluim,* from the lowest-ranking soldier all the way up to the battalion commanders, concurred that they were the actual dupes at Megiddo.

While neither the MPs nor the Palestinian prisoners mentioned meat as part of their narratives of victimization, lack of meat was the primary complaint of the reserve soldiers, who repeatedly grumbled about the abysmal quantities and low quality of the meat allocated to them. Moreover, many of them made an intentional point of comparing the quantity and quality of the reserve soldiers' meat to that allocated to the MPs and the prisoners, insisting that the men of the other groups were served more and better meat. In line with the perceptions of meat at Independence Day barbecues, which I described in chapter 2, the reserve soldiers framed their victimhood in terms of their inability, due to lack of adequate provisions and especially of meat, to achieve hegemonic ideals of masculinity and to be virile and strong soldiers.

Beyond meat, food and eating in general were important topics within the reserve soldiers' narrative of victimization. They argued that the food they were served was not fresh, that there was very little variety of products and dishes, and that the cooked meals were often served either half-frozen or scorched. They argued that the MPs siphoned off the better products (e.g., chocolate Milki) and left the reserve battalion with products of lesser quality (e.g., vanilla Milki), older bread, vegetables and fruits that were not fresh, and cooked dishes made of inferior ingredients, such as canned meat. While these were fair descriptions of the food, and while the MP dining room did, in my opinion, serve better food, this was standard operating procedure in the IDF, where combat soldiers, and especially reserve combat soldiers, are at the bottom of the food chain, for practical and sociological reasons.

Some of the reserve soldiers also argued that our dining room staff, comprised of soldiers from our battalion, were doing their job poorly by failing to ensure that we had better food. To a certain extent, this was also true. The dining room attendants had to deal with the low-quality food that they were allocated, but they didn't go out of their way to improve it. Moreover, the battalion soldiers were envious of the dining room staff because they were exempt from guard shifts, didn't work as hard, and had more leave. Because of the severe manpower shortage, the fact that some battalion soldiers were not sharing the full burden of duty became a real issue, which I will return to shortly.

Beyond food, many of the reserve soldiers' grievances had to do with the physical conditions at the prison. Megiddo was extremely hot during the summer, and the supposed upgrade of our living quarters from tents (in which we slept during our first week of *miluim*) to brand new mobile units turned out to be a curse rather than a blessing. The corrugated iron structures lacked air conditioning and were much warmer than the tents, which could be manipulated to allow fresh air inside. Though a new common room featuring satellite television and comfortable armchairs had been set up just prior to our arrival, its air conditioning system didn't function properly, and many of the soldiers complained that the television often failed.

When it came to military discipline, the reserve soldiers felt bullied by the MPs, who routinely inspected their guard posts and filed complaints for seemingly minor breaches of conduct, such as improper uniforms or unkempt watchtowers. There was also a paradox that stemmed from the spatial arrangement of the prison. The reserve battalion soldiers—the official prison guards—were stationed in a pen just like the Palestinian prisoners, while the prison's headquarters was located in the Tegart fort at the center of the prison grounds. Megiddo was a version of Bentham's panopticon, a prison designed so that the inmates can be observed by the guards at all times but cannot see their sentinels. The reserve soldiers, who functioned as the prison guards, were themselves subject to the gaze of the MPs, as if they were prisoners too. In the reserve soldiers' narrative, constant oversight by the MPs emasculated them, compounding the victimization that they attributed to the meat situation.

Another factor in the reserve soldiers' narrative of victimhood was the strict monitoring of the prison's gate. The reserve soldiers were allowed exit the prison grounds only with passes signed by their officers, even when they only wanted to go to their cars, which were parked by the gate. These rules, which are typical in prisons, were rare in regular *miluim* duties, exacerbating the soldiers' sense of disempowerment. One of them bitterly told me: "We are the real prisoners at Megiddo."

Physically surrounded by their prisoners, the reserve soldiers were also being constantly surveyed by the detainees, who kept a watchful eye on the guards. The prisoners were very sensitive to the reserve soldiers' activities and reacted swiftly to any changes. During one alert drill, in an extreme case of power reversal, the prisoners commented loudly on the reserve soldiers' awkward performance, jeering things like "run fatso," and imitated the aging and not-particularly-fit guards. This further contributed to the reserve soldiers' sense that they were being bullied and victimized by the Palestinian prisoners, who, they said, were "keeping us waiting for hours in the sun," "laughing in our faces," and generally "had an attitude." Because the MPs, and especially the MP officers, wanted a "quiet" tenure, the reserve soldiers were forced to simply accept these indignities.

The reserve soldiers, feeling victimized by all aspects of prison life, also took issue with their own officers, who issued demands that would have seemed reasonable were it not for the soldiers' already entrenched notions of victimhood. For example, they were commanded to stay awake during guard shifts and to wear their gun belts crossed over their shoulders while on duty. The reserve officers themselves complained about "difficulties" and power struggles with the MPs and with their superiors in the Home Front Command, who were often perceived as acting arbitrarily and inconsiderately so as to "cover their own asses."

With the mindset that all aspects of the prison were conceived to punish and emasculate them, the reserve soldiers also protested the length of *miluim* and the number and length of their leave. All of the soldiers wanted longer leaves, and everyone carefully noted the leaves of others while constantly comparing the length of their individual tours of reserve duty. Many of them requested a shortening of their service for a variety of reasons, and only about half of the soldiers actually served the entire thirty-two days. They all complained that they were not being treated fairly by the regimental adjutant, who handled leave requests. The adjutant, for his part, bitterly criticized the ungrateful soldiers, who, he said, "swarm like bees, demanding impossible leaves and making up all kinds of excuses in order to go home."

The persistent attempts by the soldiers to shorten their service and obtain more leaves reflected the general resentment felt by most *miluim* soldiers toward the well-known fact that only 20 percent of IDF reserve soldiers were recruited for periods exceeding twenty days per year and that 30 percent of all reserve soldiers performed more than 90 percent of the total reserve days. All of the reserve soldiers at Megiddo felt that they had been charged with the responsibility of securing the nation while the overwhelming majority of Israelis managed to evade duty. Consequently, many of the *miluim* soldiers and officers described themselves as *frayerim* (suckers), and, as I argued in chapter 1, being a sucker is one thing Israelis can't stand.

Even though the soldiers' complaints may seem negligible and even childish, especially when compared to those of the prisoners (no satellite television versus detention for years in overcrowded tents; vanilla Milki versus bogus judicial processes; and thirty-two days of *miluim* versus forty years of military occupation), the soldiers strongly felt that they were the ones suffering the most at the prison. They described the prisoners' pens as "holiday camps" and "five-star hotels" despite the grim realities observable from the watchtowers. Almost all of these arguments were tied to the indignity of the reserve soldiers' relative lack of meat and built off the narrative of emasculation caused by the meat issue. Thus, the argument that they were receiving less meat and that the meat was of lesser quality was both the main reason for and the main confirmation of their other complaints and their sense of victimization.

All in all, a single master narrative of victimization prevailed at the prison, narrated with only slight differences by members of all three groups of men (Palestinians, MPs, and reserve soldiers) that made up its population: "This place is terrible. I shouldn't have been here in the first place. The others here mistreat me constantly for no reason. All I want is to get out of here and go home. I am the real and only victim of the situation." This common narrative exposes the paradox that characterizes not only the prison setting but also the Israeli occupation of Palestinian territories at large. Wardens and their prisoners, the occupiers and occupied—they all feel very much the same about the situation: trapped and desperate. One of the soldiers summed up his feelings about the prison in these words: "What can you expect? It's a prison."

## MEAT, MASCULINITY, AND THE LOGIC
## OF THE OCCUPATION

About two weeks into my *miluim,* feeling that I was taking part in military activities that were clearly undermining Israeli interests and that might also be illegal, I asked my battalion commander to appoint me to a mission that would include no contact with the Palestinian prisoners. The commander responded that he had the perfect job for me: escorting Palestinian prisoners to civilian hospitals for treatment. He argued that this mission was about the prisoners' well-being and that I had no reason to object since I was supporting their human rights.

The next morning, four of us—a reserve medic, a reserve soldier, an MP escort sergeant, and myself, serving as the officer in charge—got into the back of a light truck. We were taking a Palestinian prisoner who had had a mental breakdown to a nearby hospital. The handcuffed prisoner, empty-eyed and inert, was slumped on the floor between us.

At the hospital's reception, we were instructed to take the prisoner to the office of the psychiatrist on duty. Our entourage—a barely walking prisoner surrounded by four armed soldiers—went through the emergency room to the psychiatric ward. The psychiatrist was a recent migrant from the former USSR and could hardly speak Hebrew. The prisoner couldn't speak Hebrew either and was hardly able to talk at all. The medical examination was short and included handing in the prison physician's report, which the psychiatrist quickly read. He then wrote a prescription for medication and handed it to the MP. I asked him whether we should uncuff the prisoner so that he could examine him. The psychiatrist looked at me as if I were mad and told us that we could leave.

On our way back to the prison, the MP sergeant and the reserve medic discovered that they shared a passion for American antiwar and freedom songs of the 1960s. They talked about Bob Dylan, Joan Baez, Leonard Cohen, and Pete Seeger. When they started to discuss the book *Zen and the Art of Motorcycle Maintenance,* I asked how they could talk about freedom and human rights while the lethargic, handcuffed Palestinian prisoner lay by their feet. They looked at me in utter surprise. It was obvious that they didn't see any contradiction between their interest in protest music, human rights, universal peace, and the brotherhood of all men and the fact that they were soldiers in the IDF who were clearly mistreating a sick human being.

18. *A View from the Watchtower*

What was going on? How was it possible that these nice, positive men, who loved music and were inspired by the freedom movement of the 1960s and its intellectual ideas and humanistic messages, wouldn't acknowledge a possible resemblance, as slight as it might be, between the struggle for universal equality, compassion, and peace and the Palestinian quest for independence? How could they ignore the obvious discrepancy between the calls of those singer-songwriters for universal human equality and rights and the fact that they were treading a legal and moral gray space when it came to the human and legal rights not only of the prisoner they were escorting but also of the thousands of other prisoners at Megiddo. And more generally, how could it be that the reserve soldiers guarding the prison, all normative adult men, perceived of themselves as the victims of their prisoners? The answers to these queries could serve as a key to unlocking the question posed at this chapter's introduction: How is it that the Jewish citizens of Israel, a state established to liberate Jews from millennia of persecution and abuse, take part in the systematic victimization of the Palestinians?

Here, I would like to argue that despite Israel's significant social, economic, and scientific achievements and its proven military might, Israeli Jews cultivate a self-image of the eternal victims, as if they were still the weak and persecuted minority and the ultimate scapegoat. This sense of victimization is actively widened to include all scopes of social life. Alon Gan (2014, 9), in his analysis of Israeli victimhood discourses, writes: "In recent years, victimization is the fashion. Thinkers, writers, artists, and academics use their victimization to their advantage. Everyone presents their victimized existence publically. Many wish to add their share to the ever increasing hall of Israeli victimization, which is at the point of becoming a Tower of Babel of 'survivors' competing over who has suffered the most."

Indeed, in contemporary Israel, everyone claims victimization. Mizrahi Jews feel victimized by the Ashkenazi; immigrants from the former USSR are mistreated and discriminated against by (more) veteran Israelis; black Jews from Ethiopia are victimized by white Jews. Israeli Jews feel victimized by cellular companies, large retailers, and car importers. They also feel abused by their own elected government, which levies heavy taxes but seems to return very little when it comes to state services and quality of life. Israeli Ashkenazi Jews point to the numbers tattooed on their grandparents' arms as a symbol of their victimization by the Nazis. Recently, as the numbers of Holocaust survivors is quickly decreasing, a trend has emerged of tattooing one's grandparent's number on one's hand.[10] Honoring their grandparents and turning their bodies into living cenotaphs, these young Israeli Jews are also claiming an eternal and absolute victim status.

In his study of Israeli Jewish high school trips to Holocaust sites in Poland, Jackie Feldman (2008) shows that these popular tours are planned to turn the participating youth into Holocaust "witnesses" charged with keeping and passing on the Holocaust memory. A few months after their return from the trip, most of these kids join the IDF, shortly after being commissioned with the Holocaust memory and embedded with a strong sense of Jewish victimization.

This sense of Israeli Jewish victimization is encouraged by Israeli politicians, who insistently claim that Israel's existence is threatened by its enemies, whose sole desire is to destroy it. These enemies have changed over the years, with "the Arabs," and more specifically the Egyptians, Syrians, and Jordanians, having been replaced by the more distant Iraqis and Iranians and by nonstate militias such as the Palestine Liberation Organization, Hamas, Hezbollah, and ISIS. Yet "the enemy" is always presented as an imminent, existential threat, and Israeli politicians do not stop their fearmongering even when the real or imagined enemy is substantially weakened or gives up some of its power, as in the recent case of Iran.

The Palestinians, whose paramilitary forces in the West Bank and Gaza do not have a single warplane, gunboat, or tank, turned as of recently to sending individuals to carry out sporadic stabbings, which generally end with the individual being "neutralized" (killed) by Israeli security forces or armed civilians. These desperate attempts were nicknamed by General Eizenkot, Israel's chief of staff, "the scissor's uprising," attesting to the low level of threat he attributed to such attacks.

Yet despite the Palestinians' military, political, and economic marginality and weakness, they are repeatedly portrayed by Israeli Jewish politicians and media as mighty enemies, threatening the very existence of the State of Israel. Benjamin Netanyahu, Israel's long-standing prime minister, established his political career on such claims, but most Israeli politicians and many of the state's military leaders resort to this strategy in their quest for power. Yet the cultural mechanism that facilitates the self-transformation of a regional superpower into a victim is seldom explained. At Megiddo Prison, I had the rare chance of witnessing this cultural mechanism in action.

In the masculine setting of the military prison, the transformation of armed soldiers, the epitome of hegemonic masculinity, into self-perceived victims of their own prisoners was not simple or straightforward. This cognitive and emotional leap was activated, unexpectedly but effectively, by meat. Since meat is such an important marker and maker of power and masculinity, the fact that the soldiers received small amounts of low-quality meat made them feel weak and unfit for their military mission. This was summarized in their desperate call for help during the "meat mutiny," when the soldiers refused to guard the prison unless they were provided with meat. The soldiers were not threatening to revolt but rather just the opposite—they were arguing that they were unable to perform their military duties due to lack of meat. The next step in the process of substantializing the reserve soldiers' victimization entailed comparison. By claiming that the two other groups of men at the prison—the Palestinian prisoners and the MPs—had more and better meat, the reserve soldiers were able to support their argument of relative weakness. Once it was established that the Palestinians had larger quantities of better meat, it became possible for the soldiers to address the prisoners as the prison's powerful rulers, the MPs as the prisoners' servants and collaborators, and themselves as everyone's punching bags.

The soldiers, convinced that they were at the bottom of the prison power structure because they had less meat of lesser quality could now passionately argue that they were being bullied by the Palestinians, who made them "wait for hours in the sun" and "had an attitude"; that the prison was like a "holiday camp" or a "five-star hotel" for the prisoners; that the MPs, unarmed and unfit for combat and thus far removed from the Israeli hegemonic masculine model of the combat soldier, were bullying and abusing them too; and that they were actually "the real prisoners at Megiddo." Lack of meat became the pretext and proof that they were the actual victims of the situation.

It should therefore come as no surprise that almost none of the reserve soldiers expressed doubts regarding the justification or wisdom of the military mission they were taking part in, the obvious injustices inflicted upon the Palestinian prisoners, or the potential negative consequences of participating in a coercive system that was producing ever more committed and indoctrinated enemies. Here, the cognitive and emotional mechanisms that justify the occupation were fully exposed: since the Israeli Jewish soldiers felt that they were the real and only victims of the situation, even when the State of Israel and the IDF had devised and structured the institution that was victimizing them, they felt both victimized and justified in their actions. And even when the soldiers themselves pointed out that they were acting in unjust and unproductive ways (for example, one said that they were running "a university for terrorists under the auspices of the Israeli army" and another admitted that the juridical process was "twisted and looked like a [television] show"), they still felt that they were doing the right thing because the Palestinians had forced them to take such measures. "It's their fault," said one of the soldiers when I confronted him about the fact that many of the Palestinian prisoners went through judicial procedures that would be deemed unacceptable by Israeli legal standards. "They shouldn't have started the terror attacks in the first place," he continued. "And if their leaders are to blame, they should change them." The fact that Israel conquered Gaza and the West Bank thirty-six years prior to the events described in this chapter (which took place in 2002) and kept the Palestinians under a coercive military regime ever since has hardly had an impact on the Israeli Jewish sense of victimization and self-righteousness.

This incredible shift of perceived power at Megiddo Prison was the result of meat. While the soldiers pointed to quite a few other aspects of their victimization, mainly various military procedures, when it came to the Palestinian prisoners, lack of meat was their main conduit for claiming victimization. The soldiers also used meat to prove that the Palestinians were better off in the prison than back home. Thus, though the reserve soldiers had a point when they argued that they were victimized by the military system and by Israeli society at large, the only way that they could justify their sense of victimization at the hands of the Palestinian prisoners was by arguing that the prisoners had more meat.

I have argued elsewhere (Avieli 2005b) that food bridges the gap between the theory and praxis of nationalism, with national dishes concretizing the abstract ideas members of national groups tell themselves about themselves. At Megiddo Prison, meat was both a material and a symbolic means of attaining power. It bridged the gap between the self-perception of victimization harbored by many Israeli Jews and the actual power structure of the jail, in which Israeli Jews overwhelmingly had the upper hand. The perceived lack of meat translated into a total and complete sense of weakness, which in turn confirmed the reserve soldiers' sense of victimization. As victims, they could hardly be expected to take responsibility for the situation. As far as the reserve soldiers were concerned, the larger quantities of better meat that they believed the Palestinian prisoners were eating elevated the prisoners to the top of the prison power structure and left the soldiers feeling that they were simply resisting, as much as they could, Palestinian abuse.

Food, though an important component in the relations between Israelis and Palestinians, is hardly the only thing that can affect such power reversals. The logic of the occupation—that is, the ability of Israelis to redefine any engagement with the Palestinians as an expression of Israeli weakness and victimization—finds its expression in many cultural contexts. Yet the fact that food is both a symbolic and a material means of attaining power facilitated these processes of hierarchy reversal even in the extremely rigid power structure of the prison.

# SIX

# Thai Migrant Workers and the Dog-Eating Myth

Dog eating is an international urban legend with some truth to it. Everybody knows that Asians eat dogs.

FRANK WU, *Professor of law at Harvard University (Wu 2002, 40)*

IT IS A WELL-ESTABLISHED ISRAELI total social fact that Thai migrant workers, who make up the bulk of the agricultural workforce in Israel, systematically hunt and eat Israeli pet dogs. Canine flesh, however, is rarely eaten in Thailand, and my investigations of reported cases of dog-meat eating by Thai migrant workers in Israel repeatedly led to the conclusion that the specific events I was examining did not actually involve the consumption of dog meat. My follow-up of media reports on dog-meat consumption by Thai migrant workers produced similar results: despite the bold headlines and condemning readers' comments, the reports accusing Thai migrant workers of hunting and eating dogs regularly turned out to be ambiguous texts in which the question of whether dog meat was actually eaten by Thai migrant workers remained unclear. Why is it, then, that Israelis are so adamant that Thai migrant workers eat the flesh of their pet dogs?

In this chapter, I turn from Israeli culinary preferences to Israeli beliefs about the culinary preferences of others. I argue that dog hunting and dog eating are myths made up by Israelis to define the Thais, members of the new global class of cheap laborers, as subhuman and to relegate them to the bottom of the Israeli power structure, thereby justifying their economic exploitation.

I collected some of the data presented in this chapter during the late 1990s. I gathered further ethnographic data over the years in different contexts. While the early data may seem outdated and irrelevant, my argument in this chapter is that at a specific moment in time, in the mid-1990s, Israelis had to deal with the arrival of a significant number of migrant workers and with the dilemmas they posed for a nation that was still upholding, at least rhetorically, a socialist ethos and that was still venerating self-sufficiency, hard work, and especially agriculture. The arrival of significant numbers of non-Jewish immigrants to the country also challenged Israel's ethnocratic (Yiftachel 2006) and orientalizing (Khazzoom 2003) organizing principles. Once the accusation that Thai immigrants ate dog meat was established as a total social fact in the late 1990s, these dilemmas were solved, at least to a certain extent, and called only for occasional "maintenance," which, as I will show, is ongoing.

## THAI MIGRANT WORKERS AND ISRAELI DOGS

The first Thai migrant workers arrived in Israel in 1993.[1] During the 1990s, increasing numbers of migrant workers came to Israel to replace the Palestinians, who had provided the bulk of cheap manpower for the Israeli economy since the 1967 occupation (Bartram 1998). In 1995, Palestinian suicide attacks by organizations opposing the Oslo Peace Accords led Prime Minister Rabin's government to impose *sgarim* (literally "closures") on the occupied territories, which resulted in manpower shortages and had an immediate negative impact on various segments of the Israeli economy, most importantly on agriculture, construction, and caregiving. Rising pressure from employers and a failure to attract Israeli Jews to these jobs (Rosenhek 2000) led to a government decision to import migrant workers. 10,000 work permits were issued in 1993; 70,000 in 1995; 100,000 in 1996; and 80,000 in 1998 (Rosenhek 2000).

The actual numbers of legal and undocumented migrant workers in the country is unclear and contested. According to a Knesset report, there were 70,000 migrant workers employed in the construction industry, 22,500 migrant workers employed in agriculture, and 55,000 migrant workers with jobs in nursing and caregiving in the country in 2014.[2] According to the Immigration Authority, in late 2015 there were 77,000 legal migrant workers and 16,000 undocumented migrant workers in Israel; 22,000 legal migrant workers and 650 undocumented workers were legally employed in agriculture. Since only Thais are employed in agriculture, the total number of Thais employed in Israeli comes to roughly 23,000.[3] Other estimates suggest a total of 100,000 legal workers and another 100,000 undocumented ones, though most sources state that there are only a small number of undocumented Thai workers.

The Ministry of Interior officials charged with handling the influx of migrant workers decided that workers from specific countries would be employed only in specific economic sectors. Erik Cohen (1999) argues that the Thais were relegated to agriculture because of their assumed background as farmers and because they came from a tropical country and were thus expected to be able to handle the heat. Romanian workers were relegated to construction (they were later replaced by Turkish and Chinese builders). Workers from the Philippines were mainly consigned to nursing, caregiving, and domestic help (they were later joined by small numbers of Nepali, Sri Lankan, and Eastern European caregivers).

Cohen and his colleague Zeev Rosenhek, both from the Department of Sociology and Anthropology at the Hebrew University of Jerusalem, initiated the first study on migrant workers in Israel in 1995 (E. Cohen 1999). Cohen was my PhD advisor, and he recruited me as a research assistant. I was charged with organizing his research on Thai workers. I established contacts and sought permission for and arranged interviews with employers, workers, and other people with connections to Thai migrant workers and the industry. I joined Cohen on these field trips, participated in the interviews, took notes and pictures, and collected data. Between 1996 and 1998, we made dozens of trips to different agricultural communities in Israel: kibbutzim, moshavim, private farms, nurseries, and other farming operations that employed Thai migrant workers.

While we were conducting our study, the Israeli Jewish populace was gripped by a severe wave of moral panic. Multiple media reports accused Thai migrant workers of stalking protected wild animals and of systematically hunting and eating pet dogs. This surge of accusations culminated with the publication of a double-page story by journalist David Regev in Israel's leading newspaper, *Yediot Ahronot,* on June 9, 1996, with an extra-large bold headline announcing: "The Target: Dogs" (Hamatarah: Klavim). The different sections of the article included a small photo of an Asian-looking man holding a knife and a text that read: "The Hunters: Special Inquiry."

The bold subheads read: "Thai workers are not satisfied with the food provided by their employers, and so they go on hunting trips"; "As if in a military raid, they operate in small units: dog catchers, spice gatherers [*melaktei tavlinim*], skin removers [*poshtei or*], barbecue cooks, and watchers [*tazpitanim*]"; "They raid groves and neighborhoods, set cruel traps, slaughter man's best friend, and feast over its flesh around the barbecue"; "Testimony:

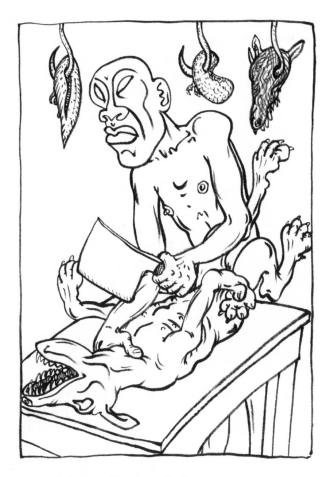

19. *Everybody Knows That Asians Eat Dogs*

I saw a Thai turning a huge spit; I was horrified to realize that he was roasting a dog with its legs chopped off."

The article explained that as complaints over the disappearance of dogs in areas where Thai migrant workers were employed amassed, the reporter and photographer began a six-month investigation. According to the article, Thai migrant workers ate "modest, meatless meals" during the week but went on hunting sprees during the weekends, trapping birds, wild animals, and domestic pets—specifically dogs. The text described an orgiastic celebration of killing, dismembering, and roasting dogs, whose flesh was consumed with large quantities of alcohol.

The text was accompanied by five large, blurry photos, each with its own caption. The main photo was of a human figure with its head covered, holding what looked like a plastic bag and squatting by a small fire of branches and weeds, and there was a little arrow pointing at the bag. The caption read: "A recipe for dinner: Thai takes dog out of plastic bag." Next was a picture of a miserable-looking dog whose head was trapped in a plastic container attached to a pole. The caption read "The trap: Chocolate is placed as bait in the plastic container. This stray dog managed to push his head into the container but couldn't get it out. The dog was released by the photographer, badly injured and infested with parasites." Finally, there was a set of three adjacent photos: the first pictured two Asian-looking men walking in a field, with the caption "The lookout"; the second showed two men who were standing under a clothesline with laundry hanging over their heads and pulling something out of a bucket, with the caption reading "The preparations"; and the third was a picture of an improvised barbecue with some pieces of unclear matter, with the caption "The leftovers: Last night the Thais feasted over the barbecue, these are the morning's leftovers."

In what follows, I examine the report critically for its journalistic short-comings without making any assertions as to the integrity, professionalism, and ethics of the writer or photographer. In many ways, the article is a jour-nalistic masterpiece: it weaves images and words into a powerful and con-vincing message that is not evident in the photos and is not substantiated by any additional evidence presented in the text.

There are six photos altogether: an Asian-looking man holding a knife; a human figure with a covered head squatting by a fire and holding a bag; a dog whose head is trapped in a plastic container; two Asian-looking men walking in a field; two human figures bent over a bucket; and some unrecognizable material on an improvised grill. Not one of the humans is clearly Thai, not one of images clearly involves food preparation, and none of the photos that pur-port to depict cooking clearly involve dog meat, or for that matter any kind of meat or even the practice of cooking. As for the dog, there is no evidence in the picture that can support the claim that it was purposefully trapped by Thai migrant workers. In fact, there is no evidence that the dog was purposefully trapped by anyone, let alone by Thai migrant workers. All in all, the photos do not provide evidence that Thai migrant workers were hunting and eating dogs. The bold headlines and text, however, weave a coherent story out of the images, convincing readers that they are observing hard evidence of Thai migrant workers hunting, butchering, cooking, and eating dogs.

The article attracted significant public attention and media reaction and elicited heated discussions and condemnations on the radio and television. While most readers didn't notice the article's shortcomings, some professional commentators did point out that there was a problem with this journalistic project. On the day the article was published, the reporter and photographer were interviewed on the popular television program *Erev Hadash* (*New Evening*), where they were confronted by the host, a senior journalist, who accused them of making claims despite very little supporting evidence in the photos. The reporter responded that they had graphic pictures of the slaughtering and cooking of dogs but felt that these were too explicit and might hurt the public feelings.

The authors must have anticipated this kind of criticism because they took measures to confront it within the text itself. In a box dedicated to their methodology, with the heading "How the inquiry was conducted," they wrote: "[We] amassed extremely disturbing photographic evidence. We didn't publish most of it. The sights are horrifying." Such care for the public's feelings was unexpected considering that the same newspaper published a close-up photograph of a dismembered hand on its front page in the aftermath of a suicide bombing just a few months earlier. Moreover, the photos' captions and vivid descriptions left little to the imagination. The journalists might have been genuine in their wish to spare the public's feelings, but the outcome was a deceitful text. Nevertheless, despite its shortcomings, this article was seminal in cementing the image of Thai migrant workers as cruel dog-meat eaters.

During the following two years, while we were conducting our research on Thai migrant workers, many of our interviewees and people with whom I happened to discuss the study made frequent references to this article and to dog-meat eating among Thais. It is interesting to note that farmers who employed Thai workers as well as manpower agents involved in hiring Thai workers vehemently rejected these accusations. Other people, who had little or no contact with Thai workers, passionately argued that Thais did eat dogs, both in Thailand and in Israel. When I asked some members of the latter group whether they had personally seen Thais hunting or eating dogs or whether they had seen dogs eaten in Thailand, the most common response was that although they had never personally witnessed it, they knew a cousin, friend, neighbor, or friend of a friend who had. I was facing yet another "riddle of food and culture" (Harris 1998): Why were Israelis accusing Thai migrant workers of hunting and eating dogs even though this practice was denied by the Thais and by their Israeli employers and was never substantiated by real evidence?

A disclaimer is due here. It might very well be the case that some dogs were caught in traps set by Thai migrant workers. It might also be the case that an extremely hungry Thai worker did hunt, cook, and eat a dog. However, such events have never been confirmed, and there is a huge discrepancy between the acknowledgment that such an event *might* have happened and the common Israeli belief that Thai migrant workers routinely and systematically kill and eat pet dogs.

## THAI DOGS

While conducting the research on Thai migrant workers in Israel, I was employed as a tour guide by an Israeli travel agency to lead tours to East and Southeast Asia. Thailand was almost always included in the itinerary as a destination or as a springboard to neighboring countries. This allowed me to observe how dogs were treated in Thailand and whether they were eaten or treated as practical or potential food.

It was hard to ignore the miserable state of the dogs that I observed in Thai public and semipublic spaces. In urban Thailand, dogs were part of the street scene, laying by the stairs and thresholds of houses in the narrow *sois* (urban alleys), roaming the streets, and congregating in wat (Buddhist temple) yards. The dogs rarely had collars or other markings of human ownership, were skinny, and often had observable injuries, rashes, and skin diseases. They didn't look as if they were being groomed as pets or working dogs, or for that matter as food. In fact, they looked extremely unhealthy and unappealing, and I seriously doubt that anyone would consider eating, let alone craving, their flesh.

When I inquired about their presence in temple yards, I was told that these Buddhist temples were safe havens for stray animals. Urban wats often had monkeys and sometimes horses and even elephants on their grounds. Most commonly, however, they had packs of dogs. I saw visitors to these temples giving food to the dogs, and I was told that this was a meritorious practice similar to the food alms given to Buddhist monks. Yet the dogs at the temples were as skinny and miserable as the rest of the dogs visible in urban settings. Their congregation in wat yards suggested that they were treated badly and needed protection, but I was assured that they were threatened by neglect, disease, and hunger, not by hungry hunters.

In the countryside, dogs were used as guards; they were kept on leashes or left loose to run around at farmyards, barking loudly at passersby. They looked better fed than urban dogs, had healthier fur, and rarely had observable skin diseases. While traveling in Vietnam and China, I did observe dog merchants, dog-meat restaurants, and dog meat sold at markets, but I never saw dog-meat merchants in Thailand. Furthermore, I never saw dog meat on offer at any of the dozens of fresh-produce markets I visited in different parts of Thailand, nor did I see restaurants in Thailand that served dog meat.

The local tour guides who accompanied my tour groups in Vietnam and China often mentioned dog meat, pointed to dog meat sold at markets, and referred to restaurants that specialized in dog meat. This was a way of engaging the tourists and provoking their orientalist stereotypes and fears, amusing and horrifying them at once. This, however, was never the case in Thailand.

The only exception was the occasional mention by Thai tour guides that the Akha, one of Thailand's ethnic groups, ate dogs (Maneeprasert 1989). Ethnic minorities, however, are considered by most ethnic Thais to be of low status (Leepreecha 2005), and the Akha are considered to be one of the most backward ethnic groups in the country (Trupp 2015). My sense was that when ethnic Thai guides pointed out that the Akha ate dog meat, they were depicting them as exotic and primitive savages, and through this distinction they defined their own ethnic group as civilized, sophisticated, modern, and Western. These guides were clearly disgusted by the idea of eating dog meat, and the fact that the inferior Akha craved this flesh made it all the more repulsive.

However, these were obviously superficial observations. But I found it very hard to locate relevant scholarly works on human-dog relations and on dog-meat eating in Thailand. I consulted anthropologist Eugene Anderson, an expert on Asian foodways, who responded: "There is nothing in the literature about Thais eating dogs, for the very good reason that they don't do it. At least I never heard of it, and my wife and I have done a lot of work there."[4]

The major exception is Stanley Tambiah's (1969) authoritative ethnographic analysis of human-animal relations in Phraan Muan, a village in northeastern Thailand, which pays specific attention to dogs and their social status. Tambiah begins by pointing out that the dog is one of the ten animals whose flesh is forbidden in Buddhism, the others being humans, elephants, horses, snakes, lions, tigers, leopards, bears, and hyenas. While some of these creatures are forbidden for their royal status (horse and elephant) or what they consume (hyenas), Tambiah argues that the dog is forbidden due to its proximity to human beings. While some Buddhist sources put forward that dog is man's best friend and that eating it thus verges on cannibalism, Tambiah points out that dogs in Theravada Buddhist Thailand are tolerated but loathed. The Thais, he argues, perceive of dogs as humanlike creatures that breach two of the most fundamental human taboos: they are incestuous and they eat their own feces. He explains:

> The dog is in one sense a friend of man, but it is not a "pet" as understood by the English. It is treated casually, given great license and little care. It is, in fact, an animal that arouses paradoxical attitudes which are symptomatic of its close bearing on human relationships. *The dog is not edible; this is not simply a neutral attitude but a definite taboo.* . . . This animal, though close to man, is viewed as a "low creature"; it eats feces and is therefore unclean and inedible. The dog is regarded as the incestuous animal par excellence; canine parents and children copulate. . . . The dog is treated as a "degraded human"; its inedibility corresponds to notions of uncleanliness and incest. . . . One of the strongest insults that one villager can hurl at another is to say that a dog has had intercourse with his paternal and maternal ancestors. Other animals do not figure so effectively in insulting language. (Tambiah 1969, 435; emphasis mine)

It should be clear from Tambiah's analysis that dogs are considered disgusting in Thailand and that eating their flesh would be unthinkable for most Thais. Tambiah's understanding of the Thai taboo against consuming dog meat is very much in line with the attitude of Thai tour guides and other Thais with whom I discussed the practice of eating dog meat: they found it repulsive.

Beyond the scant academic literature, Thai and international newspapers have reported on the dog-meat trade in Thailand, specifically in Isan (northeast Thailand), where most Thai migrant workers in Israel come from. These reports describe a lucrative export of dog meat to Vietnam (and, to a lesser extent, southern China) but do not report that dog flesh was consumed in Thailand or by Thais. In 2013, Kate Hodal reported in the *Guardian*: "Every year, hundreds of thousands of pets are snatched in Thailand, then smuggled into Vietnam."[5] Peter Shadbolt, reporting for CNN, described a similar situation: "As many as 200,000 live dogs every year are smuggled from northeast

Thailand across the Mekong River destined for restaurants in Vietnam."[6] Reports of actual consumption of dog meat in Thailand, however, usually attribute the practice to Vietnamese immigrants. In 2014, *New York Times* correspondent Thomas Fuller explained: "Eating dog, by no means a mainstream tradition in Thai cuisine, is confined to isolated pockets of aficionados, mostly in northeastern Thailand. The practice has existed for decades, chiefly among communities of ethnic Vietnamese."[7]

Even though there is ample evidence of trade in dog meat in Thailand, especially in the northeast, the meat is not consumed locally. The relatively few media reports of dog-meat eating in Thailand usually involve ethnic Vietnamese, who in many cases are also involved in exporting dog meat to Vietnam. These reports further support my argument that dog meat is practically taboo in Thailand, that it is rarely, if at all, eaten by ethnic Thais, and that it can hardly be described as part of the Thai foodscape. Thais shun dog meat and find it revolting. Thus, the assumption made by many Israelis that Thai migrant workers were simply maintaining their original food habits by eating dog meat in Israel has very little to do with actual Thai eating patterns.

## WORKING IN ISRAEL

In this section, I discuss some of the regulations governing the employment of Thai migrant workers in Israel and the implementation of these regulations by Israeli employers. While this section, unlike the rest of the chapter, does not focus on the foodways of Thai migrant workers, it describes the administrative and practical settings that define the working conditions of these workers. This is crucial for my argument that the allegation that Thai workers hunt and eat dogs is the cultural solution devised by Israelis to handle the ethical dilemmas posed by the exploitative nature of the employment of migrant workers in Israel.

When the Israeli government decided to allow migrant workers to enter the country in the early 1990s, it was determined that each worker would be granted a two-year working visa that could be renewed twice, for a total of up to six years. It was also decided that it would be possible to apply for a renewal only in the country of origin—that is, workers would have to leave Israel after two years, fly home, and apply for a renewal, which would be processed within three months. This turned out to be complicated and costly for workers, who had to purchase two extra tickets within their six-year working period and remain unemployed (and unpaid) for three months each time they applied for a visa renewal. Israeli farmers were also unhappy with this arrangement, which entailed many potential complications and mishaps and also meant that workers were absent for long periods of time, leaving their farms short of manpower. According to the 2015 edition of the "Foreign Workers' Rights Handbook," published by the Israeli Immigration Authority, this arrangement was replaced by a one-year working visa that could be extended in Israel for up to sixty-three months.[8]

According to this official text, migrant workers in Israel were entitled to the minimum wage, 4,300 shekels (roughly US$1,200) in 2015, for 186 working hours per month. Like all employees in Israel, they were entitled to health insurance, social security, and other social benefits and extra payment for overtime. The handbook stated that it was illegal for employers to withhold their employees' passports and other documents. Visas, however, were always allocated to employers according to their specific needs, making migrant workers dependent on their employers.

The workers were entitled to "suitable housing," defined as "at least 4 square meters sleeping space per worker, no more than 6 workers in one room, personal cupboards and bedding for each worker, heating and ventilation, reasonable lighting and electric outlets in each room, hot and cold water in the bathroom, kitchen and showers; sinks, kitchen counters and cupboards, burners, refrigerator, table and chairs, a washing machine for 6 workers. There must be reasonable access to the living quarters as well as to bathrooms."[9] This paragraph is the result of a grim reality and thus calls for some elaboration.

First, the instructions are so precisely detailed because, as Cohen, Rosenhek, and I saw while conducting our study in the late 1990s, and as I often observed in the years that followed, quite a few Israeli employers did not provide even these bare essentials and had to be forced to comply with the minimum standards. Over the years, both Israeli and international media outlets reported on cases where employers subjected Thai workers to abysmal living conditions.[10]

Second, these rules actually define very basic and crowded living conditions, allowing up to six people to share a 24-square-meter room. This means that a 48-square-meter two-bedroom mobile home, built to accommodate two adults, maybe with a child or two, can legally house *twelve* adult Thai workers. So even when employers did follow the rules, the living conditions were very basic, if not miserable. Large numbers of mainly male adults were crowded into dilapidated mobile homes (called *caravans* in Israel) and farming structures, such as sheds and chicken coops, converted into low quality, badly maintained dwellings with improvised electricity, showers, and toilets. Many of the kitchens and dining areas that I saw were of the open-air variety: a few tables and chairs, a fridge, a stove, and a sink in the yard next to the dwellings.

Furthermore, according to the official handbook, Israeli employers are entitled to deduct up to 25 percent of their workers' salaries for "housing and related expenses."[11] The handbook clearly stresses that "this is not an automatic deduction and the employer may only deduct actual expenses" and quotes a maximum deduction of 500 shekels, about 12 percent of the minimum wage.[12] However, during the research we conducted in the late 1990s, we were asked by many Thai workers why 25 percent of their salary was knocked off. When we asked the employers, they referred us to their accountants, who quoted the above-mentioned rule of deducting up to 25 percent for basic arrangements. In most cases, a flat rate of 25 percent was simply subtracted from the paychecks with no reference to the employers' actual expenses. Thus, in some cases, twelve Thais housed in a cramped and poorly maintained *caravan* would pay over 13,000 shekels (around US$3,700) of rent and related expenses per month. This was five to ten times the market rental price for mobile homes of this size (though the maintenance level of migrant workers' dwellings was often so low that no one would have rented them even for less than a tenth of this sum). In fact, for this price they could probably rent a well-maintained six-bedroom villa.

Another disturbing economic issue was the loan most Thai workers needed to pay for their initial airfare and paperwork, which was processed for a fee by Thai and Israeli manpower agencies. Our interviewees reported taking out loans of US$5,000–10,000 in the late 1990s that incurred yearly interest rates of 50–100 percent.[13] These loans were usually from Thai loan sharks who were purportedly connected to Thai criminal organizations, and the Thai migrant workers were terrified of the prospect of being unable to pay back their loans and interest, fearing that the lenders would hurt their family members.

The Thai migrant workers were practically enslaved by these loans, which took two to three years to repay, but only if they worked a substantial number of extra hours. In fact, most Thai workers reported working twelve hours a day, seven days a week, at least until they repaid their loans. The employers, many of whom knew about these debts, told us that their Thai employees insisted on working so many hours. One of them explained that if he didn't allow his Thai employees to work unlimited extra hours, they would leave. Many Thais worked as many as 370 hours per month, roughly twice the number of hours stipulated by the law.

The main reason Thai migrant workers came to Israel was financial: they wanted a chance to earn more money so that they could improve the economic lot and future prospects of their families. Workers and their families were willing to go through some hard times. When a child, spouse, or parent leaves for a very long period of time, there are substantial emotional, practical, and financial consequences. The families back in Thailand were expecting, and often depending on, remittances, and they put heavy pressure on the workers to earn more money to send home.

As a consequence, Thai migrant workers employed in Israeli agriculture were confined to the countryside and to their employers' farms, where many toiled twelve hours a day, seven days a week. Some 25 percent of their salary was deducted from their paychecks for housing, despite the cramped and poorly maintained quality of their dwellings. Many of them spent as much as 50 percent of their salary to repay the loans they had taken out to come to Israel. Internal and external pressures to send more money home further aggravated their financial situation.

According to a 2015 Human Rights Watch report titled "A Raw Deal: Abuse of Thai Workers in Israel's Agricultural Sector," Thai migrant workers "were paid salaries significantly below the legal minimum wage, forced to work long hours in excess of the legal maximum, subjected to unsafe working conditions, and denied their right to change employers. . . . Thai workers were housed in makeshift and inadequate accommodations. Only workers in one of the 10 groups Human Rights Watch interviewed were able to show us salary slips, and these were written in Hebrew, and did not accurately reflect the hours that workers had worked."[14]

It is important to bear in mind that Thai migrant workers chose to work in Israel of their own free will. It is also important to remember that the structural abuse of migrant workers is universal and shaped by global forces, that Israel is probably not the worst place in the world for migrant workers, and that Israeli employers are probably not the worst employers. In fact, many of the Thai workers I met over the years managed to create warm and intimate Thai-style patron-client relations with their employers (an extremely interesting topic that is not directly relevant to this chapter) that improved their financial, material, and emotional conditions. It is also true that for most

Thais, working in Israel eventually turned out to be profitable. However, working in Israel was also physically grueling and emotionally exhausting.

## THE FOODWAYS OF THAI MIGRANT
## WORKERS IN ISRAEL

Most of the Thai migrant workers in Israel come from Isan, in northeast Thailand. Located on the Khorat Plateau, Isan is the most arid region of Thailand, with substantially lower amounts of rainfall than other parts of the country. It also features distinctive wet and dry seasons, receiving very little rain for six months a year. These conditions make farming, and specifically subsistence rice cultivation, more difficult and precarious than it is in other regions of the country. Consequently, Isan has long been the country's poorest region and the main exporter of both domestic and international migrant workers.

Isan is also a culturally distinct region that has more in common with Laos than with the rest of Thailand. Most prominently, the language spoken in the region is a Lao dialect that is distinct from Thai (though these languages are mutually intelligible). While the ethnic identity of Isan dwellers is a debated political and academic subject, the Thai (by nationality) migrant workers we interviewed in Israel were visibly pleased when we asked them whether they were Lao and tended to respond that they were Lao or Lao-Thai.

Specifically relevant to this chapter is the Isan's distinct cuisine, which is defined, first and foremost, by the use of *khao niew*—"sticky" or glutinous rice—which is different from the long-grain rice common in other parts of Thailand. Israeli employers we interviewed in the late 1990s often mentioned that each of their Thai employees was entitled to 25 kilos of long-grain rice per month. Israeli farmers were astonished by the amount of rice their workers consumed and often noted in awe that the workers would eat rice for breakfast, lunch, and dinner. They added that their employees also consumed sticky rice, which was not included in the employment agreement, so the workers had to purchase it. At that time, sticky rice was imported by only a few specialized shops and was quite expensive. Over the years, grocery stores and supermarkets in farming regions started selling sticky rice as well as other Isan and Thai products, and prices dropped. *Khao niew*, which is cooked in specific bamboo and metal steamers and carried to work for lunch in special bamboo baskets (these utensils are now available in many local grocery shops), has become the norm in these regions in recent years.

While rice, sticky or long-grained, is the centerpiece of Thai meals and the main source of calories and nutrients, its culinary role is that of a white canvas on which the meal is drawn. While Thai cuisine is generally aromatic and strong tasting, Isan food is by far the spiciest in the country. The compelling colors, flavors, and smells of Isan food are achieved with liberal use of seasoning and aromatic agents, including ginger, galangal root, lemongrass, kaffir lime leaves, several kinds of basil, and a large variety of chilies.

Since Isan cuisine evolved in a poor region where farming is limited to roughly six months per year, it makes use of ingredients that are rarely used in other parts of Thailand, and this is especially true for animal products. Isan cuisine uses the flesh, blood, and internal organs of a large variety of wild and domesticated mammals, birds, reptiles, insects, and aquatic creatures. Professor Erik Cohen, who spent many years conducting ethnographic research in Thailand, told me that during the dry season, subsistence farmers in Isan shift into hunting and gathering mode. They hunt, set traps in the jungle and in fallow farm lands, fish and trap aquatic animals in natural and manmade waterways, look for edible insects, and gather the leaves, roots, seeds, nuts, shoots, buds, and fruits of domesticated and wild plants.

When Thai migrant workers first arrived in Israel, most of the essential Isan spices and ingredients were not available. Many of the workers planted gardens next to their dwellings and grew their own chilies, basil, coriander, garlic, onions, spring onions, and, at times, peppers, tomatoes, and eggplants. Another plant that I have often seen in Thai kitchen gardens in Israel is the papaya, which is usually harvested green for the preparation of *som tam* (papaya salad). These kitchen gardens can be found wherever Thai workers reside.

Ginger, and to a lesser extent galangal and kaffir lime leaves, which are hard to cultivate in Israel, can be purchased in Israeli markets, supermarkets, and shops that specialize in imported food. Another extremely important taste agent is *nam plaa* (Thai fish sauce), which is also found in these specialized shops and, increasingly, in Israeli supermarkets. These imported and sometimes rare ingredients are not cheap, but they are essential to Thai cooking, so the workers had no choice but to purchase them.

Thai migrant workers often had unlimited access to the fruits and vegetables produced by their employers. Israeli agroindustry, however, is often monocrop based, so the Thai workers in one region could have as many cucumbers as they liked (as was the case in Ahituv, a moshav specializing in cucumbers—where the Thai employees told us that they wouldn't touch cucumbers any more), while those in another region could have as many peppers as they could eat, but nothing else. Thus, in most instances, they had to purchase at least some fruits and vegetables.

While some of the spices and vegetables mentioned so far were considered exotic and rare in Israel, meat was clearly the most controversial food item on Thai migrant workers' menu.

## MEAT

I have shown in previous chapters that meat is associated with physical and social qualities such as strength, potency, masculinity, wealth, and power. Furthermore, food taboos are almost exclusively focused on the flesh of animals (Fessler and Navarrete 2003; Fiddes 2004). This is especially true for the Jewish kashrut system, which is centered on meat and is extremely important in Israeli private and public spheres. In his book on the social meanings of meat, Fiddes argues that meat is "a natural symbol"—that is, "a natural metaphor for the social experience" (2004, 2). It is little wonder, then, that the kinds of meat consumed by Thai workers, a non-Jewish group of newcomers that were seen as exotic and primitive, attracted more attention and criticism than any other food item they ate.

While Thais eat relatively small amounts of animal protein, many of their dishes include some animal flesh, which significantly contributes to the taste of the food. Thai migrant workers in Israel, despite their limited income and high level of debt, were still eager to add animal protein to their diet. They devised four strategies for the acquisition of meat: farming poultry, purchasing meat, accepting meat leftovers, and stealing and hunting.

### Farming Poultry

Many of the Thai dwellings I visited had improvised coops where chickens were raised for eggs and meat. This was rarely mentioned by their employers, as chicken coops are an integral part of the Israeli agroindustry (although poultry farming without veterinary inspection is illegal in Israel). Employers and other commenters mentioned instead that Thai workers farmed fighting cocks. Illegal but widely practiced in Thailand, this activity was criticized by

Israelis for being cruel. Nevertheless, Israeli employers generally accepted cockfighting and allowed it to continue. Poultry farming enhanced the Thai workers' limited culinary and leisure options at no direct cost to the farmers, which might be the reason it was tolerated. However, the fact that Thai workers slaughtered animals for their meat and engaged in cockfighting only contributed to the negative and savage image Israelis had of them.

## Purchasing Meat

This was probably the most obvious way of acquiring meat in Israel, but it was not necessarily the most accessible method for Thai migrant workers. First, meat was relatively expensive, and certainly more expensive than most other food products. With their limited incomes and high debts, Thai workers couldn't afford a lot of meat. Second, shopping for food required means of transportation, which was a significant obstacle for the Thai workers. The Israeli periphery is badly serviced by public transportation, and Thai migrant workers in Israel rarely owned cars. Thus, most could shop for food only when their employers provided transportation. While I occasionally met Thai migrant workers at fresh-produce markets, which tend to attract significant numbers of migrant workers of various nationalities, only rarely did I have such encounters at supermarkets. Some employers reported taking their workers to shop at fresh-produce markets on a regular basis. These farmers, however, were the exception that proved the rule: shopping for meat was inaccessible to most Thai workers.

In the late 1990s, we were told by employers and workers that an Israeli entrepreneur, who had discovered the captive audience of Thai workers, was driving around in a van stocked with Thai products, such as sticky rice and fish sauce, as well as different kinds of meat, which he sold for a hefty profit. Interestingly, he had pork on offer. Pork was quite hard to find in Israel at the time, and this was probably the only source of pork available to the Thais. As far as I know, this entrepreneur is not active anymore, probably because Thai products (and pork) have become more accessible.

But even when Thais purchased meat, things could get messy. In the spring of 1997, I read a newspaper report about Thai migrant workers employed in a large nursery who ate a donkey. I contacted their Israeli employer and asked if we could meet him and his employees. He suggested that we come immediately, hoping that we might provide some advice to him. The next morning, we drove to the nursery, located in the occupied

Palestinian Territories not far from Jerusalem. When we arrived, the Israeli employer, a Modern Orthodox settler, told us that he had discovered that his Thai employees had purchased a donkey from neighboring Bedouins and slaughtered and cooked it. He was so angry that he was thinking of having the employees deported. Cohen pointed out that the Thai employees were not Jews and asked him what was wrong with eating a donkey. The employer, who was distressed to begin with, did not like the question, but he agreed that we could talk to the Thai workers first and then discuss the issue with him.

The Thai workers were on their lunch break and were visibly upset. They were very glad when they found out that Cohen could speak both Thai and Lao, and they recounted their ordeal to us. They noted that there were no donkeys in Isan. In fact, they used the Thai word *ma,* "horse," rather than *la,* "donkey," as they didn't even know how to refer to the animal. They explained that there were many donkeys in the area and that they had asked a Bedouin who was working at the farm if the animals were edible. He responded positively (even though donkey flesh is not consumed in the Middle East) and offered to sell them one. He quoted a price of 600 shekels (ten times the going price for a donkey), took the money, and provided an animal. The Thai workers realized that it was an extremely muscular beast, so they decided to strangle rather than slaughter it. Slaughtering the donkey, they explained, would toughen its meat (probably due to the secretion of adrenaline). They then cleaned and carved the donkey, but when they tried to cook it, they found that no matter what cooking technique or seasoning they employed, the meat was too tough to chew and had an unpleasant aroma. Eventually, they had to throw it away.

When their employer found out that they had killed and cooked a donkey, he was furious and threatened to deport them. This left them feeling victimized by everyone: first, their Bedouin colleague had lied to them by saying that donkeys were edible and charged them a huge amount of money for an animal he knew they would not be able to eat, and now they were facing an extremely severe punishment, deportation, even though they could not understand what they had done wrong by cooking a donkey they had paid for.

We returned to the Israeli employer and had a long conversation with him, trying to explain to him that the whole incident was a mistake. We pointed out what the consequences of deportation might be for his employees (who would still have to repay their loans even though their source of income would be gone), and he was convinced to postpone his decision. We were getting ready to leave when he told us that ever since these events had taken place (a few days earlier), his Bedouin employees refused to work alongside the Thais, and he asked us if we would be willing to talk to the Bedouins. I return to this conversation in the chapter's conclusion.

## *Leftovers*

Thai migrant workers were employed in all segments of Israeli agriculture, including farms that produced milk and dairy products, eggs, meat, and fish. Some larger employers (especially kibbutzim) farm vegetables and fruits in addition to engaging in different kinds of husbandry. Thais employed on these farms often had access to free and practically unlimited amounts of meat. This, however, turned out to be a double-edged sword when it came to their public image, as Thais became seen as people who "eat everything."

Quite a few poultry famers told us that they let their Thai employees help themselves to invalid, sick, dying, or dead birds, which could not be sold. In my village, I often witnessed Thai workers slaughtering and cleaning such birds for their own consumption. However, the very same employers who allowed and at times encouraged this practice—we were once told "A satiated Thai is a satisfied Thai" (*Thailandi saveah hu Thailandi merutze*)—were often visibly repulsed and verbally disgusted by the idea of eating such ailing or dying creatures.

At first, I found this attitude bizarre. After all, these farmers were part of a cruel and exploitative agroindustry, farming hundreds of thousands of creatures destined for violent deaths at slaughterhouses. I gradually learned, however, that animal farmers tend to distance themselves from the act of killing, which is done elsewhere and by other people, so they considered themselves life givers rather than life takers. This was in line with Carol Adams's (1990, 1998) arguments that modern individuals distance themselves physically and emotionally from the killing of the animals they eat and actively hide the relationship between the meat they consume and the living creatures that were killed to produce it. Animal flesh is processed and packaged so that it doesn't look like an animal product any more. Labeling animal flesh "beef," "poultry," and "pork" rather than "cow," "chicken," or "pig" is also a mechanism of distancing and concealing.

By killing chicken with their hands, often in sight of their employers, the Thai workers were demolishing these symbolic barriers that protected their employers from facing the violent death they were inflicting on the millions of animals they farmed. The employers' disgusted reactions reestablished the barriers between culture and nature, marking the Thai employees as cruel and savage and relegating them to the other side of the wall.

Two cases that concerned cows are especially interesting. In one case, a cowshed manager at a Modern Orthodox kibbutz told us that he gave his Thai workers a dead calf, which they proceeded to consume. Even though he was the one who had offered the dead animal to his employees, he was clearly disgusted by the act. The religious context only exacerbated the paradox, as eating the flesh of dead animals (that is, animals that have not been slaughtered ritually) is strictly forbidden in Judaism. Moreover, eating dead animals is illegal in Israel due to sanitary considerations. The employer was disgusted by a practice that *he himself had initiated*. He did not explain why he had offered the dead calf to his Thai employees, but the fact that he had breached both religious and legal prohibitions in doing so suggested that it was not only about offering them a treat. It seemed to me that he was following the "a satiated Thai is a satisfied Thai" principle, treating his employees to something that came at no cost to his operation.

In another case, a dairy farmer told us that his employees would ask for cow placentas to make soup. His expression when he told us about this exposed his utter disdain for the practice. Eating embryos and placentas is a practical taboo in Israel, perhaps because of the Jewish prohibition on consuming *ever min hachai* (the organs of a living creature), which defines edible flesh as only that of a properly slaughtered animal. It is universally forbidden by Judaism to consume organs from a living creature. This is one of the Seven Laws of Noah, which apply to the "children of Noah"—that is, not only to Jews but also to all human beings, Thais included. The employer gave the placentas to his Thai employees, most likely as a treat that cost him nothing, even though he was breaching a major taboo of his own culture. His repulsion was totally directed toward his Thai employees, even though he was the one responsible for the breach of a taboo that does not exist in Thailand.

The Thai employees later told us that placenta soup is a sought-after dish in Isan, considered nourishing and invigorating. Human and animal (mainly cow) placentas are also used in the pharmaceutical and cosmetics industries because of their regenerative properties. Placentas are rich with "hormones, growth factors, immune molecules, lipids, and nucleic acids, . . . [which] could turn out to have particular clinical applications" (Glausser 2009, 15). Placentas are also used in stem cell research, which is among the most sophisticated fields in medicine. While the Israeli employer insinuated that the practice of consuming placentas was barbaric, relegating his Thai employees to the realm of savages, stem cell research is thriving in Israel, and cosmetics that use placentas are widely available.[15]

## STEALING

While some Thai migrant workers did have access to free animal flesh, most of them did not. Considering their limited income and the economic pressures they faced, it is not surprising that some of them might have resorted to stealing animals for meat. While conducting our study, we heard rumors about Thai workers stealing and eating animals. Several events of theft were reported in the media over the years, and I will address some of them shortly. However, just like with the stories of Thai workers eating dog meat, these rumors and reports were usually vague, and the texts often questioned and even contradicted the bold headlines. While I can't argue that Thai migrant workers in Israel *never* stole animals for food, there is little evidence that they did.

Not all stealing was viewed with the same disdain. Stealing poultry, for example, was not perceived as a serious offense. Stealing chicken was a famous part of the Palmach mythology (see chapter 2). When *palmachniks*, sabra elite who fought for Israel's independence and suffered heavy casualties, stole chicken, it was tolerated and later mythicized. Thai migrant workers were certainly not seen as *palmachniks,* and it was problematic and aggravating when they stole chicken, but it did not breach cultural norms. Even when we were told about incidences of Thai workers stealing larger and more expensive animals, such as calves or lambs, the acts were perceived as illegal but not as barbaric savagery, since these animals are considered perfectly edible in Israel.

Things became more complicated when Thais stole animals that were defined as pets rather than livestock, and even more so when the animals belonged to educational and therapeutic programs. An extreme case that I investigated involved two Thai workers employed by a kibbutz who broke into a *pinat hai* (small zoo) that operated within the kibbutz's informal education system, where children with special needs had "personal pets" that they were individually accountable for as a means of encouraging responsibility and dealing with their emotional difficulties. The Thais admitted to stealing several animals, mainly rabbits, and eating them. The kids were traumatized and overwhelmed with grief, and the outraged kibbutz members made sure that the Thai workers were deported from the country. I read about this event in a newspaper and drove to the kibbutz. I couldn't talk to the Thais, who had already been deported, but one of the kibbutz members involved in the case told me in rage that the Thais "didn't even understand how terrible what they did was."

A year earlier, I had visited a zoo in Thailand with my toddler son and a friend who had been born in Isan but who had lived in Bangkok for many years and traveled to quite a few other countries. The reactions that my friend had to the animals—mainly large African mammals, such as zebras, giraffes, and African elephants, which he had never seen before—were very different from those of my son. One of my friend's first questions was whether the animal was edible: "*Kin dai mai?*" When the answer was positive, his interest grew, and he spent more time watching the animals and asking questions about them. When the answer was negative, he lost interest and went to the next exhibit. For him, it seemed, animals were food, and thus the only animals that were interesting to him were those that could be eaten. Did the Thai workers who broke into the kibbutz zoo understand that they were stealing from a zoo or, for that matter, that the animals they had stolen had specific emotional value? Did they understand the concept of a zoo at all? I can only imagine the distress these workers must have felt at being deported over what they probably perceived as a minor breach of the rules. For the Israelis who read about the event in the newspaper, however, it was yet another proof of Thai migrant workers' cruelty and savagery.

A few cases of animal theft by Thai migrant workers were reported in the media. One article, with the headline "Thai Migrant Workers Ate a Donkey," reported that two young donkeys had disappeared from a backyard in a moshav in the south of Israel. The moshav secretary, who was interviewed for the article, explained that a Bedouin working on a neighboring farm said that he saw some Thai workers beating the donkeys to death and then carving and cooking them. The secretary searched the Thais' caravan and found some meat in a plastic bag that was "presumably the donkeys' meat."

Just like the article on dog hunting, there was a huge gap between the bold headlines and the actual story. In rural southern Israel, where I have been living for ten years now, Bedouins are regularly accused of any theft that occurs and, for that matter, of any criminal or otherwise negative behavior that takes place. Accusing a Bedouin of stealing the disappearing donkeys would have been the obvious thing to do, both because they are usually accused of any theft and because Bedouins do own donkeys. In this case, the usual suspect became the accuser and managed to convince the Jewish employers that the Thai workers were the culprits. The article does not state at any point that its only actual piece of evidence, the plastic bag of meat, was never positively identified as donkey meat. In fact, the only "proof" offered was the secretary's argument that it was "presumably the donkeys' meat." Most readers, however, were sufficiently persuaded that Thais steal animals for their flesh and eat donkey meat despite the fact that it is tough and tastes disgusting.

A 2012 news report with the headline "Youth admits: Robbed Thais who ate his duck" recounts how a sixteen-year-old boy from a moshav in southern Israel broke into an apartment where Thai migrant workers lived and stole some 600 shekels (US$160).[16] When questioned by the police, he confessed and claimed it was an act of revenge against the Thais because they had stolen and eaten his pet duck a few days earlier.

Just like with the other media reports, there was a gap between the headlines and the actual article. No evidence was provided to substantiate the claim that the Thais actually stole or ate the duck. In fact, according to the report, "the Thai workers were interrogated for stealing pets and released." The claim could have been, and probably was, an excuse invented by the youth, just like the one made by the Bedouin mentioned in the previous case. The point is that the bold headlines shaped the context and mindset of the readers, most of whom did not make the effort to consider the discrepancy between the headlines and the text. Similar reports have appeared in the media every few months since the mid-1990s, reminding Israeli readers that Thai migrant workers have strange and cruel food habits that Israelis should find repulsive: they steal pets, kill them, and consume their flesh.


### Hunting

Farmers in Isan regularly hunt, trap, and fish to supplement their protein supply (Somnasang, Moreno, and Chusil 1998; Setalaphruk and Price 2007). Early in the research period, we realized that migrant workers from Isan maintained their foodways as much as they could in Israel. Rice was a staple, and they cooked their food according to Thai and Isan recipes, using Thai spices, herbs, and condiments that they farmed or purchased. They also turned to what for them was an integral part of rural life—hunting small game.

In fact, it was hunting and not the consumption of dog meat that first attracted the attention of Israeli media to Thai migrant workers' foodways. Israeli Jews very rarely hunt, and hunting is usually viewed negatively. Jews of the Diaspora rarely hunted, probably because game could not be slaughtered according to Halachic laws and was therefore not kosher. Moreover, the violent nature of hunting and the accompanying meat lust contradicted the norms and religious propensities of Diaspora Jews. In modern Israel, part of the Zionist and modernist agendas is the revival of the land, left barren for millennia, and its fauna and flora, which were perceived of as neglected and even destroyed by its non-Jewish dwellers (Naveh and Dan 1973; Yiftachel and Segal 1998). The Society for the Protection of Nature is one of Israel's most effective NGOs, and its campaign to protect wildflowers is considered the most successful educational campaign in the country's history (Furst 2012). Indeed, Israel has been described recently as "the first vegan nation," with 10 to 15 percent of Israelis defining themselves vegetarian or vegan and a similar number of people considering the option.[17]

Up until the arrival of Thai migrant workers, hunting in Israel was mainly associated with Bedouin and Druze—Palestinian subgroups that Israeli Jews generally identify with bravery and ruthlessness, attributes of the noble savage. The fact that the Thais hunted only supported such perceptions. It is little wonder, then, that Thai hunting elicited negative media attention and public response. However, just like with the other meat-obtaining strategies described so far, I quickly realized that the media reports were problematic. I found that employers and other relevant agencies were ambivalent when it came to the hunting practices of Thai migrant workers. In fact, in some cases, they were supportive and even enthusiastic.

In a visit to a Modern Orthodox kibbutz, the "Thai coordinator" (*ha'ahra'i al hatailandim*) recounted how he had dealt with the large number of wild rabbits that troubled the kibbutz lettuce fields: "We brought all of our Thais, as well as those of two neighboring kibbutzim, and in a few hours they cleaned the fields out. They walked in a line holding bags and were so quick. . . . None of the rabbits got away." He said that he didn't ask the Thais what they did with the rabbits they seized, but it was obvious that the animals were eaten.

Despite the Orthodox Jewish framework of the kibbutz, he wasn't disturbed by the idea that his employees consumed nonkosher meat. In fact, he was the employer that coined the phrase "A satiated Thai is a satisfied Thai," and he generally displayed a functional attitude when it came to his Thai employees. Despite the biblical prohibition on work on the Sabbath and the requirement to grant a day of rest to "your slave, ox, donkey, and any of your livestock, as well as the sojourner within your gates" (Deuteronomy 5:14), this employer gave no such relief to his workers. He defended himself by pointing out, "the Thais are not my slaves, or my oxen or donkeys, or the sojourners within my gates—they are Thais." In his view, the Thai migrant workers were not part of Jewish social world.

Another employer reported that once a week his Thai employees and the Thais employed by his neighbors would gather by his cowshed and use slingshots to shoot down pigeons that fed on the grains supplied to the cows. He pointed out the Thais were "slingshot masters" (*alufim be'rugatkot*) and added that this organized hunt helped lower his expenses by preventing the pigeons from stealing the cows' feed.

By contrast, I came across an action taken by an employee of the Israel Nature and Parks Authority (INPA) that caught me by surprise. The INPA is the government agency responsible for the protection of nature and endangered species. The agency's officers monitor hunting, and in that role, they have arrested numerous Thais accused of poaching.[18] On November 24, 1994, journalist Zvi Alush reported in the daily *Yediot Ahronot* that the agency's officer responsible for the Arava Valley had published a leaflet in the Thai language requesting that Thai migrant workers hunt three kinds of birds that were harming local farming. The leaflet, which had the title *ochlei hatulim vetziporim* (cat and bird eaters), was later denounced by an INPA spokesperson. A Thai worker interviewed by Alush confirmed that hunting birds was common in Thailand, but he insisted that Thai workers were warned against hunting in Israel and refrained from the practice. He added: "This is quite confusing, [hunting is] sometimes allowed and sometimes forbidden." Indeed, supportive reactions by employers and the encouragement to hunt specific kinds of wildlife by the authorities responsible for controlling hunting conveyed a mixed message and led Thai workers to engage in hunting despite the fact that it is technically illegal.

Over the years, it became clear that the hunting practices of Thai migrant workers in Israel posed a real threat to Israeli wildlife. One major problem was that their very effective traps were designed to catch any creature, regardless of whether it had a protected status. Both education and law enforcement were employed to deal with this problem, and the Israeli government even engaged the help of the Thai embassy.[19] Yet despite the substantial damage it caused, Thai hunting became a secondary issue and did not attract a lot of attention or criticism. It was the consumption of dog meat that became the focus of Israeli media and public attention in the late 1990s.

## Dog Meat

Thai migrant workers in Israel farmed poultry, purchased different kinds of meat, received meat leftovers from their employers, and stole and hunted a wide range of animals for meat. Though some of the culinary practices of Thai workers were tolerated by their Israeli employers, and while some accusations that the Thais engaged in culinary taboos were bogus, my findings support the argument that Thai migrant workers in Israel routinely transgressed Israeli Jewish culinary norms. I also realized that among Israeli Jews, none of these offenses were as disturbing as the consumption of dog meat. However, Thai workers did not eat dogs. While I cannot account for every Thai migrant worker or every animal caught in Thai traps, I can say with confidence that dog meat was not part of the diet of Thai migrant workers.

Thai migrant workers and their Israeli employers vehemently rejected the accusations of dog-meat consumption. There were good reasons for both parties to deny these accusations even if they had been true, but their passionate denials are important components of my analysis, regardless of their veracity. My observations, however, supported the claims made by Israeli employers that their Thai workers liked dogs as companions, groomed and petted their employers' dogs, and often had their own pet dogs.

In the 1996 article on Thai dog hunting analyzed at the beginning of the chapter, the journalist Regev reported: "Interesting phenomenon: some Thai workers adopt puppies and play with them affectionately. In the first few months [of their lives], they serve as guard dogs, but when they grow up, they end their lives on the grill." Regev offered no supporting evidence for this assertion. My observations confirm that many Thai workers owned dogs that accompanied them to work and returned with them to their dwellings in the evenings. Just like in Thailand, Thai migrant workers fed their dogs with their own leftovers. These dogs became important companions for the Thai workers during their long and often lonely years of working abroad. When I moved with my family to a rural community, we adopted a puppy from of a litter born to a dog owned by a Thai worker. He took good care of the mother and puppies and made an effort to ensure that all the puppies were adopted. I saw him with his dogs over the span of a few years, and when he left Israel, the dogs were given to other Thai workers. These observations may be anecdotal, but they are in line with what many employers told me, further supporting my argument that Thai workers were generally fond of dogs as companions and did not perceive of them as food.

Media reports of Thai workers eating dog meat that have been published over the years demonstrate the pattern I observed in Regev's article: they feature bold headlines proclaiming that Thai migrant workers stole, kid-napped, trapped, butchered, or ate dogs, but their vague text fails to substantiate the claim that dog meat was eaten by Thai workers.

One such headline, "Thais Skewered Dalmatian Dog with Iron Spike," was accompanied by the subheading: "Naama [a moshav in the Jordan Valley] resident released his dog in the vicinity of the workers' dwelling area. But the hungry Thais had a different use for it."[20] In the article, journalist Efrat Weiss reports that in December 2004, a dog was found speared in the Thai dwelling area of the moshav, "apparently intended for food." An image of a Dalmatian with an iron spike lodged into its back accompanies the text. The image contains no reference to Thai workers, to a butchering process, to the moshav, or even to Israel. The reporter does not explain why an owner would release his dog in the workers' dwelling area. The article states that "the Thais [130 of them lived on this moshav at the time] are the ones suspected of spearing the dog with the intention of eating it later," but this accusation is not substantiated by any forensic or journalistic evidence, and the story is quite incoherent. For instance, why would an owner release his dog near Thai housing if "everyone knows that Thais hunt and eat dogs"? And if the Thai workers were planning to eat the dog, why did they spear it rather than slaughter it, and why was it left in the open rather than hidden or processed for later consumption? The combination of headlines and image, however, turns an unsubstantiated suspicion into an unquestionable fact.

In another report of the same event, Israeli dwellers of the moshav told two reporters, "The Thais raise chickens and the dogs attack them [the chickens] and are then caught by the Thais."[21] A neighbor who was asked by the Dalmatian's owner to rescue the dog "from an attempted poisoning," purportedly carried out by Thai workers, is quoted as saying: "The [Israeli] farmers are imprisoned by the Thais. . . . Their livelihood depends on them, so they turn a blind eye." The article ignores the question of why the Thais would poison an animal meant for consumption. This article tells an alternative, more logical version of the story: A Dalmatian owned by a local resident either was let loose or ran away and got into an area where other local residents, Thai workers, were raising chickens. This was not the first time local dogs attacked chickens owned by the Thais, and the Thais protected their poultry from the attacker, first by trying to poison the aggressor and eventually by spearing it. This version is still just speculation because no evidence is provided that definitively involves the Thais in the killing. In fact, another plausible version would be that the dog was killed as the result of a dispute between neighbors. This was suggested in some of the readers' comments, and it should make sense to anyone who has lived in a small rural community, where dogs can be a source of major arguments between neighbors, some of which lead to conflict and even violence.

Even though the second report suggested that the dog had been killed because it attacked the Thais' chickens and not because the workers were after its meat, the subhead aligned with the hegemonic narrative: "Horror in Naama: A Dalmatian dog speared on an iron spike was found in the Thai dwelling area. Suspect taken for interrogation 'Whomever did this could spear a human being.'" While the report refrains from accusing the Thais of killing the dog for its meat, the headline insinuates that their cruelty toward dogs could lead to violence toward humans. According to this prevailing narrative, the Thai workers were barbaric subhumans and were to be feared and distrusted by Israelis.

A similar article, published in 2009, with the headline "Suspicion: Workers Hunt Dozens of Dogs," begins as follows:

> Oz [immigration police] inspectors faced a terrible sight in the yard of a house in moshav Amioz in the western Negev, where Thai workers reside. They discovered dozens of skulls, *seemingly* from dogs. The inspectors contacted the Nature and Parks Authority, which launched a joint investigation. Some of the skulls were taken for inspection. *If it is determined that these are the remains of dogs,* the findings will be passed on to the Ministry of the Protection of Environment, and the punishment could be imprisonment. If it turns out, however, that *these are the remains of jackals, foxes, or other animals,* the illegal hunters will be handled by the Nature and Parks Authority, which may fine and even deport them.[22]

The possibility that these were the skulls of edible animals or that the Thais might have had nothing to do with them was not mentioned in the report, leaving readers convinced that the Thais must have done something cruel to dogs or other animals.

Using the term "suspicion" in headlines is a solution employed by some reporters or editors who are trying to maintain balance. This allows them to attract the attention of readers by suggesting in the headline that Thai workers eat Israeli dogs while maintaining a (limited) measure of journalistic integrity by reporting the facts, even though the facts often have very little to do with Thais or with dogs. "Thais Suspected of Slaughtering and Eating Puppies"[23] and "Petah Tikva Police Investigate Suspicion That Thai Workers Launched a Wide-Ranging Dog Hunt"[24] are two examples of headlines that were followed by texts that did not support the bold accusations. While "suspicion" may have been the term used by the policemen and simply quoted by the journalists, the articles question the very suspicion. In the first case, the evidence was the bodies of dead puppies found a hundred meters away from a house where Thai workers lived; in the second case, the evidence was neighbors' complaints that dogs and cats "have been disappearing recently from the streets surrounding a building site where Thais are employed." As Thais could be employed only in agriculture, the workers were probably Chinese and not Thai, as Chinese migrants are permitted to be employed in the construction sector. For most Israelis, however, this distinction is insignificant. When I pointed out that dog meat is eaten in Vietnam and China but not in Thailand, a typical Israeli response would be: "Chinese, Thai, what's the difference? They all eat everything."

Yet one of the most revealing events in which Thais were accused of eating dog meat turned out not to involve dogs at all, although the media reports claimed otherwise. On May 16, 2011, the website *Walla News* published an article with the headline "Thai Worker Murdered during Argument over Dog Eating," accompanied by an illustration of a bloodstained ax:

> A foreign worker from Thailand . . . was murdered yesterday during a fight with a coworker. . . . The suspect, another Thai migrant worker, was arrested by the police. Initial interrogation revealed that *the deceased man and the suspected murderer had had an argument over hunting and eating dogs.* One of them favored dog eating and the other opposed it. It is still unknown which position each of them held. . . . *The suspect does not speak Hebrew,* and investigators are waiting for the arrival of an interpreter.[25]

Ten days later, the same website published a follow-up article titled "Indicted: Thai Worker Kills Colleague for Killing a Dog," with an image of a bloody knife on a bloody wooden butcher block. The text reads:

> Thaitikun Anuku was charged this morning in Petah Tikva provincial court with killing Paisan Utarkan, another Thai worker, ten days ago. According to the indictment, Anuku murdered Utarkan for killing a dog. Anuku denied this accusation. According to the indictment, . . . an argument evolved between Anuku and Utarkan for an unknown reason. Anuku grabbed a

20-centimeter-long butcher knife and stabbed his colleague.... According to the arrest warrant, Anuku [who doesn't speak Hebrew] admitted to the killing to the arresting officer but later denied the accusation. His [Israeli] employer said during the interrogation that Anuku approached him, used his hand to motion slaughtering by his neck, and said "Paisan dog." He then motioned again and said "I Paisan."[26]

Obviously, the conclusions drawn from the initial interrogation were hardly convincing because the suspect did not speak Hebrew. The Israeli employer interpreted the slaughtering motions and the four words uttered by the accused (two of which were in Hebrew: "I" and "dog"[27]) as "Paisan [slaughtered a] dog; I [therefore slaughtered] Paisan." Another interpretation, which is at least as plausible, would be: "Paisan [is a] dog; I [therefore slaughtered] Paisan." Yet another interpretation, which would be in line with Tambiah's (1969) argument that calling someone a dog in Isan is a major offense, is: "Paisan [called me a] dog; I [therefore slaughtered] Paisan."

Importantly, no actual dog, alive or dead, was included in the indictment or the media reports, casting doubt on whether an argument over killing and eating dog meat ever actually took place. The only reason for the employer, the police, the prosecution, and the reporters to assume that a fight over eating dog meat was the reason for the murder, despite the suspect's denial, a complete lack of evidence, and more plausible interpretations of the event and the alleged four words spoken by the suspect, was the fact that in Israel everybody believes that Thai workers hunt and eat dogs.

Several other media channels reported the event, with similarly problematic interpretations. Ma'ariv reporter Avi Askenazi wrote: "The police investigation revealed that the murder was instigated by a quarrel between the coworkers, Thai citizens, who couldn't decide who would be the first to eat the dog they had hunted earlier. The quarrel escalated and ended in one of the workers killing the other."[28] By now, we know that there was no evidence for this allegedly hunted dog. This undermines the reporter's main argument, but since Israelis believe that Thais eat dogs, the reporter expected that his unsubstantiated interpretation would be accepted by his readership.

There are countless other articles supporting my argument that these stories were sustained by societal misconceptions rather than evidence. For example, consider another report of the same event, published on the Hadshot Arutz 2 (Channel 2 News) website, which also flipped the story upside down with the headline: "Suspicion: Murdered His Friend in Objection to Dog Killing." The article reads: "A foreign worker from Thailand was cruelly murdered this evening... after expressing opposition to the plan of one of his friends to hunt a dog to eat. ... Witnesses recounted how a quarrel developed between the two regarding the suspect's wish to eat a dog, during which the victim stated that this was illegal in Israel."[29]

The previous three reports of the event describe the murder as a reaction to a dog being killed for food. This fourth report states that the murder was over a plan to kill a dog in the future. This report also reverses the roles of the killer and victim. In the previous reports, the suspect was accused of killing the victim because the latter killed a dog for meat. In this report, it is the suspect who is described as wanting to eat a dog. In the Ma'ariv report, the murderer and murdered were fighting over who would get the first bite of dog meat; in the Hadshot Arutz 2 report, the killing was in response to a plan to eat dog meat. Neither Ma'ariv nor Hadshot Arutz 2 reported that the suspect denied any connection between the killing and dog meat. Moreover, despite the fact reported in the first article that the accused did not speak Hebrew, Hadshot Arutz 2 quoted witnesses who reported that the victim had stated during the argument that dog meat is illegal in Israel. It's unclear who these witnesses were, but in any case, it is unlikely that an Israeli witness could have understood such a complex argument in Thai (or Lao), or that the accused could have expressed it in Hebrew.

That a murder occurred is clear; that dog meat was its cause remained completely unsubstantiated. Despite this lack of evidence, all of the Israelis involved, including employers, policemen, prosecutors, and journalists, tied the murder to dog meat. The four stories all contain internal inconsistencies and suggest very different versions and interpretations of the event, but they share a master narrative: Thai migrant workers in Israel eat dogs. Since everybody knows that Thai migrant workers eat dogs, these reports reinforce the same total social fact that proves their veracity despite a lack of physical evidence. Israelis fall into a vicious circle of belief regarding Thai migrant workers, in line with Frank Wu's argument about the Asian dog-eating myth in the West quoted at the beginning of this chapter: "Dog eating is an international urban legend with some truth to it. Everybody knows that Asians eat dogs" (2003, 40).

WHY DOGS?

In their memorable 1970 sketch "Ha'aliyah La'aretz" (Ascending to the Land),[30] Uri Zohar and Arik Einstein perform a series of scenes that depict the arrival of Jewish members of different *ali'yot* (literally "ascends," or migration waves, a term used in modern Hebrew to convey the elevated spiritual, emotional, and material status of those Jews who chose to immigrate to Israel vis-à-vis those who chose to stay in the lowly Diaspora) and the contemptuous reaction of their predecessors. This contempt is condensed in the first scene into a poisonous remark in Arabic, "*Ina'al din babur ili jab'hum*" (damn the boat that brought them), made by a couple of Arabs wearing moustaches and *keffiyehs* and directed at the arriving Russian Jews of the First Aliyah, sometime in the late 1880s. This remark is repeated in each of the scenes and is the punch line of the sketch.

Jews of each aliyah—Russians, Poles, Yemenites, Germans, Moroccans, and Georgians—are defined by traditional outfits, exaggerated accents, and, most importantly, stereotypes: the migrants from Russia are depicted as emotional and hot-blooded; the Poles as sour and bitter; the Germans as particular and tedious; the Yemenites as religious (and the female Yemenite immigrant, the only woman in the entire sketch, is pregnant, alluding to the "primitive" tendency attributed to Yemenites and other immigrants from Middle Eastern countries to bear many children); the Moroccans as combining oriental religious traditionalism and an awkward, wannabe-French style; and the Georgians as wild Cossacks. The sketch captures two important sociological traits that are important for my argument: Each wave of immigrants to Israel is represented by a condescending stereotype, and each wave is disliked and ridiculed by its predecessors.

While the sketch ends with immigrants from Georgia, additional waves of Jewish immigrations continued to arrive in Israel, and each was assigned its own derogative stereotype intended to relegate the new arrivals to the lowest position in the Israeli social hierarchy. Thus, for example, Jews from communist Romania who arrived in Israel in the 1960s were called "Romanians" though earlier immigrants from the same geographical region had not been distinguished as such. These Romanians were stereotyped as unsophisticated quasi-Europeans and dubbed "Ashkenazi orientals," suggesting that they were less sophisticated and less civilized than previous immigrants from Eastern and Central Europe.

When it came to Mizrahi Jews, a common joke in the 1970s described a ceremony at Binayaney Ha'Uma (Jerusalem's International Convention Center, literally "the national halls"): "The Transferring of the Knife from the Moroccans to the Georgians," (*Tekes Ha'avarat Haskin MeHamarokaim LaGruzinim*). The humor came from the underlying argument that the recent arrivals from Georgia were more violent and primitive than even the Moroccans, who, until then, had been dubbed *"Morocco sakin"* (Morocco knife). People also joked that since the arrival of the Georgians, the Moroccans had started attending concerts—suggesting that both Moroccan and the Georgians were primitive but that the Moroccans had begun undergoing a civilizing process, presumably inspired by the Ashkenazi elite.

The roughly one million immigrants that arrived in Israel from the former Soviet Union in the 1990s were culturally processed in a similar way. A distinction was made between "white Russians," who came from European Soviet states, and "Caucasians," who came from former Asiatic republics (Smooha 2008). The former were historically Ashkenazi, but since they could potentially compete with the Ashkenazi elite over lucrative jobs and positions that depended on academic and cultural capital (e.g., jobs as physicians, scientists, teachers, or artists), they were defined as "Russians" and stereotyped for their "Soviet pushiness," the low quality of their academic education (despite the scientific achievements of the USSR and the distinguished academic careers of some of the newcomers), and their "Russian" dress, hygiene, and food. For various reasons, women from European Soviet republics were stereotyped as "Russian prostitutes." "Caucasians," however, were conceived of as yet another "primitive" and violent Mizrahi group and treated accordingly: they were relegated to the Israeli periphery and addressed as being in need of civilizing.

Jews from Ethiopia, many of whom reached Israel after heroic voyages and rescue operations and whose arrival was celebrated as proof that the Israeli state and society were not racist and did not discriminate against blacks, were stereotyped as extremely primitive "Stone Age people" and relegated to the lowest position in the Jewish social hierarchy. Israelis have treated the recent wave of Jewish migrants from France with similar contempt and stereotyping, mainly by denying the Europeanness of these newcomers and insisting that they are essentially North African Mizrahi pretending to be European.

In her analysis of "the great chain of orientalism," Aziza Khazzoom (2003) points out that since its inception, Zionism has been a modernizing, Westernizing project within which each Jewish Diaspora has been orientalized—that is, stigmatized as oriental by its predecessors and relegated to the lower echelons of society—the process that Uri Zohar and Arik Einstein captured so vividly in their sketch. Though Khazoom doesn't deal with Russians, Caucasians, or Frenchmen, her model explains why immigrants from Russia were not perceived as Ashkenazi, immigrants from central Asia were defined as Mizrahi, and why third-generation French Jews were dubbed *Zafrokaim* (a combination of the Hebrew words for "French" and "Moroccan") and ridiculed for what veteran Israelis felt was an attempt to disguise themselves as French and European. Each arriving group had to be orientalized to diminish its threat to the prevailing hegemonic elites and social order, which defines as "Western" only those who have gone through a civilizing process in Israel.

Khazoom's scholarly project and Zohar and Einstein's artistic critique address only Jewish immigrants (and, to some extent, Arabs and Palestinians), though small numbers of non-Jewish immigrants have also arrived in Israel over the years, most notably African Hebrew Israelites, Vietnamese "boat people," and Muslim refugees from the former Yugoslavia. These immigrants were perceived by most Israelis as marginal, exotic, and strange, but it was not felt that these groups would destabilize the Israeli social structure. The arrival of massive numbers of migrant workers in the 1990s (and tens of thousands of non-Jewish, African asylum seekers since the mid-1990s), however, could not be ignored, nor could these immigrants be dismissed as marginal and exotic. Romanian, Turkish, Chinese, Filipino, Thai, West African, South American, Sudanese, and Eritrean migrants joined Israeli society and were treated with the same cultural tools that were used so successfully in dealing with previous *olim* (literally "ascenders," or immigrants). Orientalizing and stereotyping were applied once again to relegate these newcomers to the lowest social strata.

It is important to bear in mind that the decision to import migrant workers was made by Rabin's government, which was composed of Israel's Zionist labor party, Ha'Avoda, and the progressive left-wing party Meretz. Importing non-Jewish migrant workers breached some of the fundamental values of Socialist Zionism that these parties professed to champion, Israeli perceptions of social justice, and the Israeli egalitarian ethos (Ram 1993). It is therefore not surprising that Israelis employed aggressive orientalizing and stereotyping to deal with the moral dilemmas instigated by the mass employment of migrant workers.

The first significant non-Jewish groups of migrant workers that arrived in Israel in the mid-1990s came from Romania, the Philippines, Thailand, and West Africa. The Romanians, who were employed in construction, had a stereotype waiting for them: just like the Romanian Jews discussed earlier, these Romanians were perceived as quasi-European and primitive. Special attention was paid to their beer consumption: with little money to spend, they often congregated by neighborhood grocery stores, where they would purchase cheap beer and bread, which they consumed on the spot. Very quickly, they were defined as drunkards. Thus, their low salaries and poor living conditions were judged to be appropriate and even excessive.

According to Israelis, the Filipinas employed as caregivers and domestic helpers fit the classic Western stereotype of Asian women (Chung 2011): they were gentle, submissive, confined to the private sphere, and, as I was told countless times, "born to serve" (*noldu lesharet*). Though my interviewees did not mention the opera *Madame Butterfly* and its later incarnation, the musical *Miss Saigon,* tragic descriptions of oriental women who sacrificed themselves for Westerners loomed over conversations in which Israelis described the Filipina caregivers who gave up their youths, social lives, and chances of having spouses and children (or alternatively their conjugal lives and roles as parents) to take care of ailing and elderly Israeli Jews for minimal pay. The fact that they were stereotyped as "natural servants" justified their working conditions.

Undocumented workers from West Africa congregated in Tel Aviv's poorest neighborhoods and were mainly employed as domestic helpers and cleaners by upper-middle-class Israeli families. Here as well, an obvious and effective stereotype was waiting: just like the African Americans many Israelis saw on television, in films, and on occasional visits to the United States, these Africans were deemed bodily agile, extremely masculine, intellectually limited, and dangerous. As such, the most they could aspire to would be serving white people (bearing in mind that most Israeli Jews perceive of themselves as white), obviously not as slaves, but as cleaners and domestic helpers. Just like African Americans slaves and servants of the past and athletes of the present, these African men were considered attractive and sexy, socially undesirable but physically appealing; Israeli Jews wouldn't want to leave these men alone at the house with their adolescent daughters, perhaps for fear of sexual assault but possibly also for fear of mutual attraction.[31] This stereotype was exacerbated by media reports of sexual assaults committed by undocumented African workers and later by asylum seekers, reports that were probably as biased as those describing dog eating by Thais.

When it came to Thai migrant workers, however, stereotyping was more challenging. Israelis had no prevailing stereotypes of Thais, and Thailand was (and still is) one of the most popular destinations for Israeli tourists, who rave about its beaches, jungles, temples, palaces, wonderful food, and smiling people. Moreover, Thais were employed by members of the agricultural

20. Homo Homini Canis Est *(Man Is Dog to Man)*

sector, the epitome of Israeli Zionism—the ideology of self-reliance, a strong work ethic, and a socialist ethos. Members of this social echelon, composed mainly of kibbutz and moshav members, dubbed *hahityashvut haovedet* (the working settlement), were considered by many Israelis to be "the salt of the earth" and a model for ideal lifestyle and moral standards. It is thus of little wonder that Israelis found the exploitation of migrant workers by members of this social group difficult to accept.

The potential defamation of those perceived by many as Israel's moral elite and the lack of existing stereotypes for Thais prompted the cultural mechanism described in this chapter. At first it was hunting, specifically that of wildlife, that drew negative attention to the Thais and caused them to be depicted as a risk to Israeli nature (though Israeli farming itself is nature's most dangerous enemy). Hunting and gathering further defined them as people who "eat everything," primitive savages that did not develop sophisticated categorization systems to define edibility, inedibility, and food taboos. As primitive savages, their poor living conditions in Israel were believed to be much better than those in Thailand, and their Israeli salaries were imaged to be legendary in comparison with Thai standards.

But at a certain moment, perhaps but not necessarily because dogs were caught in traps set by Thai migrant workers, a new stereotype emerged—that of Thais being dog-meat eaters. The ensuing moral panic—initiated, exacerbated, and reflected by the media—suggested that accusations of dog eating were much more effective than complaints about hunting when it came to convincing Israelis that Thai migrant workers were worthy of exploitation. Thus, even though the hunting practices of Thai migrant workers posed a real threat to the Israeli nature, and even though it remains to be proven that Thai workers ever hunted or ate dogs, Israeli media and public attention shifted to reports of dog eating. The question that remains is why allegations of dog eating proved to be so effective and convincing. This question has nothing to do with Thailand and can be understood only in Israeli terms.

According to a Ministry of Industry and Commerce report, 12 percent of Israeli households had dogs in 2011, and the total number of dogs in the country was 270,000. Israeli dogs belong in most cases to the category of pets.[32] According to the report, Israelis were committed to caring for their dogs for extended periods of time (an average of 7.8 years) and to spending significant amounts of money on dog food, grooming, and health (almost US$1,00 per year). Dogs are perceived by Israelis as loyal and friendly and considered "man's best friend," and they usually enjoy their patrons' love, protection, and resources. Dogs have first names and are attributed the family names of their owners when medically and administratively registered.

In his analysis of the taboo on dog meat in the United States in the early 1970s, Marshal Sahlins argues that "America is the land of the sacred dog" (1991, 282) and explains that "dogs and horses participate in American society in the capacity of subjects. They have proper names, and indeed we are in the habit of conversing with them. . . . Dogs and horses are thus deemed inedible. . . . But as domestic cohabitants, dogs are closer to man than are horses. . . . They are 'one of the family'" (284). In her recent study of human-dog interactions in Israel, Dafna Shir-Vertesh (2012, 420) depicts a more nuanced understanding of these relationships. Dogs in Israel, she argues, are "loving and loved members of the family, very similar to small children."[33] Her research makes it very clear that Israeli dogs are important and meaningful family members. Eating them would therefore not be seen just as breaching a food taboo but also as murder and cannibalism.

The supposed murderous and cannibalistic nature of Thai migrant workers was also the implicit subject of most media reports of alleged dog eating, exposing the stereotype's meaning and might. As hunters-gatherers, Thai migrant workers were perceived as primitive and uncivilized, but as dog eaters, they were redefined as murderous and cannibalistic. As such, the moral dilemmas that surrounded their exploitation and ill treatment dissolved: those who kill and eat man's best friend are hardly human and hardly deserve human treatment. Once dog-meat eating by Thai migrant workers was established as a total social fact, Israelis didn't have to bother any more with ethical dilemmas. It was the food myth that redefined the power relations between Israelis and Thais and sent the latter to the bottom of the social hierarchy, where their exploitation was obvious.

Finally, let me return to the event in which Thai workers killed, cooked, and tried to eat a donkey. We were getting ready to leave the farm when the Israeli employer asked me if I could assist him with another problem he didn't know how to approach. "Ever since the Thais ate the donkey," he said, "the Bedouin employees refuse to work with them."

I approached the Bedouin employees, who were having their lunch break. I told them who I was and asked about the donkey affair. After some embarrassed smiles and jokes, they gave an account of the event that was similar to the version we had heard from the Thai workers. After confirming some of the details, I asked them whether it was true that they refused to work alongside the Thais ever since the donkey event had taken place. A few seconds of silence ensued, and then one of them said: "Don't you know? Thais eat Bedouins!"

Here again, a culinary practice was used to depict Israeli power hierarchies and relations. By way of a food metaphor, the Bedouins were telling me that in Israel's symbolic power structure, dogs and Bedouins occupy a similar position.

# *Conclusion*

## FOOD AND POWER IN ISRAEL—
## ORIENTALIZATION AND AMBIVALENCE

IF I WERE TO CHOOSE A SINGLE DISH to represent all of contemporary Israeli cuisine, I would suggest schnitzel in a pita. Breaded chicken breast is fried and packed into a pita along with a fresh vegetable salad and some French fries. A dash of tahini adds another dimension to this complex culinary creation. The server always asks the indispensable Israeli culinary question: "Hummus? *Harif* [spicy sauce]?" Served in virtually all school, university, and workplace cafeterias as well as in most fast-food joints; packed for lunches, picnics, and other outings; and considered an exciting treat when prepared at home, schnitzel in a pita is a favorite of Israeli adults and children alike.

Schnitzel in a pita is one of Israel's most authentic local specialties. While the original Viennese schnitzel is made of veal or pork, Israeli schnitzel is made of chicken breast. Puffy and elastic yeasted pocket-pita that can be stuffed with goodies is one of Israel's main contributions to the Middle Eastern foodscape (traditional Middle Eastern flatbreads are unleavened and less elastic, and they are usually used as wraps rather than pockets). The fresh, finely chopped vegetable salad that Israelis call "Israeli salad" and consume at all meals is another Israeli contribution to the dish (at least as far as Israeli Jews are concerned; Israeli Palestinian restaurants serve it as "Arab salad"). What is also very Israeli about schnitzel in a pita is the combination of ethnic foods of different origins with a local twist (see chapter 1): a kosher version of European schnitzel is stuffed into an Israeli version of Middle Eastern pita along with hummus, spicy sauce, American-style French fries, and salad made of vegetables produced by the Israeli agroindustry.

There is also a commercial version of the dish: a prefabricated, nugget-style cutlet made of processed meat, additives, and substitutes is reheated and packed into a mass-produced pita with industrial hummus, tahini, spicy sauce, and reconstituted French fries. It is a contemporary junk food, a product of Israel's increasing commercialization and McDonaldization. This version is often served in Israeli schools, army mess halls, and other total institutions, where the food is distributed to captive audiences, as well as in some cheap eateries.

This popular Israeli dish may also be approached as an example of some of the sociological issues and dilemmas discussed throughout this book. First and foremost, it is a value-for-money dish, of the sort discussed in the chapter 1. Diners appreciate the level of satiety the dish provides for a low cost. Its inexpensive ingredients also make it possible for home and professional cooks to produce big portions cheaply. Schnitzel in a pita allows both diners and cooks to feel that that they have cracked the system and become nobody's suckers.

The dish is also based on animal flesh, and, as such, it is culturally defined as wholesome and filling and considered to be a proper lunch that keeps the diner going for a full day of work, study, or play. Nevertheless, this dish is not considered really "meaty" because its defining component, the schnitzel, is made of chicken. This corresponds with the Israeli preference for lighter, "softer," arguably healthier, and certainly cheaper meat. Oddly enough, schnitzel is eaten by quite a few Israeli vegetarians who define themselves as "tzimhonim hutz mi'schnitzel" (vegetarians except for schnitzel). I have discussed this with several practitioners and critics, and their explanations for the phenomenon draw on the whiteness of chicken breast, which allows diners to tell themselves "it has no blood," and on the profound processing and coating that turns the schnitzel into something that does not look like meat. Tuchman and Levine (1993, 389) suggest that New York Jews were willing to consume non-kosher food at Chinese restaurants precisely because Chinese cooking manipulated shrimp and pork to such an extent that they no longer resembled shrimp or pork, making them "safe *treyf*." Carol Adams (1990) describes the general tendency of distancing meat cuts from the original animals by renaming them "beef," "pork," and "poultry" instead of "cow," "pig," and "chicken," a semiotic transformation that also exists in Hebrew. Israeli vegetarians seem to adhere to the same principles when it comes to schnitzel: pale, breaded, and termed "schnitzel," it is perceived by many as being less than meat.

Another possible explanation for the Israeli tendency to consider schnitzel as less than meat despite its definition as *besari* ("meaty") in contemporary kashrut terms has to do with the way in which the prohibition to mix meat and dairy evolved in Judaism. This ban stems from the original biblical command: "You shall not boil a kid [young goat] in its mother's milk"

(Deuteronomy 14:21). What was originally understood as an ethical taboo was later expanded by Halachic interpretations to include all kosher mammals and, according to some, all kosher birds. The status of chicken as meat that should not be mixed with dairy remained contested up until the early twentieth century, with some Jewish Diasporas, notably in the Balkans and Ethiopia, boasting chicken and dairy dishes up until their members immigrated to Israel. While observant Jews now consider chicken to be meat and do not prepare chicken and diary dishes, schnitzel's status as less than meat might reflect previous kashrut conventions.

As a less-than-meat dish, schnitzel expresses the complex Israeli Jewish engagement with the symbolism of meat and power. In chapter 2, I argue that if red meat—bull's muscle and blood—is the epitome of physical strength, masculinity, and power, the tender white flesh of chicken can hardly express heroism, maleness, and domination precisely because its "meaty" nature is contested. Adams (1990, 189) and Counihan (1992, 61) suggest that in the United States, beef is considered masculine while chicken is associated with femininity. My male interlocutors at Jerusalem's Sacher Park also associated chicken with tenderness and femininity. However, while suggesting that women and children prefer chicken because they like their meat soft and cooked quickly, these men were devouring chicken wings and *pargiot* (spring chicken) skewers.

In my analysis of these barbecues, I suggested that the centrality and importance of the tender and feminine flesh of chicken, and specifically of *pargiot*, the most popular item at these food events, expresses the ambivalence of Israeli Jews when it comes to their own power. The power reversal in an Israeli military prison for Palestinian detainees that was explained by lack of meat in chapter 5 further indicates that Israeli Jewish meat symbolism is often concerned with weakness and ambivalence rather than pure power, an idea to which I will return shortly.

The other salient symbolic aspect embedded in schnitzel in a pita has to do with ethnic relations in contemporary Israel. Schnitzel, as its name clearly indicates, is a Central European dish. Pita, hummus, tahini, and spicy sauce are all Middle Eastern staples. However, each of these ingredients was significantly modified to fit Israeli Jewish preferences, and their ethnic origins are now ignored. The Austro-Hungarian roots of schnitzel, the Shami (greater Syrian) or Palestinian origins of pita and hummus, and the provenances of the various distinct spicy sauces, such as Tunisian harissa, Libyan *filfelchuma*, Yemenite *schug*, and Palestinian *shatta*, that are simply grouped under the term *harif* (spicy) are practically disregarded, leaving a dish that highlights only two broad categories: Ashkenazi and Mizrahi.

In fact, schnitzel in a pita is an accurate representation of contemporary Israel's ethnic power structure and interethnic relations. For one, this iconic Israeli dish embodies only the two hegemonic ethnic groups in Israel: Ashkenazim and Mizrahim. The two other significant ethnic categories in Israel, "Russians" (immigrants from the European countries that were formerly part of the USSR, as opposed to the "Caucasians," who immigrated from the Caucasus region of the former USSR) and "Arabs," are not expressed in the dish, despite the ethnic and culinary affinities between Russians and Ashkenazim and between Arabs and Mizrahim. Russian and Arab food—just like that of other nonhegemonic ethnic groups in Israel, such as the "Caucasians" or "Ethiopians"—is limited to marginal enclaves and is not manifested in iconic or popular "all-Israeli" dishes such as schnitzel in a pita.

The social relations between Ashkenazi and Mizrahi ethnicities are both acknowledged and questioned by the dish's structure. Schnitzel, the core of this dish and its main marker, is Ashkenazi. This core, however, is complemented by layers of *mizrahiyut* (orientalness)—hummus, tahini, spicy sauce, and pita—that deeply influence its taste, aroma, and looks and practically conceal the Ashkenazi component, as central as it may be. As such, schnitzel in pita raises the following question regarding the ethnic relations it expresses: Is the Ashkenazi schnitzel the principal component of the dish, with Mizrahi hummus and pita serving as its exotic decorations, or do pita, hummus, and *harif*, the Mizrahi components, transform the schnitzel to such an extent that the dish is hardly Ashkenazi anymore?

## THE CULINARY ORIENTALIZATION OF ISRAEL

In a recent visit to an American campus where I presented my research on food and power in Israel, one of the listeners, who was originally from Israel but had spent almost fifty years in America, approached me after the talk and asked: "Why is it that on my recent visits to Israel I can't find even a single restaurant that serves Jewish food?"

For the uninitiated, this may sound like an odd question. Throughout this book, I have presented dozens of Israeli Jewish dishes. I have also pointed out that much of the culinary sphere in Israel is kosher and most food is prepared according to Jewish dietary laws. So why did this Israeli expatriate say that she couldn't find Jewish food in Israel in recent years? The answer has to do with the definition of "Jewish food" in Israel. What this woman was actually looking for was Ashkenazi food, something she confirmed when I asked her what she meant by "Jewish food." Why, then, did she identify Jewish food with Ashkenazi food? And why had she had a hard time finding restaurants serving Ashkenazi food in contemporary Israel given Ashkenazi socioeconomic dominance and cultural hegemony?

The first question reflects the historical processes that have shaped Israeli ethnic power relations. The term "Jewish food" was attributed to Ashkenazi fare such as chicken soup, gefilte fish, chopped liver, kugel, cholent, and the like during the British Mandate period,[1] when almost all Jews in Palestine were Ashkenazi. These immigrants brought with them Ashkenazi culinary traditions and preferences, and their food was labeled "Jewish" to distinguish it from the food eaten by the non-Jewish majority at the time, which was predominantly Arab (at this time, "Palestinian" was the inclusive term for all citizens of British Palestine, including both Arabs and Jews).

In modern Israel, even though Ashkenazi Jews are not the majority,[2] this mundane category entails power and hegemony: Ashkenazi fare is still termed "Jewish food," and in this way Judaism is identified with *Ashkenaziut*. Non-Ashkenazi Jewish food is usually given national labels, such as Moroccan, Iraqi, Kurdish, or Persian, but not Jewish. This terminology demonstrates the Ashkenazi claim for exclusivity over Judaism and the dismissive attitude Ashkenazi Israelis exhibit toward non-Ashkenazi. It also expresses Ashkenazi hegemony because, up until recently, the term "Jewish food" was used casually for both Ashkenazi and non-Ashkenazi fare, as if it were a natural category.

Increasing awareness and criticism made most restaurant columns and reviews replace the category of "Jewish food" with the supposedly neutral term "Eastern European food," bringing an end to, as it were, the Ashkenazi claim to exclusivity over Judaism. However, a web search for *ochel Yehudi* (Jewish food) in March 2016 revealed that "Jewish food" and "Eastern European food" remained overlapping categories on quite a few websites, including the progressive Achbar Ha'Ir (*City Mouse*), the printed version of which was among the first to replace "Jewish food" with "Eastern European food."[3] These labels certainly overlap when it comes to restaurant websites[4] and are routinely used interchangeably in daily conversation. The ongoing perception of Ashkenazi food as "Jewish food" in Israel maintains an enduring association of Judaism with Ashkenazi ethnicity and reflects ongoing Ashkenazi cultural hegemony.

However, as the woman at my talk observed, Ashkenazi food has disappeared from the Israeli public sphere in recent years, with only a few restaurants still serving it, mainly in ethnically segregated Haredi (Ultra-Orthodox) neighborhoods with large Ashkenazi enclaves. Years of engagement with the public and private dimensions of the Israeli culinary sphere lead me to further conclude that, with the exception of schnitzel, Ashkenazi classics are rarely eaten in private homes as daily fare and are mainly prepared for special and festive occasions.

In fact, the data presented in this book suggests that the Israel culinary sphere has been orientalized to a great extent. As different people mean different things when they talk about orientalization, or *mizruah,* let me first explain how I define this term. In various contexts throughout the book, I have asserted that Mizrahi ethnicity was created in Israel in the 1950s and '60s—an argument that now calls for some elaboration.

Jewish immigrants with very different national backgrounds, socioeconomic classes, professions, and levels of education were grouped in Israel into an undifferentiated mass, relegated to the Israeli periphery, and subjected to the "melting pot" ideology (an interesting culinary metaphor). In practice, this required all immigrants to Israel to be recast into an Ashkenazi, supposedly Western and modern, mold. Ashkenazi Jews determined that Mizrahi Jews were traditional, conservative, rigid, irrational, emotional, submissive, childish, and, to a certain extent, exotic and sensual. Most importantly, Mizrahi Jews were in dire need of modernization and civilization, a job taken on by the predominantly Ashkenazi-run state apparatus of the time.

The process of creating a single Mizrahi ethnicity was swift and effective. Within a generation, the huge socioeconomic gaps between immigrants from different countries in the Middle East and North Africa were virtually erased, with conditions in the Israeli periphery relegating everyone into the lower socioeconomic echelons. Sociologist Shlomo Swirski (1981) has described these immigrants as "not backward, but made backward" (*lo neh'shalim ela menuh'shalim*)—that is, that they have been denied resources in order to be made weaker. The consolidation of a Mizrahi political identity was also fast: by the mid-1970s, this state-created ethnic group was instrumental in the political *mahapah* (turnover) that forced the labor party, Ha'Avoda, the longstanding dominant political faction, to share power with the Likud. While the former was accused of representing only hegemonic Ashkenazi interests, the latter was perceived as standing for Mizrahi interests (even though it was always led by Ashkenazi politicians and despite the fact that its liberal and neoliberal economic and social policies rarely benefited Mizrahi Jews).

During the 1980s and '90s, Mizrahi identity continued to consolidate, gaining increasing political, religious, and cultural prominence. Intense conflicts emerged between Mizrahi public figures (writers, artists, politicians, academics) and their Ashkenazi counterparts over the quality and value of Mizrahi participation in the Israeli public sphere. This ongoing process is currently enduring yet another period of heated conflict, with Minister of Culture Miri Regev having launched a full attack on Ashkenazi cultural elites and those whom she perceives as yielding to Ashkenazi hegemony. While her political interests may be questioned, her demands—that Mizrahi culture be addressed as a rightful component of Israeli society, that discrimination against Mizrahi Jews be stopped, and that common resources be distributed evenly—are sound. It is also clear that Regev, as well as many of her supporters and opponents, champion and debate what they feel is a coherent and clearly defined ethnic group: the Mizrahim. Thus, what was originally an invented and disparaged ethnic category created by the State of Israel and the Ashkenazi community has become a total social fact in contemporary Israel.

Returning to my understanding of orientalization in contemporary Israel, *mizruah* is the process by which Mizrahi values, norms, and practices, created in Israel since the 1950s through an active, and at times violent, dialogue with the Ashkenazi, are gradually becoming hegemonic. Let me emphasize an important point: I do not argue (in the orientalist fashion) that the values, norms, and practices of the Jews from the Middle East and North Africa are becoming hegemonic in contemporary Israel. Rather, I argue that the values, norms, and practices of the Mizrahi ethnic group, *which is an Israeli creation,* are becoming popular and increasingly hegemonic. Addressing the entire range of social changes that make up the orientalization of Israel is beyond the scope of my academic expertise. However, while writing this book and examining the entire range of ethnographic data that I collected over the past two decades, I realized that the Israeli culinary sphere has been deeply orientalized. When Israeli Jews, regardless of where their grandparents emigrated from, are wondering what to cook and eat, when they think about food, and when they long for "Israeli food" while traveling abroad, they imagine falafel and hummus, *pargiot,* shawarma in a pita, tahini and *harif, kubeh,* couscous, Turkish coffee, and many other Middle Eastern and North African dishes, which may never have been part of their grandparents' culinary repertoire but are essential components of their own diets and eating preferences. I have met very few Israeli Jews who longed for classic Ashkenazi dishes such as chopped liver, gefilte fish, or *kishke* (stuffed intestines). Indeed, schnitzel is the exception that proves the rule: served in a pita with hummus, spicy sauce, and salad, its Ashkenazi nature is all but lost.

In addition to discussing dishes and tastes, I have shown throughout this book how kosher extended-family meals and an emphasis on large cheap portions are essential markers of contemporary Israeli cuisine. These culinary practices are associated in contemporary Israel with *mizrahyiut*: kashrut is considered an aspect of Mizrahi *masortiut* (conservative traditionalism), a flexible and selective interpretation of Judaism that involves, among other things, particular attention to Halachic dietary laws. Extended family meals are associated with *mishpahtiyut, shivtiyut,* and, *hamimut* (literally "family-ism," "tribalism," and "warmth"), orientalist (according to Edward Said's definition) terms that connote "primitive" society and loyalty to premodern entities rather than the modern nation-state. Getting large portions of food for cheap and avoiding suckerhood at all costs are also associated in contemporary Israel mainly with *mizrahiyut*.

Needless to say, none of these tendencies and preferences is particularly Mizrahi. In fact, it could be argued that they are all Ashkenazi: kashrut, the body of Jewish religious laws concerning the suitability of food, is supervised in Israel mainly by Ultra-Orthodox Ashkenazi and by Mizrahi Jews educated in Ashkenazi religious institutes and thus adhere to Ashkenazi standards; extended families are as important to Ashkenazi Jews as they are to Mizrahi Jews, as pointed out in the chapter dedicated to kibbutz dining rooms (Israeli Ashkenazi families were relatively small in the past, especially in the aftermath of the Holocaust, but this has radically changed in recent years[5]); large and cheap portions and a "getting by" attitude are universal Israeli qualities, with the very term *freier* ("sucker," see chapter 1) coming from German and Yiddish. While both Ashkenazi and Mizrahi Jews associate these things with *mizrahiyut*, and while the Ashkenazi association is often condescending, these tendencies are actually the main markers of Israeli cuisine. In this sense, the Israeli culinary sphere has indeed been orientalized. In chapter 2, dedicated to Independence Day barbecues, I suggested that the events at Sacher Park were celebrations of Mizrahi identity. At this point, I would like to argue that my research shows that Israelis of all ethnicities celebrate the culinary victory of *mizrahiyut*.

And yet Israeli Jews, whether they identify as Ashkenazi, Mizrahi, or other, express some ambivalence about this process. As pointed out in my analysis of Israeli adoration for Italian food in chapter 3, for example, Mizrahi restaurants, though popular, are considered cheap and mundane, inadequate for festive or remarkable events, such as birthday celebrations or marriage proposals. This ambivalence also stems from the affinity between Mizrahi and Arab/Palestinian food (discussed in the introduction and chapter 3). Ambivalence toward Mizrahi foodways is also evident in the way that the supposed Mizrahi penchant for excess is ridiculed by the very same people who practice it (see chapter 1). It is also evident in kibbutz dining rooms, whose operators regard the idea of serving spicy food as outrageous, pointing out that "after all, this is still a kibbutz," alluding to the Ashkenazi nature of the kibbutz movement and the movement's reluctance to embrace Mizrahi foodways to their full extent (see chapter 4). Ambivalence toward prevailing trends is the main observable quality of the Israeli culinary sphere, especially as it relates to power.

## FOOD, POWER, AND AMBIVALENCE

In the introduction, I outlined several modes for theoretically engaging with power in the culinary sphere: the Weberian top-bottom approach, where control over food is a means of exercising power; the Gramscian notion of hegemony, where the elite's foodways are perceived as if they are naturally the right culinary preferences for everyone (Bourdieu has a similar take, but his main point is that elites continuously change their tastes to ensure distinction from those in lower social strata); the idea that food practices can be forms of resistance, as defined by Scott—that is, that food can subvert, undermine, and bypass imposed social, political, and culinary arrangements; and the Foucauldian approach, whereby power is seen as omnipresent, multidirectional, and both detrimental and creative, with food as a perfect example for this complicated and fluid mode of energetic flows (Vester 2015, 5–9).

Throughout this book, I used these theoretical approaches to analyze specific culinary situations, events, and institutions. The Israeli preference for large cheap portions, the sequence of meats roasted at Israeli barbecues, the Mediterranean dream harbored by Israeli Jews when dining in Italian restaurants, the meal structures in kibbutz dining rooms, and the patriarchal identification of meat with masculinity as it materialized in an Israeli military prison were all discussed as manifestations of hegemonic Israeli food ideologies, devised by the elites and accepted as natural by the other members of society, along with the social structure they entail. Kashrut is another hegemonic food system taken for granted by most Israeli Jews and accepted as proper.

Resistance is an immediate and inevitable consequence of hegemonic power. Modes of culinary resistance were therefore discussed as part and parcel of every case or setting that involved culinary hegemony. The Israeli demand for large portions and low prices, which led McDonald's Israel to offer the largest Quarter Pounder (locally termed the McRoyal) in the world, was discussed not only as an Israeli Jewish hegemonic standard but also as a subversive response to global power structures and Western hegemonic culinary arrangements. The demand for kashrut and Mizrahi dishes in kibbutz dining rooms or the practice of adding North African spicy sauces to pizza were examples of subversive Mizrahi culinary preferences taking aim against Ashkenazi hegemonic foodways.

The blunt exercising of state power was discussed in chapter 5, which dealt with the ways in which a perceived lack of meat in an Israeli military prison led to self-defined emasculation and victimization, and in chapter 6, which was dedicated to the widespread belief among Israelis that Thai migrant workers eat their pet dogs. In both cases, however, eating practices were also modes of resistance to institutional top-bottom rules and directives. The "beefing up" of the Palestinian prisoners' diet by the Palestinian Authority, the constant attempts by Israeli Jewish reserve soldiers to enhance their meat supplies, and the attempts by Thai migrants to add meat to their own diets by farming, stealing, and hunting are all examples of such culinary resistance to the Weberian-style implementation of power within the culinary sphere.

Each of the chapters, and the book as a whole, demonstrates how well the Foucauldian notion of power as the energy within the system, working in all directions at all times, explains positions and processes within the culinary realm. In some ways, this book is all about Foucauldian biopolitics, which perceive of "the population as a political problem, as a problem that is at once scientific and political, as a biological problem and as power's problem" (Foucault 2003, 245). Food and foodways in Israel are precisely that: a material means and a set of practices that mediate between the Israelis as "populations"—that is, members of different social groups—and Israelis as biological beings who must eat and enjoy eating.

Power, however, is conceived of and approached in yet another form in the Israeli culinary sphere, which has barely been addressed in the existing literature: it entails ambivalence and is treated with ambivalence. While ambivalence is an expected outcome of hegemonic situations when power is resisted and acted against, it may be understood in such instances as a byproduct rather than the core of social relations. Ambivalence played a central role in the Israeli culinary cases discussed in this book.

Chapter 1, "Size Matters," was dedicated to the Israeli demand for cheap, large portions and the general tendency of Israelis to consider quality as secondary to quantity and price.[6] While food quantity was presented in the chapter as an expression of social, economic, and physical power, a sense of ambivalence permeated the culinary practices described in the text and in the critique of some of the commentators of this tendency—such as, for example, when a prominent journalist commented that "Israelis are the biggest pigs ever." Ambivalence was clearly evident when it came to Israeli definitions of satiety, with many of the Israelis quoted in the chapter expressing awe, admiration, and disgust regarding the practice of stuffing oneself. The tendency to vigorously avoid suckerhood while considering it a positive quality was, to my mind, the clearest expression of ambivalence when it comes to the discussion of power in this chapter.

Chapter 2, dedicated to Independence Day barbecues, and chapter 5, dedicated to meat and masculinity in a military prison, were all about food and power, or, to be more precise, about meat, masculinity, and power. In both chapters, however, Israeli Jews were shown to perceive of power ambivalently. First, it seems that the association of meat with power does not work smoothly in these contexts, with meat embedding weakness and power concomitantly. Second, Israeli Jews expressed ambivalence toward their own power and might, and this was conveyed in meat metaphors.

Throughout the chapters, I have argued that Israeli Jews are ambivalent when it comes to their sense of power, oscillating between perceiving their country as a regional superpower populated by supermen and superwomen *and* seeing themselves as the eternal and absolute victims, a widely held Israeli Jewish belief. At this point, I would like to suggest that another possible source of ambivalence might be the "enemy": the Palestinians (or "Arabs," as they are referred to by most Israeli Jews), who are perceived as bloodthirsty, dangerous, and murderous as well as morally, physically, and intellectually inferior.[7] Thus, the Palestinians are perceived by Israeli Jews as both *powerful* and *powerless*. This was clearly evident in the Israeli military prison, where the presumed fact that the Palestinian prisoners had more meat than the armed reserve soldiers was enough to make the latter feel vulnerable and victimized while simultaneously practicing total control over the former.

Ambivalence was also central in Israeli Jews' partiality for Italian food, in the ways in which socialism and communality were discussed by kibbutz members in regard to their dining rooms, and in the way that ethics and social justice were interpreted in the case of Thai migrant workers. I suggested that Israeli Jews like Italian food precisely because it lets them get away, even if only in their imagination, from the Middle East and from their Arab neighbors. Thus, many Israeli Jews, especially those who are better off and can afford to dine in relatively expensive Italian restaurants, would like to get away, at least for a while. The historical and ethnographic analysis of kibbutz dining practices exposed the ambivalence of kibbutz members when it came to their utopian settings: some members struggle to maintain the purity of their kibbutzim and others fight against the very idea of collectivism and emphasize alternative loyalties.

When it comes to the dog-eating accusations aimed at Thai migrant workers in Israel, I argued that this culinary myth was devised to solve the unease caused by ambivalence and excessive implementation of power. Israeli employers and Israelis in general wanted to pay as little as they can for their fruits and vegetables, and this necessitated a workforce that was paid as little as possible. Israelis, and especially those working in the farming sector, perceived themselves, however, as just, kind, and generous. Some of them still argue that they are ethically committed to an egalitarian ethos. These contrasting demands led to inevitable tension and unease, which was solved with the help of a culinary myth. Accusing the Thais of eating what Israelis deem inedible relegated the Thais to a less-than-human status, that of murderous cannibals, and this status, along with the fear and contempt that accompanied it, served to justify the exploitation of these workers.

Ambivalence permeates the Israeli culinary sphere, especially when it comes to the sense of power and the uses of power. When I decided to write this book, I was hoping that approaching power from the culinary perspective would permit a better understanding of one of the most observed, researched, and commented on aspects of modern Israel: the ways in which power works. My final argument is therefore that the Israelis I have studied during the past two decades in numerous culinary settings and contexts were increasingly confused, worried, and upset; increasingly unsure about Israel and the path it was taking; and, most importantly, increasingly ambivalent about Israel's power. The point is that the Israelis whose foodways I was studying were not just the leftist Ashkenazi upper-middle-class elites—that is, they were not the usual suspects for such tendencies. What I have shown throughout this book is that ambivalence toward Israel and its power is sensed, at least to a certain extent, by members of all social echelons and ethnic groups in Israel, including the most vociferous advocates of right-wing politics. While this may sound somewhat apocalyptic, I actually feel that ambivalence about power is positive. First, it seems to me that it always makes sense to be careful when dealing with power. Second, and more importantly, the Israeli culinary sphere demonstrates that ambivalence creates opportunities, enhances rethinking, and allows for the emergence of new directions. Power in the Israeli culinary sphere is not only a destructive force; it is also regenerative, progressive, and innovative.

# NOTES

## INTRODUCTION: THE HUMMUS WARS

Unless otherwise noted, all translations in this book are my own.

1. "Guinness Record for Israeli Hummus," *Israel Today,* March 15, 2006, www .israeltoday.co.il/NewsItem/tabid/178/nid/6840/Default.aspx.

2. A Middle Eastern salad made of bulgur, tomatoes, parsley, onions, olive oil, and lemon juice.

3. Gideon Lichfield, "Food Fight," *Foreign Policy,* January 15, 2010, www .foreignpolicy.com/2010/01/15/food-fight-4/.

4. Ilanit Adler, "The World's Largest Jerusalem Mix," *Hadshot 2,* November 30, 2009, www.mako.co.il/news-israel/local/Article-bbeb277c6e54521004.htm.

5. "Another Victory for Israel: Record in Jerusalem Mix." *Walla!News,* November 30, 2009, news.walla.co.il/?w=//1616594.

6. "Israelis Seek World Record with 'Jerusalem Mix,'" *Al Arabiya,* November 30, 2009, www.alarabiya.net/articles/2009/11/30/92799.html.

7. Didi Harari, "Abu Gosh Restaurant Owner to Break Lebanese Guinness Record," 103FM website, November 8, 2009, www.103.fm/programs/Media.aspx?Z rqvnVq=ELLMGD&c41t4nzVQ=EG.

8. The term "good Arab" is routinely used in Israeli Jewish discourse to describe Arabs (mainly Palestinians) who behave in ways that please Israeli Jews. Journalist Gideon Levi, for example, wrote the following about the former radio broadcaster and current Knesset member Zouheir Bahloul: "All his life he tried to be a good Arab. . . . He was still proud of himself for realizing the dream of an Arab boy from Nazareth who wanted to meet Benjamin Netanyahu. . . . Only two months ago, he participated in a Hebrew language conference in Rishon Letzion" (Gideon Levy, "There's No Place in Israel for an Honest Arab," *Haaretz,* April 09, 2016, www. haaretz.com/opinion/.premium-1.713607).

9. "Profile of Local Councils," publication no. 1451, Central Bureau of Statistics, 2009, www.cbs.gov.il/publications11/local_authorities09/pdf/348_0472 .pdf.

10. Tani Goldstein, "Jawadat Ibrahim: Abu Gosh Is Not Just Hummus" *Ynet*, January 20, 2006, www.ynet.co.il/articles/1,7340,L-3202839,00.html.

11. A video of the speeches can be found at www.mako.co.il/news-israel/local/Article-a960951ce5a0621004.htm.

12. Bahloul joined Ha'Avoda (the Israeli Labor Party) and was elected to the Knesset a few years after the events described here.

13. He was referring to a famous statement made by Israeli-American basketball player Tal Brody, "We are on the map, and we shall remain on the map," which he made immediately after Maccabi Tel Aviv's historic victory over CSKA Moskva in 1977, an event that was perceived in Israel as an almost biblical triumph over the Soviet Union's anti-Semitic and anti-Israeli communist regime.

14. Omri Meniv, "Syrian TV Features: Fighting in Israel—Over Hummus," *Nana News,* December 5, 2013, news.nana10.co.il/Article/?ArticleID=1022262.

15. Take, as one example among many, the Palestinian journalist Muhammad Al-Qeq's hunger strike, started on November 24, 2015, that put him close to death. Al-Qeq's protest against administrative detention rallied supporters across the occupied territories. After ninety-three days, the Israeli government decided to release him from detention. See "Muhammad Al-Qeq Reportedly Close to Death," *Middle East Monitor,* January 27, 2016, www.middleeastmonitor.com/news/middle-east/23570-muhammad-al-qiq-reportedly-close-to-death.

16. For a discussion of the shift from fieldwork to homework in anthropology as a decolonizing and emancipating project, see Kamala Visweswaran's (1994, 101) call for "homework, not field-work." Visweswaram rejects the dichotomy between home and field and argues that doing ethnographic homework does not mean literally staying at home or studying one's own community but rather "cutting across locations of race, gender, class, [and] sexuality, . . . a locus of critical struggle that both empowers and limits the subject whenever she or he conducts formal research" (quoted in Clifford 1997, 213).

17. Addressing the huge and complex debate regarding the meanings and manipulative nature of visual images in anthropology is beyond the scope of this section, but I am well aware of the fact that images and videos are hardly objective representations. They are ethnographic artifacts produced and constructed by ethnographers to convey ideas the wish to emphasize.


## CHAPTER 1. SIZE MATTERS

1. The false belief that the Chinese will eat anything is one of the meanest food stereotypes because it insinuates that "they" do not have eating rules and food taboos, which makes "them" hardly human and certainly not civilized. I return to this perception in chapter 6.

2. The words cholent (an Eastern European Sabbath stew made from meat, beans, and potatoes) and shakshouka (a Tunisian dish of eggs poached in a tomato

and pepper sauce) are used in modern Hebrew to refer to social processes where intensive mixing and fusing takes place.

3. H. Gourfinkel, "HaBishul BeIsrael: Kavim Lidmuto" [Israeli cooking: Some characteristics], *MaarivNRG*, November 9, 2008, www.nrg.co.il/online/55 /ART1/729/549.html. Emphasis mine.

4. Doron Halutz, "Hasipur Haisraeli derech matkonim vesifrei bishul mereshit hamedina vead yameinu" [The Israeli Story through recipes and cookbooks from the establishment of the states till now], *Haaretz,* September 1, 2011, www.haaretz.co .il/hasite/spages/1159044.html.

5. Sirkis explained to me in a recent conversation that this specific picture was chosen for technical and aesthetic reasons and that she never thought about it in terms of cultural fusion, "at least not consciously." Later, in an e-mail, she added: "At that time, I used to publish international recipes that were completely new in the Israeli foodscape, inclusive of new poultry dishes such as 'Hawaiian Chicken with Pineapple,' 'Far East–style Chicken with Soy Sauce, Wine and Honey,' 'French Chicken in Wine,' 'Chicken with Almonds,' 'Chinese Sweet-and-Sour Chicken'— and also Israeli-style chicken in orange sauce [oranges were at the time Israel's most famous export]. The recipe [for the Israeli-style chicken] included cumin [characteristic of falafel], and its photo was chosen for the cover [of the book]." It seems that Sirkis chose this specific dish because it was a fusion dish.

6. Orit Harel, "Sefer Bishul Hadash: Hamitbach HaIsraeli" [New cookbook: The Israeli Cuisine, *Motke,* May 1, 2010, www.motke.co.il/index.php?idr= 400&p=2005590.

7. Rika Lichtman, "Haprovokator shehafah lebustanai" [Provocateur turned orchardist]. *Stemazki,* 2005.

8. Most probably because television cooking shows had not yet been introduced to Israel.

9. A term developed by Robert Kozinets (1998, 2002) to describe " a new qualitative research methodology that adapts ethnographic research techniques to study cultures and communities that are emerging through computer-mediated communication" (Kozinets 2002, 63).

10. I couldn't locate professional texts that defined the average weight of a salad bar serving. The point, however, is not the actual weight but the chef's belief that Israelis were taking so much more food than diners elsewhere—presumably in Europe and the United States.

11. In mid-1990s prices. In 2017, the wholesale price for 10 kilos of medium grade pasta is 50 to 80 shekels.

12. He later mentioned that many restaurants, particularly Italian ones, followed suit and adopted these unusually large plates.

13. Rol Editorial Board, "Chefim Medabrim: Shaul Ben Aderet Medaber al Kimmel" [Chefs talk: Shaul Ben Aderet talks about Kimmel], *ROL* (online restaurant portal), accessed August 24, 2017, www.rol.co.il/index/chef-secrets/kimeli-shefim.html.

14. Similar to the "American breakfast," as its called in the tourism industry, the Israeli breakfast features all-you-can-eat buffets with Western breakfast items and emblematic local dishes. The Israeli breakfast differs from its American counterpart in two respects. First, it features a large array of dairy products but no meat because of kashrut considerations. Second, it includes a variety of fresh vegetables and salads, which are consumed in Israel thrice daily but are not an integral component of most Western breakfasts.

15. The lyrics to this song can be read at http://shironet.mako.co.il/artist?type =lyrics&lang=1&prfid=1132&wrkid=13814.

16. Tahel Blumenfeld, "Lamekomot, Hikon, Esh" [Ready, steady, fire], *Yediot Ahronot,* April 24, 2007, www.ynet.co.il/articles/0,7340,L-3408000,00 .html.

17. Shoshana Chen, "Aruhat Boker Plus Laila" [Breakfast plus night], *Ynet,* January 17, 2005, http://www.ynet.co.il/articles/0,7340,L-3153985,00.html.

18. Ibid.

19. Ibid.

20. Ibid.

21. I have been collecting data on Israeli backpackers since the mid-1990s. Backpackers' myths are emblematic stories that are repeated by Israeli (and other) backpackers year in and year out yet attributed immediate space and time, similar to urban legends. Often, the narrators admit that they did not personally witness the events but only heard about them.

22. A moshav is an Israeli agricultural community with some socialist features. Both moshav and kibbutz members are reputed to be corpulent, physically strong, and in possession of an impressive capacity for food intake, somewhat reminiscent of American truckers. This reputation probably stems from their uniqueness as Israeli Jews who do physical labor and therefore need a lot of energy.

23. Bama Editorial, "Shuk Taam Ha'Ir Hozer leTel Aviv" [Taste of the City market returns to Tel Aviv], *Habama,* May 25, 2011, www.habama.co.il/Pages /Description.aspx?Subj=8&Area=1&ArticleId=14919. Note that the importance of size is again being used as a marker of quality for Israelis.

24. Orna Yefet, "Mashehu lo meriah tov beshuk 'taam ha'ir'" [Something doesn't smell good at the "Taste of the City" market], *Calcalist,* May 29, 2008, www .calcalist.co.il/local/articles/0,7340,L-3078682,00.html.

25. Achbar Ha'Ir, "Taam Ha'Ir hozer: Ma mehake lachem" [Taam Ha'Ir returns: What is waiting for you], *Achbar Ha'Ir,* March 29, 2012, www.mouse.co.il/CM .articles_item,582,209,61237,.aspx.

26. Melamed, Dana. "Ta'am ha'ir 2011: hashefim hagdolim hosfm et hasodot" [Ta'am ha'ir 2011: The big chefs exposing the secrets], *Achbar Ha'Ir,* 2014.

27. Ibid.

28. Yefet, "Mashehu lo meriah tov beshuk 'taam ha'ir'."

29. I have decided not to include a link to this website as my point is not to criticize the restaurant but rather to point out that Israeli customers prefer large portions at low prices.

30. Sagi Cohen, "Tortuga: Sof sof osim kan tapas kmo shetzarich" [Tortuga: At long last they make tapas here as they should], *Haaretz,* February 4, 2011, www .haaretz.co.il/hasite/spages/1213264.html.

31. "Sushi History and Sushi Today," SushiNow.com, accessed August 24, 2017, http://sushinow.com/history.htm.

32. "Eich mechinim sushi inside out" [How to make sushi inside out], Sushi avuri: Madrich hasushi haIvri [Sushi for me: The Hebrew sushi guide], accessed August 24, 2017, www.sushi4me.com/index.php/%D7%9E%D7%93%D7%A8% D7%99%D7%9B%D7%99%D7%9D/%D7%90%D7%99%D7%A0%D7%A1%D7 %99%D7%99%D7%93-%D7%90%D7%90%D7%95%D7%98.html.

33. Judaism does not forbid raw flesh but rather the consumption of blood, which is believed to contain the soul, which belongs to God (Leviticus 17:11). Traditional Jewish cooking therefore involves thoroughly draining blood from an animal's carcass, absorbing any remaining blood with salt, and, in some situations (e.g., when cooking liver), searing the raw meat to burn away any remaining blood. As a consequence, raw flesh is practically avoided in all Jewish culinary traditions. This has remained a powerful taboo among most Israeli Jews, with very few willing to eat steak tartare, for example, or raw fish.

34. James Watson (1997) and other anthropologists have shown that despite the claims for universal standardization, McDonald's branches are always adjusted, at least to a certain extent, to local culture and local culinary demands.

35. Bronski Hagit, "McDonald's magdila et ha 'Mc-Royal'" [McDonald's increases the McRoyal], *Globes,* March 12, 2001, www.globes.co.il/news/article .aspx?did=475849. See also Ilana Barash, "McDonald's magdila et ha 'Mc Royal'" [McDonald's increases the McRoyal], *Ynet,* March 11, 2001. www.ynet.co.il /articles/0,7340,L-589789,00.html.

36. I feel that it would be unethical to disclose the restaurant's name.

37. Hagit Evron, "Shirat Sfarad" [Spanish poetry], *Mako,* December 6, 2009, www .mako.co.il/food-cooking_magazine/restaurants_review/Article-2315772cc394521004 .htm.

38. I believe that this article did not get the attention and appreciation it deserved because of its misleading title and terminology. The authors titled it "The Freier Culture and Israeli identity," but the article is all about the *non-freier* culture and *not* about being a *freier.*

39. In a terrible twist of fate, my friend and colleague Dr. Michael Feige was murdered in a terror attack in a Tel Aviv restaurant in June 2016, embodying suckerhood to the fullest extent. This chapter is dedicated to his memory.


CHAPTER 2. ROASTING MEAT

1. *Mangal* is a Turkish term for a metal utensil that contains burning charcoal and is used for heating or cooking. In contemporary Israel, *mangal* is used as a noun to refer to a charcoal grill but also as a verb to mean barbecuing.

2. The Palmach was an elite, prestate Jewish militia that became a legendary component of Israel's national ethos, "symbolizing not just valorous struggle for independence but also a [n egalitarian, hard-working, self-sacrificing] way of life which shaped the traits and characteristics of the future Israeli" (Segal 2003, 251).

3. For a discussion of biblical sandals, see El Or 2012.

4. Every Independence Day, the park's lawns are heavily damaged by charring.

5. This sense of affinity and identification with the United States was significantly eroded following the election of Barack Obama, who was initially perceived by many Israelis as an "Arab lover," someone sympathetic to the Palestinian cause and hostile to Israel, and even an Arab and a Muslim himself. In 2010, I saw no American flags on sale for Independence Day, but in 2011, with Obama's "softening" toward Israel in the context of the approaching US elections, the American flag was again available for purchase.

6. In an academic event held at Ben-Gurion University in December 2010, a senior American-Israeli anthropologist said of the comprehensive adoption of the American model by Israeli anthropologists: "That's how it is in all American colonies."

7. Mimouna is a North African Jewish festival that marks the end of Passover and the week of abstention from *hametz* (leavened bread). Though it is meant to celebrate bread, Mimouna festivities in contemporary Israel involve major barbecues.

8. Rabbi Shimon Bar Yochai was a second-century Jewish sage and a disciple of Rabbi Akiva, and he is believed by many Orthodox Jews to be the author of the Zohar, the chief work of Kabbalah. The anniversary of his death is Israel's largest religious event, attracting hundreds of thousands of pilgrims.

9. Rabbi Israel Abuhatzera, known as Baba Sali, was an important Moroccan Jewish *kadosh* (saint) and Kabbalist. His grave in Netivot is an active pilgrimage site, especially on his death anniversary, popular mainly among Jews of Moroccan descent.

10. Netivot is a so-called development town in southern Israel, part of the Israeli periphery, established during the 1950s to settle mainly Mizrahi immigrants.

11. Sderot is a southern development town with a large Mizrahi population.

12. *Combina,* from the Latin term meaning "combine" or "unite elements," is used in contemporary Israel to denote manipulation and trickery. It is not necessarily negative, as it always involves a measure of shrewdness and wit, which is appreciated in a society of survivors.

13. Since the mid-1980s, Israel has absorbed some two hundred thousand Ethiopian Jews. Members of this community, who are referred to as Ethiopians, face ongoing discrimination based on the color of their skin.

14. Backpacking, or simply traveling to developing countries, is very popular among Israeli Jewish youth and has been the object of substantial academic attention.

1. Gil Gutkin and Shiri Maymon, "North to South: Best Pizza in the Land," *Haaretz,* October 16, 2015, www.haaretz.co.il/food/.premium-1.2708490. The original text was revised on June 8, 2017.

2. *Achbar Ha'Ir,* www.mouse.co.il. This website changed its format and does not feature restaurant numbers per category any more.

3. Dapei Zahav, www.d.co.il.

4. These numbers are probably inaccurate due to overlapping categories and to other considerations Dapei Zahav and *Achbar Ha'Ir* might make. Deviating from the convention that "anthropologists don't count" (double meaning intended), I present these numbers because they demonstrate a tendency: both Dapei Zahav and *Achbar Ha'Ir* in Tel Aviv, Jerusalem, and nationwide feature similar proportions of these restaurants and thus support my claim that Italian food is the most popular cuisine in Israel even if the exact numbers are inaccurate.

5. The community has no website, and my attempt at contacting community officials failed. The numbers here are quoted from *Wikipedia,* s.v. "Yahadut Italia" [Italian Jewry], last modified July 24, 2017, http://he.wikipedia.org/wiki/%D7%99%D7%94%D7%93%D7%95%D7%AA_%D7%90%D7%99%D7%98%D79%C%D7%99%D7%94. The number of non-Jewish Italians in Israel is very small.

6. Though Italy had (and still has) both Sephardi and Ashkenazi communities, most Italian Jews practiced "Italian style" (*nusah italia*) prayer. As they come from Europe, they are considered Ashkenazi in practice if not in name.

7. For similar reasons, Chinese, Japanese, and Spanish cuisines were also imported to Israel mainly from the United States.

8. Oz Almog, "Ochel Italki beIsreael" [Italian food in Israel], Anashim Israel website, October 8, 2010, www.peopleil.org/details.aspx?itemID=30073. This website is managed by Oz Almog, a professor of Israel studies at Haifa University, and features pseudoacademic coverage of core Israeli issues and terms.

9. See the restaurant's website, www.pronto.co.il.

10. Trained, among other places, in Copenhagen's Noma, widely considered to be one of the best restaurants in the world, Frankel has won several prestigious culinary prizes in Israel.

11. Halacha is the collective body of Jewish religious laws derived from the written and oral Torah. While kashrut is most obvious in kosher meat and the separation of meat and dairy products, there are hundreds of Halachic food rules, which have been translated into thousands of practices.

12. "Holchim al kasher" [Opting for kosher], *MaarivNRG,* September 25, 2006, www.nrg.co.il/online/1/ART1/428/415.html.

13. Hagit Evron, "Haim haheh hatelavivi shone mehaheh hashkeloni—madrich lamisadan heperipheriali" [Is the Tel Aviv palate different from the Ashkelon palate—A guide to the peripheral restaurateur], *Globes,* June 1, 2008, www.globes.co.il/news/article.aspx?did=1000350943.

14. One of my relatives, an ordained rabbi and Chinese herbalist who treats mainly Ultra-Orthodox patients (note the potential tensions and apparent paradoxes), told me that, as far as he was concerned, the official kashrut permit issued by the office of the chief rabbinate is sufficient for him to eat in a restaurant, and he will not question even though he knows this institute is plagued with corruption and malpractice.

15. Avidan, Maya. "Pizat hazahav: Hapizot hahi tovot baaretz" [The golden pizza: Best pizzas in the country], *Mako*, December 31, 2013, www.mako.co.il/food-food-week/Article-31714a19281e241006.htm.

16. "Selected Data for the International Child Day 2015," Central Bureau of Statistics, November 17, 2015, www.isoc.org.il/wp-content/uploads/2015/11/11_15_312b.doc.

17. "Hata hamishpahti beIsrael behashvaa lemdinot ha OECD" [The Israeli family in comparison to the OECD nations], Central Bureau of Statistics, www.cbs.gov.il/publications09/rep_02/pdf/1_box3_h.pdf.

18. "Ehud Banai - Mahari Na (The kid is 30) - Subtitles," YouTube video, 5:18, posted by "Orly Yahalom Photography & Israeli Music," November 11, 2015, www.youtube.com/watch?v=z_0NN60I7Oc.

19. Rita Goldstein, "Italkit lemathilim: Lama anhnu hahi ohavim ohel italki" [Italian for beginners: Why we like Italian food the best], *MaarivNRG*, January 26, 2012, www.nrg.co.il/online/55/ART2/330/599.html.

20. Barak Ravid, "Netanyahu: We'll Surround Israel with Fences 'To Defend Ourselves Against Wild Beasts,'" *Haaretz*, February 9, 2016, www.haaretz.com/israel-news/.premium-1.702318.

21. There are two other Mediterranean cuisines that one might think would provide Israelis a similar sense of escape: Greek (and, perhaps more broadly, Balkan) and Turkish. My interviewees did not mention these cuisines, so this is therefore a learned speculation. While Italy is clearly regarded in Israel as a Western, European nation, Greece is not. Michael Herzfeld (1989) described Greece as located at the geographical and social margins of Europe, and Israelis perceive Greece as Mediterranean but not European. The Balkans are understood in Israel as backward and violent. Turkey, a Muslim country that was not accepted as a member of the European Union despite its efforts and one that falls politically between Western Europe and the Muslim world, is even less of an option when it comes to the European fantasy sought after by my interviewees. Thus, though Greece and Turkey are popular destinations for Israeli tourists and though these tourists love the food when visiting the countries, Greek and Turkish restaurants in Israel do not allow diners to imagine being in Europe in the way that Italian restaurants do. Rather, they are seen as liminal spaces between Europe and Asia and between modernity and backwardness. In many ways, Turkey and Greece are much more similar to Israel than Italy, but this is exactly why such restaurants do not allow Israelis the "great escape" they seek.

22. Shlomo Svirski, "Peripheria: Kama margia" [Periphery: How soothing], *Haoketz*, November 9, 2011, www.haokets.org/2011/11/09/%D7%A4%D7%A8%D

7%99%D7%A4%D7%A8%D7%99%D7%94-%D7%9B%D7%9E%D7%94-
%D7%9E%D7%A8%D7%92%D7%99%D7%A2.

23. In nonreflexive, day-to-day discourse in Israel, Palestinians living in the occupied territories are not perceived as part of Israeli society, but Israeli Jews who live in these territories are. Ultra-Orthodox enclaves such as Beitar Illit are therefore considered part of the Israeli periphery but the neighboring Palestinian village Battir is not despite the socioeconomic resemblances between the two places.

24. Though these social spaces are of much ethnographic and culinary interest (and quite a few pizza parlors are located there), they were beyond the scope of my ethnographic study.

25. Doron Lavih, an economist at Tel-Hai College, estimates the average family income in the periphery at 11,500 shekels per month, compared to 18,000 shekels in the center. He estimates the average monthly expenditure for family in the periphery to be 12,500 shekels, leaving families in an average deficit of 1,000 shekels each month. Families in the center, however, end the month with a surplus income of 2,000 shekels. "Madad haperipheria: Kenes mehkarei hagalil h 15 betel hai" [The Periphery Index: The Fifteenth Galilee Research Conference at Tel Hai], Hasifa Latzafon (blog), April 30, 2013, http://blog.telhai.ac.il/news/6902.

26. Haim Rivlin, "Sheker hapizza: Kama gvina yesh beemet al habatzek" [The pizza lie: How much cheese there really is on the dough], *Mako,* November 5, 2013, www.mako.co.il/news-money/consumer/Article-7ccd613e7d92241004.htm.

27. Josef Federman, "Ex-Employee of Israeli PM Sues over Alleged Abuse," CNSNews.com, March 20, 2014, www.cnsnews.com/news/article/ex-employee-israeli-pm-sues-over-alleged-abuse.

28. "Lakohot boharim: 'Pizza Tonino' hahi teima bair" [Customers choose: Pizza Tonino tastiest in town], *Erev Erev BeEilat,* December 1, 2010, www.ereverev .co.il/article.asp?id=9075.

29. Manhattan's original Jewish neighborhood was the Lower East Side, bordered by Little Italy and Chinatown.


CHAPTER 4. THE MCDONALDIZATION OF
THE KIBBUTZ DINING ROOM


1. "Hakibbutzim veochlusiatam: tmurot demographiot bashanim 1961–2005" [Kibbutzim and their population: Demographic changes 1961–2005], Central Bureau of Statistics, 2008, www.cbs.gov.il/publications/kibo5/pdf/h_print.pdf.

2. Shiri Saidler, "Habhirot lemazkal hatnua hakkibutzit" [Elections for the chairman of the kibbutz movement], *Haaretz,* June 24, 2015, www.haaretz.co .il/1.2667806.

3. According to Palgi and Reinharz (2014, introduction), though kibbutz members make up only about 2 percent of Israel's population, kibbutzim produce 40 percent of the country's agricultural crops, 7 percent of the industrial output,

and 9 percent of the industrial exports, and they account for 10 percent of the tourism market.

4. I changed the names of all kibbutzim and kibbutz members to preserve anonymity.

5. Nahal is the acronym for Noar Halutzy Lohem (literally "fighting pioneer youth"), a military unit formed after prestate Palmach (see chapter 2). Youth movement graduates may volunteer in this unit and spend their compulsory military service with their peers in a *garin* (group, literally "core"). Originally, Each *garin* was associated with an "absorbing kibbutz," in which the members spent roughly a year of their extended military service of forty-two months, and which they were expected to join as full members once their military service was over. Since the 1980s, *garin* members have been able to choose alternative social goals and locations during and after their military service. Nowadays, many of them opt for peripheral towns and neighborhoods as well as peripheral moshavim instead of kibbutzim. In any case, the number of *garin* members has been steadily declining.

6. The term "individualism" is highly contested. In this chapter, I use this term as a reference to the "self-sufficient individual," a person who, according to Beck and Beck-Gernsheim (2005, xxi), lacks any sense of mutual obligation toward other members of society. I use this definition not because I find it accurate but rather because it is most reminiscent of the ways in which the kibbutz members I interviewed conceived of individualism.

7. I have argued elsewhere (Avieli 2005b) that when the members of very large social groups, such as the modern nation, eat the same food item simultaneously (e.g., eating the national dish on the national day), a sense of commensality and shared identity emerges and overcomes the murkiness characteristic of the imagined nature of modern communities (Anderson 1983).

8. For instance, kibbutzim affiliated with the left-wing Hashomer Hatzair movement had a culinary legacy of purposely violating kashrut laws, mixing meat and milk and feasting publically on rabbits and pork.

9. Shira Harpaz-Pomerantz, Mike Livne, and Oz Almog, "Hadar Haochel bakibbutz" [Kibbutz dining room], *Anashim Israel,* March 17, 2008, www.peopleil .org/details.aspx?itemID=7670.

10. It is tempting to suggest that the dining room is the watchtower of Bentham's panopticon. However, kibbutz members are not hidden behind one-directional windows watching other inmates. Rather, they are both watching and being watched in the dining hall, which is accessible to anyone. Furthermore, my research is actually focused on dining room interactions, that is—interactions with (and within) the "watchtower."

11. Eight is a "magic number" in most kibbutz dining rooms that was maintained after the shift to self-service, though the long tables were replaced by pairs of tables for four, which allowed for more flexibility.

12. The private kettle was one of the earliest end-of-the-kibbutz anecdotes (Spiro 2004), and it was mentioned repeatedly by my interviewees. Private teakettles

allowed members to have tea in the privacy of their rooms. It is interesting to note how brewing a cup of tea, a trivial and mundane culinary activity, can be endowed with such social and ideological meanings, some of them as ominous as the end of kibbutz. Just like in Zen stories, it is precisely the taken-for-granted nature of the cup of tea that makes it such a powerful symbol. The importance given to the cup of tea also expresses the extent of ideological commitment that governed the most minute, trivial, and private activities of kibbutz members.

13. In the self-service system, when specific dishes are more attractive, whether because they are tastier or because their amount is limited (e.g., meat dishes or the more luxurious desserts), diners are expected to be considerate and show restraint so that there will be enough left for other diners. However, as social control is weaker when food is served buffet style, it is often the case that an attendant is charged with portioning such dishes. This demonstrates that there is a need for increasing institutional control when informal social control is weakened.

14. The communal budgets were a method of pooling resources that allowed kibbutzim to invest relatively large sums of money in specific projects and offer some high-quality services to their members. Swimming pools are the emblematic example, and these were the focus of Likud criticism of kibbutzim in the 1981 parliamentary elections. But kibbutzim also pooled their resources (money and manpower) and invested in education, medicine, and community infrastructure. Most kibbutzim, however, did not invest in housing or other forms of personal and family consumption such as clothing, home appliances, cosmetics, and tourism. Much of the internal demand for privatization concerned such forms of individual consumption as well as a general demand for personal choice. Accommodating such demands meant that fewer resources were available for communal use. Swimming pools were once again an emblematic case: many had to be shut down or privatized, just like the dinning rooms.

15. Though mechanisms were established to prevent large income gaps, the outcome of privatization has been the emergence of a small but rich managerial class and an increasingly large echelon of mainly older kibbutz members who are poor and lack socioeconomic support.

16. During the research period, there was a large group of Israeli Palestinians that dined in Mishmar every Thursday. According to the dining room manager, they were an important source of income. While I didn't get to interview them, their choice to dine at the kibbutz is extremely intriguing. My guess is that much of the appeal of the kibbutz dining room for Israeli Palestinians is the opportunity to access to what is perceived as one of the holiest spaces of Zionism as well as the possibility to purchase and consume the sense of modernity and sophistication of these spaces.

17. One exception is military dining rooms, where the food is often very spicy. I guess, though I have no empirical data to support this claim, that the predominantly Mizrahi cooks relegated to kitchen positions, which hold extremely low prestige in the Israeli army, spice up the food as a mode of resistance and subversion.

CHAPTER 5. MEAT AND MASCULINITY
IN A MILITARY PRISON

1. Nir Yahav, "Asor lemehumot october: Haherem hayehudi" [A decade to the October riots: The Jewish boycott], *Walla!News*, October 1, 2010, news.walla.co.il /item/1737069.

2. Fortress-like police stations planned by British police officer Charles Tegart. They were built throughout Mandatory Palestine.

3. Interestingly, as soon as the foreign rulers, whether British or Israeli, moved out, the former detainees became the detainers. The jails presently run by the Palestinian Authority are the same Tegart forts that were built by the British to detain both Jews and Arabs in British Palestine. Once the British left, the Israelis used them to detain Palestinians insurgents, and following the Oslo Accords, the Palestinians themselves use these forts to detain their own opponents.

4. Megiddo Prison was taken over by the Israeli Prison Service in 2005, three years after the events described in this chapter.

5. One of the ongoing demands of the Palestinian prisoners and the Palestinian Authority is that the prisoners be allowed to cook their own food. As noted in chapter 4, control over food and eating is an important venue for exercising control over inmates in total institutions. The Palestinian prisoners at Megiddo and other Israeli military prisons are not *required* to cook; rather, they *demand* this right and see it as a privilege worth struggling for.

6. See also Israeli artist Dan Allon's 2014 project *The Shawish of Section Four,* exhibited at the Hayarkon 19 Gallery in Tel Aviv, which featured a recreation of a *shawish* hut at Kzioth Jail, www.danallon.com/the-shawish-of-section-four.

7. Note the Jewish Israeli orientalizing discourse that relegates Arabs to villages. Within Israel, state authorities are reluctant to define Israeli Palestinian settlements as cities even if they are large, crowded, and urban. I don't have exact data regarding where the prisoners lived prior to their being incarcerated, but most Palestinians in the occupied territories live in cities and towns.

8. My father-in-law would often brag about his *luf* cooking skills. According to a family legend, he cooked a dish of *luf,* eggs, and onions with a leftover can of *luf* when he returned from the October War. His toddler son loved it so much that he had to continue to buy cans of *luf* to cook the praised dish, which was embedded with heroism and male bonding. A recent article notes that the late prime minister and former general Ariel Sharon enjoyed *luf,* preferably fried with eggs, stressing again its mythological aura as warriors' fare. Boaz Wollinitz, "Luf keyad hamelech" [Royal luf], *Walla!News,* April 21, 2015, http://food.walla.co.il/item/2847869.

9. In the IDF, carrying a gun is the ultimate expression of being a combat soldier, and different guns mark specific units and ranks. MPs, however, rarely carry guns during policing missions. The MPs at Megiddo Prison would enter the pens unarmed, escorted by the armed reserves soldiers. We were told that they were not allowed to carry weapons for fear that their guns would be snatched by the prisoners. Quite a few MP officers, however, would arrive every morning at the prison

carrying large pistols. IDF soldiers are rarely armed with pistols, and it was clear that these were the officers' personal sidearms. As they were not allowed to perform their prison missions armed, these officers would check their pistols at the prison's armory every morning and collect them at the end of the day on their way home. For a reason that was never explained to me, they kept their empty pistol holsters hanging on their belts throughout the day. Perhaps this was one way for them to express their potential masculinity: "I may be unarmed now, but I do have a large pistol." I couldn't help wondering, however, what Sigmund Freud would have said if he had seen these officers openly demonstrating their own castration.

10. Shai Gal, "Dor shlishi im mispar" [Third generation with a number], *Mako*, October 12, 2012, www.mako.co.il/news-israel/local/Article-53e99d149965a31004 .htm; Jodi Rudoren, "Proudly Bearing Elders' Scars, Their Skin Says 'Never Forget,'" *New York Times*, September 30, 2012, www.nytimes.com/2012/10/01/world /middleeast/with-tattoos-young-israelis-bear-holocaust-scars-of-relatives.html.

## CHAPTER 6. THAI MIGRANT WORKERS AND THE DOG-EATING MYTH

1. Agriculturalists in the Arava and Jordan Valleys started to employ Thais in the mid-1980s. Employing migrant workers was illegal at the time, and these Thais were defined as volunteers or trainees and paid significantly less than the minimum wage (E. Cohen 1999). This arrangement, devised to bypass the prohibition on migrant labor, is ongoing at the Arava International Center for Agricultural Training, where hundreds of Vietnamese, Burmese, Tibetan, Laotian, Cambodian, Nepali, and Thai nationals, defined as "students," live and work alongside Thai migrant workers and dedicate a day per week to classes. On a recent visit, I was told that these classes were taught mainly by members of the local community and not by academics or professional teachers. As both the students and teachers speak very basic English, which is the only language that they can use to communicate with one another, it seems to me that these classes are more about socializing than learning and that the project's main objective is to increase the volume of imported manpower and circumvent the restrictions on the numbers of migrant workers. See Liat Natovich-Kushitski, "Baim lilmod haklaut vehofhim le 'ovdim zarim'" [Coming to study agriculture and becoming "foreign workers"], *NRG*, July 31, 2015, www.nrg.co.il/online/1/ART2/713 /622.html.

2. "Ofen haasakat ovdim zarim bebinyan, behaklaut ubesiud" [Employment mode of foreign workers in construction, agriculture and care-giving], Hakneset Merkaz Hamehkar Vehameida [Knesset Center for Research and Information], June 2015, http://main.knesset.gov.il/Activity/Info/MMMSummaries19 /Foreign_3.pdf.

3. "Ovdim zarim beIsrael" [Foreign workers in Israel], Population and Immigration Authority, 2016, www.gov.il/BlobFolder/reports/foreign_workers_in_ israel_2016_report/he/foreign_workers_march_2016_report_0.pdf.

4. Eugene Anderson, e-mail message to author, January 24, 2016.

5. Kate Hodal, "How Eating Dog Became Big Business in Vietnam," *Guardian,* September 27, 2013, www.theguardian.com/world/2013/sep/27/eating-dog-vietnam-thailand-kate-hodal.

6. Peter Shadbolt, "Smugglers Drive Thailand's Grim Trade in Dog Meat" CNN, June 3, 2013, www.cnn.com/2013/06/02/world/asia/thailand-dogs.

7. Thomas Fuller, "Dog Meat Trade in Thailand Is under Pressure and May Be Banned," *New York Times,* November 1, 2014, www.nytimes.com/2014/11/02/world /asia/dog-meat-trade-in-thailand-is-under-pressure-and-may-be-banned.html?_r=0.

8. National Service and Information Centre, "Foreign Workers' Rights Handbook," Population and Immigration Authority and the State of Israel, January 1, 2017, http://mfa.gov.il/MFA/ConsularServices/Documents/ForeignWorkers2013 .pdf.

9. Ibid., 10.

10. Camilla Schick, "Israel's Thai Farmworkers Tell of Grim Plight," BBC, January 30, 2015, www.bbc.com/news/world-middle-east-31001525; Or Kashti, "Bikur Atzuv etzel ovdei haklaut mitailand shemegadlim et mezonenu" [A sad visit to the Thai agriculture workers that grow our food], *Haaretz,* June 20, 2013, www.haaretz .co.il/news/education/.premium-1.2051826.

11. National Service and Information Centre, "Foreign Workers' Rights Handbook," 12.

12. Ibid., 13.

13. Raijman and Kushnirovich (2015, 10) point out that prior to the implementation of the bilateral agreements with Thailand in 2010, "the recruiting agencies' fees were exorbitant: slightly over $9,000." The agreements led to reduced expenses of US$2,000–3,000 in 2012–13. This remains a high sum by Thai standards, and the outrageous interest rates make it even higher.

14. "A Raw Deal: Abuse of Thai Workers in Israel's Agricultural Sector," Human Rights Watch, January 21, 2015, www.hrw.org/report/2015/01/21/raw-deal /abuse-thai-workers-israels-agricultural-sector.

15. That Israelis refuse to eat placentas but are comfortable with using cosmetics that contain them may be explained first by the fact that when the organs are used in cosmetics, they have been heavily processed into homogenous pale creams with pleasant aromas that are far removed from the bleeding placentas. Second, the power of food lies precisely in the process of incorporation, whereby matter crosses the body boundaries and breaches the world-self dichotomies (Fischler 1988). In this sense, applying a cream made with processed placenta to the outer surfaces of the body is nothing like cooking and eating the actual organ.

16. Ilana Koriel, "Naar hoda: Shadad tailandim shebishlu et habarvaz shelo" [Youth admits: Robbed Thais who ate his duck], *YNET,* October 2, 2012, www.ynet .co.il/articles/0,7340,L-4287586,00.html.

17. See, for example, Sivan Pardo Renwick, "Is Israel Going to Be the First Vegan Nation?" *Vegan Woman,* January 10, 2014, www.theveganwoman.com/israel-going-first-vegan-nation.

18. Tamar Nahari, "Dorban bamekarer" [A porcupine in the fridge], *News!Walla,* October 21, 2001, http://news.walla.co.il/item/129878; Adi Hashmonai, "Berashut hateva vehaganim nilhamim bazaid habilti huki" [Nature and Parks Authority combats illegal hunting], *NRG,* December 27, 2009, www.nrg.co.il/online/1 /ART1/998/014.html; "Lishmor al hayot habr beartzenu—Malkodot shel poalim zarion meaymot al olam hahai shel Israel" [Protecting wildlife in our country—Foreign workers' traps threaten Israel's wildlife], Nature and Parks Authority, December 15, 2009. www.parks.org.il/ConservationAndheritage/Science/Pages/hayotBar.aspx.

19. Erez Erlichman, "Hatailandim mehaslim et hayot habar" [The Thais exterminate wildlife], *YNET,* January 30, 2008, www.ynet.co.il/articles/0,7340,L-3500242,00.html.

20. Efrat Weis, "Tailandim shipdu kelev dalmatic al mot barzel" [Thais skewered Dalmatian dog with iron spike], *YNET,* December 13, 2004, www.ynet.co.il /articles/0,7340,L-3018037,00.html.

21. Gil Horev and Yemin Wolpowich, "Kelev meshupad belev hayeshuv" [Dog skewered in village center], *NRG,* December 13, 2004, www.nrg.co.il/online/1 /ART/836/910.html.

22. Yonatan Golan, "Hashad: Poalim tzadu asrot klavim" [Suspicion: Workers hunt dozens of dogs], *YNET,* September 15, 2009, www.ynet.co.il/articles /0,7340,L-3777009,00.html. Emphasis mine.

23. Yoav Itiel, "Hashad: Tailandim shahtu gurei klavim veachlu otam" [Thais suspected of slaughtering and eating puppies], *Gefen Magazine Hamoshavot,* February 10, 2014, www.magazin.org.il/inner.asp?page=179781.

24. Tamar Nahari, "BePetah Tikva yesh tailandim reevim" [Petah Tikva police investigate suspicion that Thai workers launched a wide-ranging dog hunt], *News!Walla,* May 16, 2001, http://news.walla.co.il/item/62189.

25. "Oved tailandi nirtzah bevikuah al ahilat klavim" [Thai worker murdered during argument over dog eating], *News!Walla,* May 16, 2011, http://news.walla .co.il/item/1823616. Emphasis mine.

26. Gilad Grossman, "Ishum: Poel tailandi ratzah havero ki harag kelev" [Indicted: Thai worker kills colleague for killing a dog], *News!Walla,* May 26, 2011, http://news.walla.co.il/item/1826916.

27. Israeli employers and Thai workers have devised a functional language made of basic Hebrew and Thai with which they convey quite complex instructions and ideas—but in the very limited register of the farming activities taking place at specific farms. Both employers and workers rarely speak fluent English.

28. Avi Ashkenazi, "Ktata bein ovdim zarim histayma beretzah" [Fight among foreign workers ends in murder], *NRG,* May 15, 2011, www.nrg.co.il/online/1 /ART2/240/972.html.

29. Azri Amram, "Hashad: Ratzah et havero ki hitnaged leachilat kelev" [Suspicion: Murdered his friend in objection to dog killing], *Mako,* May 15, 2011, www. mako.co.il/news-law/crime/Article-9afcbea2a45ff21004.htm.

30. "Arik Einstein & Uri Zohar (Aliyah w/Subtitles)," YouTube video, 7:08, posted by "NyJazzGuit," November 27, 2013, www.youtube.com/watch?v=

MBNWHTipwEA. Zohar was a legendary film director before he became a born again Ultra-Orthodox rabbi. Einstein went on to become Israel's premier singer.

31. West African migrant workers termed their line of employment *gumi* (rubber), after the rubber bands fixed on Israeli-style mops. But just like "rubber" in English, *gumi* is also a nickname for condoms, further adding to the sexual aura of these workers.

32. The ministry of Industry and Commerce was replaced by the Ministry of Economy and Industry, and this report is no longer available online.

33. Shir-Vertesh points out that these loving relationships may sometimes transform: changing circumstances, and especially the birth of a child, may dramatically change a dog's position, sometimes to the extent of their being moved outside of the home.

CONCLUSION: FOOD AND POWER IN ISRAEL—
ORIENTALIZATION AND AMBIVALENCE

1. Ronit Vered, "Maka afora: Haochel hayehudi hamizrah eiropi shav mehagalut" [Gray strike: Jewish Eastern European food returns from the Diaspora], *Haaretz,* September 2, 2013, www.haaretz.co.il/food/dining/.premium-1.2112505.

2. "Statistical Abstract of Israel 2012," Central Bureau of Statistics, 2012, www .cbs.gov.il/shnaton63/st02_24x.pdf.

3. "Ochel Yehudi" [Jewish food], *Achbar* Ha'Ir, accessed August 24, 2017, www .mouse.co.il/Tags/7963.aspx.

4. See also Keton Jewish Bistro, www.keton.co.il; Hashaked, www.hashaked .co.il; and Eatery, eatery.co.il/he/place/3116/%D7%A9%D7%98%D7%99%D7%91 %D7%9C%D7%A2/?gclid=CKi_87vJ6csCFYEehgodeVoJmg.

5. According to a 2015 Central Bureau of Statistics report, Ashkenazi fertility rates are as high, if not higher, than Mizrahi fertility rates. "Sheurei pirion, gil memutsa shel haem, veyahas minim baleida lefi tchunot nivharot shel haem 2014" [Fertility rates, average age of mothers and gender ratio at birth according to selected mothers' features 2014], Central Bureau of Statistics, September 10, 2015, www.cbs .gov.il/shnaton66/st03_14x.pdf.

6. While I was visiting the European Institute for the History and Cultures of Food at Francois Rabelais University in Tours, France, my hosts kept suggesting that I purchase my food at the city market, Les Halles: "The food there is expensive," they pointed out, "but very good." My hosts in Paris also suggested that I buy food at shops that were expensive but offered high quality products. In Israel, the routine advice would be to go to whichever store was the cheapest, to which the comment "and they offer pretty merchandise" might be added—referring to the looks of the products rather than their culinary quality and taste. Culinary quality is rarely mentioned in Israeli daily discourses.

7. This is implied, for example, by the deprecating term *avoda aravit,* or "Arab work," the manual and physical labor done by Israel's wood choppers and water bearers, whether they are Israeli Palestinians, Palestinians from the occupied territories, or migrant workers. This work is considered cheap and of low quality but is widely relied on by all sectors of the Israeli economy.

# REFERENCES

Adams, C. J. 1990. *The Sexual Politics of Meat: A Feminist-Vegetarian Critical Theory.* Cambridge: Polity.

———. 1997. "'Mad Cow' Disease and the Animal Industrial Complex: An Ecofeminist Analysis." *Organization Environment* 10 (1): 26–51.

———. 1998. "Eating Animals." In *Eating Culture,* edited by R. Scapp and B. Seitz, 60–75. Albany: State University of New York Press.

Adar, G. 2009. *Demographic Growth in the Kibbutzim 2009.* Haifa: Institute for Study and Research of the Kibbutz, Haifa University. http://kibbutz.haifa.ac.il /index.php/he/new-pub-hebrew/20-2009.

Adar, R. 2010. *Pronto: Ochel, Tarbut, Ahava* [Pronto: Food, cooking, love]. Tel Aviv: Kinneret.

Agar, M. H. 1996. *The Professional Stranger: An Informal Introduction to Ethnography.* New York: Academic Press.

Albala, K. 2011. "The Historical Models of Food and Power in European Courts of the Nineteenth Century." In *Royal Taste: Food, Power and Status at the European Courts after 1789,* edited by D. De Vooght, 13–29. Burlington, VT: Ashgate.

Alfino, M., J. S. Caputo, and R. Wynyard. 1998. *McDonaldization Revisited: Critical Essays on Consumer Culture.* Westport, CT: Praeger.

Almog, Oz. 2000. *The Sabra: The Creation of the New Jew.* Berkeley: University of California Press.

Alon-Mozes, T., H. Shadar, and L. Vardi. 2009. "The Poetics and the Politics of the Contemporary Sacred Place: Baba Sali's Grave Estate in Netivot, Israel." *Buildings and Landscapes: Journal of the Vernacular Architecture* 16 (2): 73–85.

Anderson, B. 1983. *Imagined Communities: Reflections of the Origins and Spread of Nationalism.* London: Verso.

Anderson, P. 2004. "'To Lie Down to Death for Days': The Turkish Hunger Strike, 2000–2003." *Cultural Studies* 18 (6): 816–846.

Appadurai, A. 1988. "How to Make a National Cuisine: Cookbooks in Contemporary India." *Comparative Studies in Society and History* 30 (1): 3-24.

Ariel, A. 2012. "The Hummus Wars." *Gastronomica* 12 (1): 34–42.

Ashkenazi, M., and J. Jacob. 2000. *The Essence of Japanese Cuisine: An Essay on Food and Culture.* Richmond, Surrey: Curzon.

Avieli, N. 2005a. "Roasted Pigs and *Bao* Dumplings: Festive Food and Imagined Transnational Identity in Chinese-Vietnamese Festivals." *Asia Pacific Viewpoint* 46 (3): 281–293.

———. 2005b. "Vietnamese New Year Rice Cakes: Iconic Festive Dishes and Contested National Identity." *Ethnology* 44 (2): 167–187.

———. 2007. "Feasting with the Living and the Dead." In *Modernity and Re-Enchantment: Religion in Post-War Vietnam,* edited by P. Taylor, 121–160. Singapore: ISEAS Press.

———. 2012. *Rice Talks: Food and Community in a Vietnamese Town.* Bloomington: Indiana University Press.

———. 2013. "Grilled Nationalism: Power, Masculinity and Space in Israeli Barbeques." *Food, Culture and Society* 16 (2): 301–320.

Avieli, N., and R. Grosglik. 2013. "Food and Power in the Middle East and in the Mediterranean: Practical Concerns, Theoretical Considerations." *Food, Culture and Society* 16 (2): 181–195.

Aviezer, O., M. Uzendoorn, A. Sagi, and C. Schuengel. 1994. "'Children of the Dream' Revisited: 70 Years of Collective Early Child Care in Israeli Kibbutzim." *Psychological Bulletin* 116 (1): 99–116.

Azaryahu, M. 2000. "McIsrael? On the Americanization of Israel." *Israel Studies* 5 (1): 41–64.

Bahloul, J. 1995. "Food Practices Among Sephardic Immigrants in Contemporary France: Dietary Laws in Urban Society." *Journal of the American Academy of Religion* 63 (3): 485–496.

Baloglu, S., and M. Mangaloglu. 2001. "Tourism Destination Images of Turkey, Egypt, Greece, and Italy as Perceived by US-Based Tour Operators and Travel Agents." *Tourism Management* 22 (1): 1–9.

Barabas, S. 2003. "'I'll Take Chop Suey': Restaurants as Agents of Culinary and Cultural Change." *Journal of Popular Culture* 36 (4): 669–686.

Bartram, D. 1998. "Foreign Workers in Israel: History and Theory." *International Migration Review* 32 (2): 303–325.

Bar Yosef, E. 2013. *A Villa in the Jungle: Africa in Israeli Culture.* Jerusalem: Van Leer Institute.

Bates, T.R. 1975. "Gramsci and the Theory of Hegemony." *Journal of the History of Ideas* 36 (2): 351–366.

Beardsworth, A., and T. Keil. 1996. *Sociology on the Menu: An Invitation to the Study of Food and Society.* London: Routledge.

Beck, U., and E. Beck-Gernsheim. 2005. *Individualization.* London: Sage.

Ben Amotz, D., and H. Heffer. 1956. *The Pack of Lies.* Tel Aviv: Hakibbutz Hameuhad.

Ben-Porat, G., and Y. Feniger. 2009. "Live and Let Buy? Consumerism, Secularization, and Liberalism." *Comparative Politics* 41 (3): 293–313.

Ben Rafael, E. 1996. *Non-Total Revolution.* Ramat Efal: Yad Tabenkin.

————. 1997. *Crisis and Transformation: The Kibbutz and Century's End.* Albany: State University of New York Press.

Ben Ze'ev, E. 2004. "The Politics of Taste and Smell: Palestinian Rites of Return." In *The Politics of Food,* edited by M. E. Lien and B. Nerlich, 141–160. New York: Berg.

————. 2011. *Remembering Palestine in 1948.* Cambridge: Cambridge University Press.

Bettelheim, B. 1969. *The Children of the Dream: Communal Child Rearing and American Education.* London: Macmillan.

Bilu, Y. 1988. "The Inner Limits of Communitas: A Covert Dimension of Pilgrimage Experience." *Ethos* 16 (3): 302–325.

Blasi, J. 1978. *The Communal Future: The Kibbutz and the Utopian Dilemma.* Chicago: Norwood.

Blumenfeld, T. 2007. "Lamekomot, Hikon, Esh" [Ready, steady, fire]. *Yediot Ahronot,* April 24.

Bornholdt, C. 2010. "What is a Gaúcho? Intersections between State, Identities and Domination in Southern Brazil." *(Con)Textos,* no. 4: 23–41.

Bourdieu, P. 1984. *Distinction: A Social Critique of the Judgment of Taste.* London: Routledge and Kegan Paul.

————. 1996. *The Rules of Art: Genesis and Structure of the Literary Field.* Stanford, CA: Stanford University Press.

————. 2001. *Masculine Domination.* Stanford, CA: Stanford University Press.

————. 2005. *The Social Structures of the Economy.* Cambridge: Polity.

Bove, C. F., J. Sobal, and B. S. Rauschenbach. 2003. "Food Choices among Newly Married Couples: Convergence, Conflict, Individualism, and Projects." *Appetite* 40 (1): 25–41.

Brillat-Savarin, J. A. 1999. *The Physiology of Taste, or Meditations on Transcendental Gastronomy.* Washington: Counterpoint.

Buerkle, C. W. 2009. "Metrosexuality Can Stuff It: Beef Consumption as (Heteromasculine) Fortification." *Text and Performance Quarterly* 29 (1): 77–93.

Caine-Bish, N., and B. Scheule. 2009. "Gender Differences in Food Preferences of School-Aged Children and Adolescents." *Journal of School Health* 79 (11): 532–540.

Caldwell, M. 2004. "Domesticating the French Fry: McDonald's and Consumerism in Moscow." *Journal of Consumer Culture* 4 (1): 5–26.

Calo, N.. 2005. "Taste Changes in Israeli Food: The Case of Italian food 1980–2000." Master's thesis, Tel Aviv University.

Cavanaugh, J. 2007. "Making Salami, Producing Bergamo: The Transformation of Value." *Ethnos* 72 (2): 149–172.

Charles, N., and M. Kerr. 1988. *Women, Food and Families: Power, Status, Love, Anger.* Manchester: Manchester University Press.

Chua, B. H. 2003. *Life Is Not Complete without Shopping.* Singapore: Singapore University Press.

Chung, T. I. 2011. "The Transnational Vision of Miss Saigon: Performing the Orient in a Globalized World." *MELUS: Multi-Ethnic Literature of the US* 36 (4): 61–86.

Chyutin, M. 1979. "Planning in a Communal Society: A Comparison between Physical Planning in the Kibbutz and in the City." *Socio-Economic Planning Sciences* 13 (6): 289–295.

Clark, D. 2004. "The Raw and the Rotten: Punk Cuisine." *Ethnology* 43 (1): 19–31.

Clark, P., and A. Bowling. 1990. "Quality of Everyday Life in Long Stay Institutions for the Elderly." *Social Science and Medicine* 30 (11): 1201–1210.

Clifford, J. 1997. "Spatial Practices: Fieldwork, Travel, and the Disciplining of Anthropology." In *Anthropological Locations: Boundaries and Grounds of a Field Science,* edited by A. Gupta and J. Ferguson, 185–222. Berkeley, CA: University of California Press.

Cohen, A. 2010. "Mehkar: Hamarvihim Hagdolim Mehafratat Hakibutzim hem Hamenahaim uvnei Mishpehoteihem" [Study: The big winners of kibbutzim privatization are the managers and their families]. *TheMarker,* August 18. www.themarker.com/misc/1.586462.

Cohen, E. 1999. "Agricultural Workers from Thailand in Israel." In *The New Workers, Wage Earners from Foreign Countries in Israel,* edited by R. Nathanson and L. Achdut, 155–204. Jerusalem: Hakibbutz Hameuchad.

Connell, R. W., and J. W Messerschmidt,. 2005. "Hegemonic Masculinity: Rethinking the Concept." *Gender and Society* 19 (6): 829–859.

Counihan, C. M. 1992. "Food Rules in the United States: Individualism, Control, and Hierarchy." *Anthropological Quarterly* 65 (2): 55–66.

———. 1998. "Food and Gender: Identity and Power." Introduction to *Food and Gender: Identity and Power,* edited by C. M. Counihan and S. Kaplan, 1–10. Amsterdam: Gordon and Breach.

———. 1999. *The Anthropology of Food and Body: Gender, Meaning, and Power.* New York: Routledge.

———. 2004. *Around the Tuscan Table: Food, Family and Gender in Twentieth-Century Florence.* New York: Routledge.

Cusack, I. 2000. "African Cuisines: Recipes for Nation Building?" *Journal of African Cultural Studies* 13 (2): 207–225.

Cwiertka, K. J. 2002. "Popularizing a Military Diet in Wartime and Postwar Japan." *Asian Anthropology* 1 (1): 1–30.

Davidoff, L. 1995. *Worlds Between: Historical Perspectives on Gender and Class.* New York: Routledge.

Davies, C. 1989. "Goffman's Concept of the Total Institution: Criticisms and Revisions." *Human Studies* 12: 77–85.

Denny, R., P. Sunderland, J. Smart, and C. Christofi. 2005. "Finding Ourselves in Images: A Cultural Reading of Trans-Tasman Identities." *Journal of Research for Consumers* 8: 1–24.

Deutsch, J., and R. D Saks. 2008. *Jewish American Food Culture.* Westport, CT: Greenwood.

De Vooght, D., and P. Scholliers. 2011. Introduction to *Royal Taste: Food, Power and Status at the European Courts after 1789,* edited by D. De Vooght, 1–12. Burlington, VT: Ashgate.

Douglas, A., J. Mills, and R. Kavanaugh. 2007. "Exploring the Use of Emotional Features at Romantic Destination Websites." In *Information and Communication Technologies in Tourism 2007: Proceedings of the International Conference in Ljubljana, Slovenia,* edited by M. Sigala, L. Mich, and J. Murphy (Wien: Springer-Verlag), 331–340.

Douglas, M. 1972. "Deciphering a Meal." *Daedalus* 101 (1): 61–81.

———. 1975. *Implicit Meanings.* London: Routledge and Kegan Paul.

———. 1978. "Culture." In *Annual Report 1977–1978,* 55–81. New York: Russell Sage Foundation.

Dunevich, N. 2012. *A City Dines: One Hundred Years of Dining in Tel Aviv.* Tel Aviv: Ahuzat Bait.

Eichfeld, I. 2010. "The 2nd Hummus War." *Yediot Ahronot,* January 28. www.ynetnews.com/articles/0,7340,L-3839025,00.html.

Elias, N. 1978. "Norbert Elias and 'The Civilizing Process.'" *Theory and Society* 5 (2): 219–228.

Elizur, J. 2001. "The Fracturing of the Jewish Self-Image: The End of 'We Are One'?" *Israel Affairs* 8 (1–2): 14–30.

Ellman, M., and S. Laacher. 2003. *Migrant Workers in Israel: A Contemporary Form of Slavery.* Edited by S. Han and K. Vanfasse. Copenhagen: Euro-Mediterranean Human Rights Network and International Federation for Human Rights.

El Or, T. 2012. "The Soul of the Biblical Sandal: On Anthropology and Style." *American Anthropologist* 114 (3): 433–445.

Farb, P., and G. Armelagos. 1980. *Consuming Passions: The Anthropology of Eating.* Boston: Houghton Mifflin.

Fast, H. 2000. Forward to *The Kibbutz: Awakening from Utopia,* edited by D. Gavron, ix–x. Boston: Rowman and Littlefield.

Feige M. 2009. "Midbar, Shmama and Garbage Can." In *The Desert Experience in Israel: Communities, Art, Science and Education in the Negev,* edited by A. P. Hare and G. M. Kressel, 27–32. Lanham: University Press of America.

Feldman, A. 2003. "Strange Fruit: The South African Truth Commission and the Demonic Economies of Violence." In *Beyond Rationalism: Rethinking Magic, Witchcraft and Sorcery,* B. Kapferer, 234–265. New York: Bergham.

Feldman, J. 2008. *Above the Death Pits, Beneath the Flag: Youth Voyages to Poland and the Performance of Israeli Identity.* New York: Berghahn.

Femia, J. 2005. "Gramsci, Machiavelli, and International Relations." *Political Science Quarterly* 76 (3): 341–349.

Fessler, D. M., and C. D. Navarrete. 2003. "Meat Is Good to Taboo: Dietary Proscriptions as a Product of the Interaction of Psychological Mechanisms and Social Processes." *Journal of Cognition and Culture* 3 (1): 1–40.

Fiddes, N. 1991. *Meat: A Natural Symbol.* London: Routledge.

Fischler, C. 1988. "Food, Self and Identity." *Social Science Information* 27 (2): 275-292.

Fogiel-Bijaui, S. 2007. "Women in the Kibbutz: The 'Mixed Blessing' of Neo-Liberalism." *Nashim: A Journal of Jewish Women's Studies and Gender Issues,* no. 13: 102–122.

Fogiel-Bijaui, S., and A. Egozi. 1985. "From East to West—and Back: On the Awakening of Ethnicity among Kibbutz Oriental Members." In *Communal Life: An International Perspective,* edited by Y. Gorny, I. Paz, and Y. Oved, 533–539. Efal: Yad Tabenkin; NJ: Transaction.

Foucault, M. 2003. "Lecture 11, 17 March 1976." In *Society Must Be Defended: Lectures at the Collège de France,* 239–264. London: Picador.

Frenkel, M., and Y. Shenhav. 2003. "From Americanization to Colonization: The Diffusion of Productivity Models Revisited." *Organization Studies* 24 (9): 1537–1561.

Furst, B. 2012. "Environmental Activism as Motive for Cultural Change: Israel's Campaign for Protecting Wild Flowers." *Horizons in Geography,* no. 78: 26–47.

Gabaccia, D., and J. Pilcher. 2011. "'Chili Queens' and Checkered Tablecloths: Public Dining Cultures of Italians in New York City and Mexicans in San Antonio, Texas, 1870s–1940s." *Radical History Review,* no. 110: 109–126.

Gal, S. 1995. "Review: Language and the 'Arts of Resistance.'" *Cultural Anthropology* 10 (3): 407–424.

Gan, A. 2014. *Korbanutam Umanutam: MeShiah Korbani LeSiah Riboni* [From victimhood to sovereignty: An analysis of the victimization discourse in Israel]. Jerusalem: Israeli Institute for Democracy.

Garfinkel, A. 2010. "The Meeting of the Kibbutz and Corporate Capitalism: A Case Study." Master's thesis, Ben-Gurion University. http://in.bgu.ac.il/icqm/DocLib1/%D7%90%D7%91%D7%99-%D7%92%D7%A8%D7%A4%D7%95%D7%A0%D7%A7%D7%9C.pdf.

Gavron, D. 2000. The Kibbutz: Awakening from Utopia. Boston: Rowman and Littlefield.

Geertz, C. 1973. *The Interpretation of Cultures.* New York: Basic Books.

Gelfer, J. 2013. "Meat and Masculinity in Men's Ministries." *Journal of Men's Studies* 21 (1): 78–79.

Gerber, H. 2003. "Zionism, Orientalism, and the Palestinians." *Journal of Palestine Studies* 33 (1): 23–41.

Getz, S. 2011. *Shitot Tagmul Bakibuttzim 2011* [The remuneration system in the kibbutzim 2011]. Haifa: Institute of Kibbutz Research, Haifa University. http://kibbutz.haifa.ac.il/index.php/he/new-pub-hebrew/17-2011.

Gilon, M. 2011. "Lefazer et ha'ashan (me'al hamangal)" [Removing the smoke (over the mangal)]. Clalit website, last updated May 4. www.clalit.co.il/he/lifestyle/nutrition/Pages/cook_out_fest.aspx.

Girardelli, D. 2004. "Commodified Identities: The Myth of Italian Food in the United States." *Journal of Communication Inquiry* 28 (4): 307–324.

Glausser, A. 2009. "The Placenta's Second Life." PhD dissertation, Massachusetts Institute of Technology. http://cmsw.mit.edu/placentas-second-life.

Godderis, R. 2006. "Food for Thought: An Analysis of Power and Identity in Prison Food Narratives." *Berkeley Journal of Sociology*, no. 50: 61–75.

Goffman, E. 1968. *Asylums: Essays on the Social Situation of Mental Patients and Other Inmates*. New York: Anchor Books

Goody, J. 1982. *Cooking, Cuisine and Class: A Study in Comparative Sociology*. Cambridge: Cambridge University Press.

Griffin, J., and Soskolne, V. 2003. "Psychological Distress among Thai Migrant Workers in Israel." *Social Science and Medicine* 57 (5): 769–774.

Grosglik, R. 2011. "Organic Hummus in Israel: Global and Local Ingredients and Images." *Sociological Research Online* 16 (2). doi:10.5153/sro.2339.

Grosglik, R., and U. Ram. 2013. "Authentic, Speedy and Hybrid: Representations of Chinese Food and Cultural Globalization in Israel." *Food, Culture and Society,* 16 (2): 223–243.

Gvion, L. 2005. "Humus-Couscous-Sushi." In *Al Beten Melea* [Over a full stomach], edited by A. Kleinberg, 32–78. Jerusalem: Keter.

———. 2006a. *At Stomach Level: Social and Political Aspects of Arab Cuisine in Israel*. Jerusalem: Carmel.

———. 2006b. "Cuisines of Poverty as Means of Empowerment: Arab Food in Israel." *Agriculture and Human Values* 23 (3): 299–312.

———. 2009. "Narrating Modernity and Tradition: The Case of Palestinian Food in Israel." *Identities: Global Studies in Culture and Power* 16 (4): 391–413.

Hage, G. 2005. "A Not So Multi-Sited Ethnography of a Not So Imagined Community." *Anthropological Theory* 5 (4): 463–475.

Halfin, T. 2016. "Shitufi: Yomyom Utopi Bakibutz shel Dhnot Ha 2000" [Communal: Utopian daily life on the kibbutz in the 2000s]. PhD diss., Ben-Gurion University.

Hammershlag, R. 2008. "Balada Leozev Kibbutz" [A ballad for the kibbutz returnee]. Nana10, August 30. http://news.nana10.co.il/Article/?ArticleID=578 309&sid=126.

Handelman, D. 2004. *Nationalism and the Israeli State: Bureaucratic Logic in Public Events*. Oxford: Berg.

Handelman, D., and E. Katz. 1995. "State Ceremonies in Israel: Remembrance Day and Independence Day." In *Israeli Judaism: The Sociology of Religion in Israel,* S. Deshen, C. Liebman, and M. Shkeid, 75–86. New Jersey: Transaction.

Harris, M. 1987. *The Sacred Cow and the Abominable Pig: Riddles of Food and Culture*. Tel Aviv: Massada.

———. 1998. *Good to Eat: Riddles of Food and Culture*. Long Grove: Waveland.

Hawkes, K. 1993. "Why Hunter-Gatherers Work: An Ancient Version of the Problem of Public Goods." *Current Anthropology*, no. 34: 341–361.

Hawkes, K., J. O'Connell, and N. G. Blurton Jones. 2001a. "Hadza Meat Sharing." *Evolution and Human Behavior*, no. 22: 113–142.

———. 2001b. "Hunting and Nuclear Families." *Current Anthropology* 42 (5): 681–709.

Helman, A. 1994. "Privatization and the Israeli Kibbutz Experience." *Journal of Rural Cooperation,* no. 22: 19–32.

Herzfeld, M. 1985. *The Poetics of Manhood: Contest and Identity in a Cretan Mountain Village.* Princeton, NJ: Princeton University Press.

———. 1989. *Anthropology through the Looking-Glass: Critical Ethnography in the Margins of Europe.* Cambridge: Cambridge University Press.

Hirsch, D. 2011. "'Hummus Is Best when It Is Fresh and Made by Arabs': The Gourmetization of Hummus in Israel and the Return of the Repressed Arab." *American Ethnologist* 38 (4): 617–630.

Hirsch, D., and O. Tene. 2013. "Hummus: The Making of an Israeli Culinary Cult." *Journal of Consumer Culture* 13 (1): 25–45.

Holt, G., and V. Amilien. 2007. "Introduction: From Local Food to Localised Food." In "From Local Food to Localised Food," edited by Edited by V. Amilien and G. Holt, special issue, *Anthropology of Food,* no. S2 (March). http://aof.revues.org/index405.html.

Howell, S. 2003. "Modernizing Mansaf: The Consuming Contexts of Jordan's National Dish." *Food and Foodways* 11 (4): 215–243.

Jacobson, Y. 1997. "Secular Pilgrimage in the Israeli Context: The Journey of Young Israelis to Distant Countries." Master's thesis, Tel Aviv University.

James, R. 2004. "The Reliable Beauty of Aroma: Staples of Food and Cultural Production among Italian-Australians." *Australian Journal of Anthropology* 15 (1): 23–39.

Katriel, T. 1995. "Touring the Land: Trips and Hiking as Secular Pilgrimages in Israeli Culture." *Jewish Ethnology and Folklore Review,* no. 17: 6–13.

Katz, A. 2007. "We Have Celebrated Independence." *Israeli,* April 29, 13.

Katz, H. 2006. "Gramsci, Hegemony, and Global Civil Society Networks." *Voluntas,* no. 17: 333–348.

Kent, S. 1993. "Sharing in an Egalitarian Kalahari Community." *Man* 28 (3): 479–514.

Khazum, A. 1999. "Western Culture, Ethnic Classification and Social Enclosure: The Background of Ethnic Inequality in Israel." *Sociologia Israelit* 1 (2): 385–428.

Khazzoom, A. 2003. "The Great Chain of Orientalism: Jewish Identity, Stigma Management, and Ethnic Exclusion in Israel." *American Sociological Review,* 68 (4): 481–510.

Kimmerling, B., ed. 1989. *The Israeli State and Society: Boundaries and Frontiers.* Albany: State University of New York Press.

———. 1993a. "Militarism bahevra ha'Israelit" [Militarism in Israeli society]. *Theoria Ubikoret,* no. 4: 123–140.

———. 1993b. "Patterns of Militarism in Israel." *European Journal of Sociology* 34 (2): 196–223.

Kleinberg, A., ed. 2005. *Over a Full Stomach.* Jerusalem: Keter.

Kozinets, R. 1998. "On Netnography: Initial Reflections on Consumer Investigations of Cybercultures." *Advances in Consumer Research,* no. 25: 366–371.

———. 2002. "The Field behind the Screen: Using Netnography for Marketing Research in Online Communities." *Journal of Marketing Research*, no. 39: 61–72.

Laniado-Tirosh, M. 2011. "Not on Mangal Alone." *Haaretz Galleria*, April 22, 10.

Lanir, J. 2004. *The Kibbutz in Israeli Society: The Pathology of Crisis*. Ramat Ef'al: Yad Tabenkin.

Lapidot, A., L. Appelbaum, and M. Yehudai. 2006. "Hakibbutz besviva mishtana" [The kibbutz in a changing environment]. *Ofakim Begeographia*, no. 66: 7–27.

Lavee, Y., and R. Katz. 2003. "The Family in Israel: Between Tradition and Modernity." *Marriage and Family Review* 35 (1–2): 193–217.

Lavie-Dinur, A., and Y. Karniel. 2015. "Ha'Israeliut Hahadasha Hi Mizrahit" [The new Israeliness is mizrahi]. *Panim*, nos. 68–69. www.ruvik.co .il/%D7%A4%D7%99%D7%A0%D7%AA-%D7%A2%D7%99%D7%95%D7% 9F/2015/%D7%A7%D7%A8%D7%A0%D7%99%D7%90%D7%9C- %D7%A2%D7%9C-%D7%98%D7%9C%D7%95%D7%95%D7%99%D7%96% D7%99%D7%94.

Leepreecha, P. 2005. "The Politics of Ethnic Tourism in Northern Thailand." Paper presented at the workshop "Mekong Tourism: Learning across Borders," Social Research Institute, Chiang Mai University, Chiang Mai, February 25. www.akha .org/content/tourismecotourism/ethnictourism.pdf.

Leviatan, A., and M. Rozner. 2002. "Emuna Be'arachim veshinui arachim etzel havrei kibbutz" [Belief in values and value changes among kibbutz members]. *Mifne: Bama Leinyanei Hevra*, no. 37: 28–33.

Leviatan, U., J. Quarter, and H. Oliver. 1998. *Crisis in the Israeli Kibbutz: Meeting the Challenge of Changing Times*. Westport, CT: Praeger.

Lévi-Strauss, C. 1966. "The Culinary Triangle." *Partisan Review*, no. 33: 586–595.

Levy, A. 2015. *Return to Casablanca: Jews, Muslims, and an Israeli Anthropologist*. Chicago: University of Chicago Press.

Levy, Y. 2009. "Is There a Motivation Crisis in Military Recruitment in Israel?" *Israel Affairs* 15 (2): 135–158.

Lieblich, A. 2001. "HaKibbutz al saf ha'Alpa'im" [The kibbutz on the edge of the 2000s]. In *Medina Baderech* [A state on the road], edited by A. Shapira, 295-316. Jerusalem: Zalman Shazar Institute.

Liebman, C. S., and E. Katz. 1997. *The Jewishness of Israelis: Responses to the Guttman Report*. Albany: State University of New York Press.

Liebman, S., and E. Don-Yehiya. 1983. *Civil Religion in Israel: Traditional Judaism and Political Culture in the Jewish State*. Berkeley: University of California Press.

Light, I., and E. Bonacich. 1991. *Immigrant Entrepreneurs: Koreans in Los Angeles, 1965–1982*. Berkley: University of California Press.

Lovell-Troy, L. 1990. *The Social Basis of Ethnic Enterprise: Greeks in the Pizza Business*. New York: Garland.

Lupton, D. 1996. *Food, the Body and the Self*. London: Sage.

MacCannell, D. 1976. *The Tourist: A New Theory of the Leisure Class*. Berkeley: University of California Press.

Maneeprasert, R. 1989. "'Women and Children First'? A Review of the Current Nutritional Status in the Highlands." In *Hill Tribes Today,* edited by J. McKinnon and B. Vienne, 143–158. Bangkok: White Lotus-Orstom.

Maoz, D. 1999. "My Heart is in the East: The Trip of Young and Old Israelis in India." Master's thesis, Hebrew University of Jerusalem.

Marcus, G. E. 1995. "Ethnography in/of the World System: The Emergence of Multi-Sited Ethnography." *Annual Review of Anthropology* no. 24: 95–117.

Maron, S. 1997. *Hakkibutz behevrat shuk* [The kibbutz in a market society]. Ramat Efal: Yad Tabenkin.

Maso, I. 2001. "Phenomenology and Ethnography." In *Handbook of Ethnography,* edited by P. Atkinson, A. Coffey, S. Delamont, J. Lofland, and L. Lofland, 136–144. London: Sage.

Matejowsky, T. 2008. "Jolly Dogs and McSpaghetti: Anthropological Reflections on Global/Local Fast-Food Competition in the Philippines." *Journal of Asia-Pacific Business* 9 (4): 313–328.

McGann, P. 2002. "Eating Muscle: Material Semiotics and a Manly Appetite." In *Revealing Men's Bodies,* edited by N. Tuana, 83–99. Bloomington: Indiana University Press.

Mendel, Y., and R. Ranta. 2016. *From the Arab Other to the Israeli Self.* London: Ashgate.

Mennell, S. 1985. *All Manners of Food: Eating and Taste in England and France from the Middle Ages to the Present.* Oxford: Blackwell.

———. 1991. "Food and the Quantum Theory of Taboo." *Etnofoor* 4 (1): 63–77.

Miller, D., ed. 1995. *Acknowledging Consumption.* London: Routledge.

Mintz, S. 1985. *Sweetness and Power: The Place of Sugar in Modern History.* New York: Viking.

———. 1996. *Tasting Food, Tasting Freedom: Excursions into Eating, Culture, and the Past.* Boston: Beacon Press.

Moore, K. 1999. "Dissonance in the Dining Room: A Study of Social Interaction in a Special Care Unit." *Qualitative Health Research* 9 (1): 133–155.

Murcott, A. 1982. "On the Social Significance of the 'Cooked Dinner' in South Wales." *Social Science Information* 21 (4–5): 677–695.

———. 1997. "Family Meals—A Thing of the Past?" In *Food, Health and Identity,* edited by P. Kaplan, 32–49. New York: Routledge.

Narayan, U. 1995. "Eating Cultures: Incorporation, Identity and Indian Food." *Social Identities* 1 (1): 63–86.

———. 1997. *Dislocating Cultures: Identities, Traditions and Third-World Feminism,* New York: Routledge.

Nash, K. 2001. "The 'Cultural Turn' in Social Theory: Towards a Theory of Cultural Politics." *Sociology* 35 (1): 77–92.

———. 2009. *Contemporary Political Sociology: Globalization, Politics and Power.* Hoboken, NJ: John Wiley and Sons.

Nath, J. 2011. "Gendered Fare? A Qualitative Investigation of Alternative Food and Masculinities." *Journal of Sociology* 47 (3): 261–278.

Naveh, Z., and J. Dan. 1973. "The Human Degradation of Mediterranean Landscapes in Israel." In *Mediterranean-Type Ecosystems, Origin and Structure*, edited by F. di Castri and H. A. Mooney, 370–390. Berlin: Springer.

Navon, M. 2001. "The Kibbutz Kitchen and Privatization." *Globes,* September 11, 2000. www.globes.co.il/news/home.aspx?fid=2&did=439431&nagish=1.

Neal, Z. 2006. "Culinary Deserts, Gastronomic Oases: A Classification of US Cities." *Urban Studies* 43 (1): 1–21.

Noy, C. 2003. "Sipurim shel Gavriut Hegemonit: Guf u'Merhav Besipurei Tarmilaim Israelim" [Stories of hegemonic masculinity: Body and space in Israeli backpackers' stories]. *Sociologia Israelit* 5 (1): 74–120.

———. 2006. "Israeli Backpacking since the 1960s: A Historic-Cultural View of Institutionalization and Experience in Tourism." *Tourism Recreation Research* 31 (3): 39–54.

O'Connor, K. 2008. "The Hawaiian *Luau:* Food as Tradition, Transgression, Transformation and Travel." *Food, Culture and Society* 2 (2): 149–172.

Oberschall, A., and M. Seidman. 2005. "Food Coercion in Revolution and Civil War: Who Wins and How They Do It." *Comparative Studies in Society and History* 47 (2): 372–402.

Ohnuki-Tierney, E. 1993. *Rice as Self: Japanese Identities Through Time*. Princeton, NJ: Princeton University Press.

———. 1995. "Structure, Event and Historical Metaphor: Rice and Identities in Japanese History." *Journal of the Royal Anthropological Institute*, no. 1: 227–253.

Paarlberg, R. L. 1978. "Food, Oil, and Coercive Resource Power." *International Security* 3 (2): 3–19.

Palgi, M., and S. Reinharz, eds. 2014. *One Hundred Years of Kibbutz Life: A Century of Crises and Reinvention*. New Jersey: Transaction.

Passmore, L. 2009. "The Art of Hunger: Self-Starvation in the Red Army Faction." *German History* 27 (1): 32–59.

Peres, Y., and R. Katz. 1981. "Stability and Centrality: The Nuclear Family in Modern Israel." *Social Forces* 59 (3): 687–704.

Peterson, N. 1993. "Demand Sharing: Reciprocity and the Pressure for Generosity among Foragers." *American Anthropologist*, no. 95: 860–874.

Phillips, K. D. 2009. "Hunger, Healing, and Citizenship in Central Tanzania." *African Studies Review* 52 (1): 23–45.

Poe, T. 2001. "The Labour and Leisure of Food Production as a Mode of Ethnic Identity Building among Italians in Chicago, 1890–1940." *Rethinking History* 5 (1): 131–148.

Punch, M. 1974. "The Sociology of the Anti-Institution." *British Journal of Sociology* 25 (3): 312–325.

Raijman, R., and N. Kushnirovich. 2015. *Recruitment of Migrant Workers in Agriculture and Construction in Israel: The Impact of Bilateral Agreements*. Ruppin Academic Center and the Center for International Migration and Integration. www.justice.gov.il/En/Units/Trafficking/MainDocs/impact-bilateral%20agreements.pdf.

Ram, U. 1993. "Emerging Modalities of Feminist Sociology in Israel." *Israel Social Science Research,* no. 8: 51–76.

———. 2004. "Glocommodification: How the Global Consumes the Local—McDonald's in Israel." *Current Sociology* 52 (1): 11–31.

———. 2012. "McDonaldization." In *The Wiley-Blackwell Encyclopedia of Globalization.* Published online February 29. doi: 10.1002/9780470670590.wbeog371.

Ranta, R., and Y. Mendel. 2014. "Consuming Palestine: Palestine and Palestinians in Israeli Food Culture." *Ethnicities* 14 (3): 412–435.

Raviv, Y. 2003. "Falafel: A National Icon." *Gastronomica* 3 (3): 20–25.

Richards, A. I. 1939. Land, Labour and Diet in Northern Rhodesia: An Economic Study of the Bemba Tribe. Oxford: Oxford University Press.

Ries, N. 2009. "Potato Ontology: Surviving Postsocialism in Russia." *Cultural Anthropology* 24 (2): 181–212.

Ritzer, G. 1983. "The McDonaldization of Society." *Journal of American Culture* 6 (1): 100–107.

———. 1996. *The McDonaldization of Society.* Thousand Oaks: Sage.

———. 1998. *The McDonaldization Thesis: Explorations and Extensions.* London: Sage.

Ritzer, G., and T. Stillman. 2001. "Postmodern Ballpark as a Leisure Setting: Enchantment and Simulated De-McDonaldization." *Leisure Sciences* 23 (2): 99–113.

Roniger, L., and M. Feige. 1992. "From Pioneer to Freier: The Changing Models of Generalized Exchange in Israel." *European Journal of Sociology/Archives Européennes de Sociologie* 33 (2): 280–307.

———. 1993. "The *Freier* Culture and Israeli Identity." *Alpaim,* no. 7: 118–136.

Rosenhek, Z. 2000. "Migration Regimes, Intra-State Conflicts, and the Politics of Exclusion and Inclusion: Migrant Workers in the Israeli Welfare State." *Social Problems* 47 (1): 49–67.

Rosen-Zvi, I. 2004. *Taking Space Seriously: Law, Space and Society in Contemporary Israel.* Surrey: Ashgate.

Rosner, M. 2000. *Future Trends of the Kibbutz: An Assessment of Recent Changes.* Publication no. 83. Haifa: Institute for Study and Research of the Kibbutz, Haifa University. http://research.haifa.ac.il/~kibbutz/pdf/trends.PDF.

Rothschild, E. 1976. "Food Politics." *Foreign Affairs* 54 (2): 285–307.

Rouse, C., and J. Hoskins. 2004. "Purity, Soul Food, and Sunni Islam: Explorations at the Intersection of Consumption and Resistance." *Cultural Anthropology* 19 (2): 226–249.

Ruffle, B., and R. Sosis. 2006. "Cooperation and the In-Group-Out-Group Bias: A Field Test on Israeli Kibbutz Members and City Residents." *Journal of Economic Behavior and Organization,* no. 60: 147–163.

Sahlins, M. 1963. "Poor Man, Rich Man, Big Man, Chief: Political Types in Melanesia and Polynesia." *Comparative Studies in Society and History* 5 (3): 285–303.

———. 1976. *Culture and Practical Reason.* Chicago: University of Chicago Press.

————. 1991. "La Pensée Bourgeoise." In *Rethinking Popular Culture: Contemporary Perspectives in Cultural Studies,* edited by C. Mukerji and M. Schudson, 278–288. Berkeley: University of California Press.

Said, E. 1978. *Orientalism.* New York: Vintage.

Sasson-Levy, O. 2002. "Constructing Identities at the Margins: Masculinities and Citizenship in the Israeli Army." *Sociological Quarterly* 43 (3): 357–383.

Schlüter, R. 2000. "The Immigrants' Heritage in South America: Food and Culture as a New Sustainable Tourism Product." *ReVista: Harvard Review of Latin America*: 46–48. http://revista.drclas.harvard.edu/files/revista/files/tourism_in_the_americas.pdf?m=1436899747.

Scott, J. C. 2005. "Afterword to 'Moral Economies, State Spaces, and Categorical Violence.'" *American Anthropologist* 107 (3): 395–402.

Scott, R. 2010. "Meat My Hero: 'I have a Dream' of Living Language in the Work of Donna Haraway, or Ride 'Em Cowboy!'" *Poroi* 6 (2): 1–15.

Segal, R. 2003. "The Palmach History Museum, Tel Aviv." *Journal of Architecture* 8 (2): 251–263.

Sered, S. S. 1989. "The Religion of Relating: Kinship and Spirituality among Middle Eastern Jewish Women in Jerusalem." *Journal of Social and Personal Relationships* 6 (3): 309–325.

Setalaphruk, C., and L. L. Price. 2007. "Children's Traditional Ecological Knowledge of Wild Food Resources: A Case Study in a Rural Village in Northeast Thailand." *Journal of Ethnobiology and Ethnomedicine* 3 (1): 1.

Shafir, S. 2010. "Not Only Park Hayarkon: Great Places for BBQ." *Mouse,* accessed January 2016.

Shani, R. 2009. "A Year to Cast Lead Operation: The Sons Are Returning to the Kibbutz." Walla!News, December 27. http://news.walla.co.il/?w=/2689/1625527.

Shapira, R., and D. Navon. 1991. "Alone Together: Public and Private Dimensions of a Tel-Aviv Cafe." *Qualitative Sociology* 14 (2): 107–125.

Shenhar, A., and T. Katriel. 1992. "'I Was There': The Poetics of Narration in Tower and Stockade Personal Experience Stories." *Jewish Folklore and Ethnology Review* 14 (1–2): 32–43.

Shir-Vertesh, D. 2012. "'Flexible Personhood': Loving Animals as Family Members in Israel." *American Anthropologist* 114 (3): 420–432.

Simmel, G. 2000. "The Sociology of the Meal." In *Simmel on Culture: Selected Writings,* edited by D. Frisby and M. Featherstone, 130–136. London: Sage.

Skinner, J. D., B. R. Carruth, W. Bounds, and P. J. Ziegler. 2002. "Children's Food Preferences: A Longitudinal Analysis." *Journal of the American Dietetic Association* 102 (11): 1638–1647.

Smart, B., ed. 1999. *Resisting McDonaldization.* London: Sage.

Smith, C. 2002. "Punishment and Pleasure: Women, Food and the Imprisoned Body." *Sociological Review* 50 (2): 197–214.

Smooha, S. 1993. "Class, Ethnic, and National Cleavages and Democracy in Israel." In *Israeli Democracy under Stress,* edited by E. Sprinzak and L. Diamond, 309–342. Boulder: Lynne Rienner.

———. 2008. "The Mass Immigrations to Israel: A Comparison of the Failure of the Mizrahi Immigrants of the 1950s with the Success of the Russian Immigrants of the 1990s." *Journal of Israeli History* 27 (1): 1–27.

Sobal, J., and M. Nelson. 2003. "Commensal Eating Patterns: A Community Study." *Appetite* 41 (2): 181–190.

Somnasang, P., G. Moreno, and K. Chusil. 1998. "Indigenous Knowledge of Wild Food Hunting and Gathering in North-East Thailand." *Food and Nutrition Bulletin* 19 (4): 359–365.

Sosis, R., and B. Ruffle. 2003. "Religious Ritual and Cooperation: Testing for a Relationship on Israeli Religious and Secular Kibbutzim." *Current Anthropology*, no. 44: 713–722.

Spiro, M. 1954. "Is the Family Universal?" *American Anthropologist* 56 (5): 839–846.

———. 1963. *The Kibbutz: Venture in Utopia*. New York: Schocken Books.

———. 2004. "Utopia and Its Discontents: The Kibbutz and Its Historical Vicissitudes." *American Anthropologist* 106 (3): 556–568.

Stanford, C. B. 1999. *The Hunting Apes: Meat Eating and the Origins of Human Behavior*. Princeton, NJ: Princeton University Press.

Staples, J. 2008. "'Go On, Just Try Some!': Meat and Meaning-Making among South Indian Christians." *South Asia: Journal of South Asian Studies* 31 (1): 36–55.

Stein, R. 2003. *Itineraries of Conflict: Israeli, Palestinians and the Political Lives of Tourism*. Durham, NC: Duke University Press.

Sumpter, K. C. 2015. "Masculinity and Meat Consumption: An Analysis through the Theoretical Lens of Hegemonic Masculinity and Alternative Masculinity Theories." *Sociology Compass* 9 (2): 104–114.

Sutton, D. E. 2001. *Remembrance of Repasts: An Anthropology of Food and Memory*. Oxford: Berg.

Swirski, S. 1981. *Not Faltering but Be-Faltered: Mizrahi and Ashkenazi in Israel*. Haifa: Mahbarot Lemehkar Ulevikoret.

Symons, M. 2007. *One Continuous Picnic: A Gastronomic History of Australia*. Melbourne: Melbourne University Press.

Talmon, Y. 1972. *Family and Community in Kibbutz*. Cambridge, MA: Harvard University Press.

Tambiah, S. 1969. "Animals Are Good to Think and Good to Prohibit." *Ethnology* 8 (4): 423–459.

Taylor, K. W. 2004. "How I Began to Teach about the Vietnam War." *Michigan Quarterly Review*, no. 43: 637–647.

Tene, O. 2005. "Kah Nevashel Bait be'Israel" [Thus we shall cook an Israeli home]. In *Al Beten Melea* [Over a full stomach], edited by A. Kleinberg, 130–193. Jerusalem: Keter.

Thiel, B. 1994. "Further Thoughts on Why Men Share Meat." *Current Anthropology* 35 (4): 440–441.

Trupp, A. 2015. "Agency, Social Capital, and Mixed Embeddedness among Akha Ethnic Minority Street Vendors in Thailand's Tourist Areas." *SOJOURN: Journal of Social Issues in Southeast Asia* 30 (3): 780–818.

Tuchman, G., and H. G. Levine. 1993. "New York Jews and Chinese Food: The Social Construction of an Ethnic Pattern." *Journal of Contemporary Ethnography* 22 (3): 382–407.

Tuomi, H. 1975. "The Food Power: The Position of Main Exporting Countries in World Food Economy." *Instant Research on Peace and Violence* 5 (3): 120–137.

Turner, V. 2017. *The Ritual Process: Structure and Anti-Structure*. London: Routledge.

Twigg, J. 1983. "Vegetarianism and the Meanings of Meat." In *The Sociology of Food and Eating*, edited by A. Murcott, 18–30. Aldershot: Gower.

Tzur, M., ed. 1987. *Kol Ha'Hatchalot: 1937–1987* [All the beginnings 1937–1987]. Kibbutz Ein Gev.

Uphoff, N. 1989. "Distinguishing Power, Authority, and Legitimacy." *Polity* 22 (2): 295–322.

Van den Berghe, P. L. 1984. "Ethnic Cuisine: Culture in Nature." *Ethnic and Racial Studies* 7 (3): 387–397.

Vered, R. 2012. "The Father of All Fathers of Food." *Haaretz*, August 31, 68–71.

Vester, K. 2015. *A Taste of Power*. Oakland: University of California Press.

Visweswaran, K. 1994. *Fictions of Feminist Ethnography*. Minneapolis: University of Minnesota Press.

Watson, J. L. 1997. *Golden Arches East: McDonald's in East Asia*. Palo Alto, CA: Stanford University Press.

Weber, M. 2009. "Class, Status, Party." In *From Max Weber: Essays in Sociology*, edited by H. H. Gerth and translated by C. W. Mills, 180–195. London: Routledge.

Welz, G. 2013. "Contested Origins: Food Heritage and the European Union's Quality Label Program." *Food, Culture and Society* 16 (2): 265–279.

Wildt, M. 2001. "Promise of More: The Rhetoric of (Food) Consumption in a Society Searching for Itself; West Germany in the 1950s." In *Food, Drink and Identity: Eating and Drinking in Europe since the Middle Ages*, edited by P. Scholliers, 63–80. Oxford: Berg.

Wilk, R. 2006. *Home Cooking in the Global Village: Caribbean Food from Buccaneers to Ecotourists*. London: Berg.

Willard, B. 2002. "The American Story of Meat: Discursive Influences on Cultural Eating Practice." *Journal of Popular Culture* 36 (1): 105–118.

Winter, M. 2003. "Embeddedness, the New Food Economy and Defensive Localism." *Journal of Rural Studies*, no. 19: 23–32.

Wolf, E. R. 1990. "Distinguished Lecture: Facing Power—Old Insights, New Questions." *American Anthropologist* 92 (3): 586–596.

Wrigley, N. 2002. "'Food Deserts' in British Cities: Policy Context and Research Priorities." *Urban Studies*, no. 39: 2029–2040.

Wu, F. 2002. "The Best 'Chink' Food: Dog Eating and the Dilemma of Diversity." *Gastronomica* 2 (2): 38–45.

Yacobi, H. 2008. "From State-Imposed Urban Planning to Israeli Diasporic Place: The Case of Netivot and the Grave of Baba Sali." In *Jewish Topographies: Visions of Space, Tradition and Place,* edited by J. Brauch, A. Lipphardt, and A. Nocke, 63–82. Surrey: Ashgate.

Yair, G. 2011. *The Code of Israeliness.* Jerusalem: Keter.

Yiftachel, O. 2006. *Ethnocracy: Land and Identity Politics in Israel/Palestine.* Philadelphia: University of Pennsylvania Press.

Yiftachel, O., and M.D. Segal. 1998. "Jews and Druze in Israel: State Control and Ethnic Resistance." *Ethnic and Racial Studies* 21 (3): 476–506.

Zerubavel, Y. 1994. "The Death of Memory and the Memory of Death: Masada and the Holocaust as Historical Metaphors." *Representations* 45: 72–100.

Zimmerman, M., and Y. Hotam. 2005. "HaHistoria shel HaYehudim HaGermanim bein Merkaz Eiropa VeHamizrah Hatichon" [The history of German Jews between Europe and the Middle East]. In *Bein Hamoladot: HaYekim BiMhozoteihem* [Between homelands: The Yekes in their places], edited by M. Zimmerman and Y. Hotam. Jerusalem: Zalman Shazar.

Zycherman, A. 2008. "To Beef or Not to Beef: Defining Food Security and Insecurity in Tucumán, Argentina." *Ecological and Environmental Anthropology* 4 (1): 28–37.

# INDEX

1948 war and founding of Israel, 1, 3, 50, 63, 150, 153
1967 war, 22, 23, 75, 80, 86, 146, 166, 167, 179. *See also* occupied territories
1973 October War, 155, 242n8
1990 Gulf War, 153

Abboud, Fadi, 1
Abu Gosh, 3–4, 5, 7, 8, 18, 150
*Achbar Ha'Ir* (City Mouse), 35, 82, 221
Adar, Rafi, 87
Africans, 103, 211, 212. *See also* Ethiopian Jews; North African Jews; South Africa
agriculture, 22, 26, 75–76, 213–14; reliance on migrant labor, 11, 17, 179, 188. *See also* Thai migrant workers
Aharoni, Israel, 28, 35
Al-Aktza Intifada, 151
*Al Arabia,* 3
alcohol, 37, 39, 211–12
*al ha'esh* (grilled meat) events, 49, 50, 55, 56, 61, 81, 151. *See also* Independence Day barbecues; meat
Alkalai, Leon, 90
*All the Beginnings, 1973–1987* (Muki Tzur), 124
ambivalence, of power, 21, 23, 67, 77, 78, 81, 107, 148, 219, 224–29
Anashim Israel, 86
*Anthology of Fibs* (Dan Ben-Amotz and Netiva Ben-Yehuda), 58
anthropology of food, 10–11, 16, 27; Sidney

Mintz, 25; on taste, 83. *See also* ethnographic methods
Arabic, 5, 6, 45, 209
Arab-Palestinian food, 3, 63, 99, 100, 220, 221, 225; Arab salad, 27, 151, 217, 270; feasting, 45–46. *See also* Palestinian food
Arabs, 47, 6, 57, 61, 63, 78, 103, 105–6; as the enemy, 4, 63, 102, 175, 227; "good Arabs," 3; *hamula* (extended family), 95, 134, 145; and orientalism, 102, 106–7. *See also* Palestinians
Argentina, 53–54, 74
Askhenazi: creation of Mizrahim, 23, 60, 221, 222–24; and "great chain of orientalism," 102, 106–7, 210–11; hegemonic status of, 4, 21, 59, 60, 62, 63, 103, 110, 121, 221, 223, 228; identification as Europeans, 21, 45, 60, 79, 100, 107, 110. *See also* kibbutz
Ashkenazi food: barbecues, 60, 62; boiled chicken, 26, 136; chicken soup, 221; cholent, 26, 45, 138, 162–64, 221, 233n2; chopped liver, 136, 221, 227; gefilte fish, 26, 45, 136, 221, 224; and kashrut, 224; kugel, 221; matzo balls, 136; schnitzel, 135, 160, 162, 163, 164; synonymous with Jewish food, 107, 220–21, 222
Australia: 53, 54, 55, 74, 84, 85
Avazi, Yehuda, 67

baba ganoush, 100, 151
Baba Sali's tomb, 61

backpacking, 34, 57, 234n21; and military service, 72. *See also* youth

Bahloul, Zuhair, 5

Balkan Jews, 60, 107, 219, 238n12

Banai, Ehud, 95

Barak, Ehud, 102

Bar Shalom, Hanoch, 28

Bar Yochai, Rabbi Shimon, 61

Bedouins, 57–58, 103; relations with Thai farmworkers, 195–96, 199–200, 201, 215

beef, 51–54, 64, 150; hamburgers, 19, 25, 26, 35, 36, 41–42, 44, 59, 64, 67, 162; in India, 149–50; at Sabbath meals, 141; stew, 136; symbolism of, 53, 63–64, 65, 66, 67, 219. See also *al-haesh;* meat

beer, 211–12

Beer-Sheva, 44, 90, 95, 104, 113

Ben Aderet, Shaul, 31

Ben Gurion, David, 138

Ben Gurion University, 16, 44, 55, 95, 113

Biber, Shaul, 31

Bourdieu, Pierre, 9–10, 106, 225; *habitus,* 10, 99

Brazil, 53, 54, 74

bread, 32, 94, 117, 162, 168, 236n7; injera, 25; in kibbutz meals, 123, 135, 136; pita, 58, 59, 63, 137, 157, 160, 217

breakfast, 32–34; American vs Israeli, 234n14

Britannia Park, 68

British Mandatory Palestine, 136, 221; Arab revolt 1936–39, 75

Brockbank, Jack, 6

Buddhism, 51, 185–86

Buhnik, Ortal, 120

Bukshester, Zahi, 36

Café Italia, 99

cafés (*batei kafe,* coffeehouses), 17, 73, 74, 83; espresso bars, 28, 31, 82–83

cafeterias, 112, 129, 141, 217

Chadar Ha'ochel, 26

Chanukah, 119

cheap food, 29–31, 34, 35, 37, 40, 45, 218, 224, 227, 246n6; at barbecues, 66, 71; Italian food, 88, 93, 97–98, 104–6; in Mizrahi restaurants, 63, 100, 225; and nonsuckerhood, 48–48. *See also* kibbutz dining rooms; portions, enlargement of

cheese, 32, 39, 160; feta, 2, 106; in Italian food, 83, 87, 88, 91, 97, 105; in kibbutzim, 123, 135, 141; *knafe* (Palestinian pastry), 17; *labane* (yogurt), 27; substitutes, 105–6, 109. *See also* kashrut dietary laws

chefs and restaurateurs, 27–28, 29, 36, 42–44, 90–91, 97, 98, 132; Adar, Rafi, 87; Aharoni, Israel, 28, 35; Alkalai, Leon, 90; Arditi, Ronen, 99; Bar Shalom, Hanoch, 28; Ben Aderet, Shaul, 31; Bukshester, Zahi, 36; Cohen, Haim, 44–45; Frankel, David, 87, 88, 96, 98; Komorwski, Erez, 27; Miller, Omer, 26; Mousayof, Nechama, 28; Sasson, Yona, 99; Schor, Alex, 85; Shaul, Anat, 32–33; Sirkis, Ruth, 26, 233n5; Spiegel, Haim, 33–34; Yerzin, Yoram, 99; Zairi, Boaz, 28, 39; Zehavi, Eitan, 86

chicken, 2, 3, 26, 40, 92, 136, 196, 221, 233n5; at barbecues, 59, 64, 65; boiled, 26, 136; farming, 196–97; and femininity, 219; in Jerusalem mix, 2, 3; and kashrut, 219; in kibbutz meals, 114, 129, 135, 141; in Palmach mythology, 58, 198; *pargiot,* 64–67, 77, 78, 219; in reservists' meals, 160, 161, 166; schnitzel, 217, 218, 219; and Thai farmworkers, 193–94, 204–5

children, 32, 63, 93, 94–95, 96, 195, 217; author's, 24, 44, 46, 93, 106; at barbecues, 65, 67, 69, 71, 219; fondness for Italian food, 92, 93–94; in kibbutzim, 114, 115, 130, 132, 133, 134, 140, 198. *See also* family, the; youth

China, 38, 58; dog meat, 185, 186, 206

Chinese food, 25, 26, 27, 28, 82, 87, 90, 232–3n1; dim sum, 36, 38, 39, 42, 44; in the kibbutz, 129; New York Jews and, 109–10, 111, 218

Chinese migrant workers, 180, 206

cholent, 26, 45, 138, 162–64, 221

Christianity, 4, 149

class, 4, 21, 29, 58, 88, 102–3, 128, 212, 228

coffee, 31; and campfires, 56, 57, 58, 71; espresso bars, 28, 31, 82–83; Italian, 83, 97; in the kibbutz, 122, 135, 136, 162; Turkish, 56–57, 223. *See also* cafés (*batei kafe,* coffeehouses)

Georgians, 209–10. *See also* ex-Soviet Union, immigrants from

Germany, 25; *Yekes* (immigrant German Jews), 90, 120, 209

Goffman, Erwin, 118–19

gluttony, 32, 35

gourmet food, 28, 35, 35–36; Italian, 86–87, 88

Gramsci, Antonio, 9, 10–11, 13, 225

Greece, 2; cuisine, 238–9n21

Grosglik, Rafi, 4, 38

Guinness World Record, 1, 2, 3, 4, 6

Gvion, Liora, 11

Ha'aliya La'aretz (Ascending to the Land [Uri Zohar and Arik Einstein]), 208–9

Hadshot Arutz, 2, 2–3, 104, 207–8

Hagana, 3

Haifa, 90

Halachic rules, 89, 92, 219, 224, 237n11; on game/hunting, 201; the Sabbath, 162. *See also* kashrut dietary laws

hamburgers, 19, 35, 36, 44, 64, 67, 162; and American cuisine, 25, 26, 59; McDonald's, 36, 41–42

Haredi (Ultra-Orthodox Jews), 103, 222

*harif* (spicy/ hot sauce), 107, 217, 219–20, 223

harissa, 106, 108–9, 111, 219

Hashomer Hatzair, 240n8

Hebrew, 5, 6, 17, 29, 172, 190

Hebrew University of Jerusalem, 16, 180

Herzliya, 32, 90, 103

Hinduism, 149; and nationalism, 150

Hoi An, Vietnam, 15, 20

Holocaust, the, 23, 45, 46, 48, 85, 224; survivors, 174

*Homa u'Migdal* (Tower and Stockade), 74, 75–77

Home-Front Command (Pikud Ha'Oref), 153, 154, 159, 165, 170

home meals: 20, 34, 59, 84, 89, 106, 117, 152, 217, 222; image of Italian, 94; in a kibbutz, 129–30, 131, 134–35; kosher, 89, 91; Sabbath, 162

hummus, 56, 82, 108; Israelization of, 1, 16, 100, 117; as Lebanese national dish, 1–2; Palestinian-Arab origins of, 1, 3, 5, 151;

in schnitzel in a pita, 217, 219, 220, 223, 224

Hummus Abu Gosh, 3

Hummus Wars: Abu Gosh, 3–4, 5, 7, 8, 18, 150; Jawadat Ibrahim, 3, 4, 5–6; Jerusalem mix (*meorav Yerushalmi*), 2–3; and the Lebanese, 1–2; in the media, 2–3, 4; rotting hummus, 4–5, 6

hunger, 45, 46, 48, 98, 110

hunger strikes, 13, 14, 232n16

hunting, 14; and masculinity, 54, 148; and Thai-Isan workers, 100, 178, 180–81, 183–84, 192, 193, 200–203, 206, 226; threat to wildlife, 202, 213–14

Ibrahim, Jawadat, 3, 4, 5–6

Independence Day (Yom Ha'atzmaut), 49, 78; Yom Hamangal (Barbecue Day), 50

Independence Day barbecues: American model, 58–60; "barbecue nations," 53–54, 55, 74; chicken vs red meat, 64, 65–67, 219, 223; grabbing space, 69–72, 77; *kumzitz*, 56–58, 62, 63; *mangal*, 26, 49, 55, 59, 62; and masculinity, 63–66; as *Mizrahiyut* celebration, 60–63, 224; multivocal symbolism of, 63, 65; *Occupied* (artwork), 79–81; Palmach ethos, 57, 63, 236n2, 198; Sacher Park, 21, 55, 56, 57, 73–74, 79, 80–81, 224; Tower and Stockade, 74, 75–77; women and, 52–53, 58, 64, 65, 67. *See also* beef; meat

India, 18, 109, 149–50

International Evangelical Church, 69

Intifida, Second, 151

Iran, 175; Iranian cuisine, 107

Iraq: 45; cuisine, 45, 82, 107, 221; Iraqi Jews, 60. *See also* Mizrahim food

Islam, 4, 6, 12, 211

Israel, State of, 24, 47, 48, 50, 75, 175, 176, 223; 1948 war and founding of, 1, 3, 50, 63, 150, 153; 1967 war, 22, 23, 75, 80, 86, 146, 166, 167, 179; 1973 October War, 155, 142n8; Arab revolt, 1936–39, 75; enemies of, 63, 157, 161, 168, 175, 214, 227; ethnic composition, 137; official languages, 5; pre-state, 47, 136, 167, 221; relations with the United States, 59–60; Zionism, 12, 23–24, 47, 144, 153, 210,

69, 79, 80, 100; Hindu, 150; Lebanese, 1–2. *See also* Hummus Wars; Israel, State of; Zionism

Netanyahu, Benyamin, 102, 107, 175, 231n9

Netanyahu, Sara, 107

Netivot, 61, 236nn9–10

New York, 1, 85; Jews and Chinese food in, 109–10, 111, 218

New Zealand, 53–54, 55, 74

North African Jews, 11, 60, 99, 100–101, 103, 106, 137, 210, 222, 223, 226; cuisines, 98, 107–8, 137–38; Mimouna festival, 236n7. *See also* Middle East and North Africa; Mizrahim; *mizruah*

Notre Dame Church, Abu Gosh, 4

nutrition, 48, 50–51, 52, 65, 104, 129, 148; nutritionists, 50, 83, 85

*Occupied* (art installation), 79–81

occupied territories, 76, 151, 239n23, 242n7; 1967 War, 22, 23, 75, 80, 86, 146, 166, 167, 179. *See also* Palestinians; Tower and Stockade

*Ochel, Kadima Ochel* (Food, charge forward [Biber]), 31

October War (1973), 155, 242n8

orientalism, 23, 60, 63, 106–7, 210–11, 224

Oslo Peace Accords, 153, 179

Ottoman Palestine, 1, 75

Padan, Omri, 41

Palestine, 75–76, 136, 167, 221

Palestinian food, 11, 21, 26, 82, 99–100, 150–51, 219, 225; in Abu Gosh, 3, 4, 5, 7, 8, 18, 150; Arab salad, 27, 151, 217, 270; baba ganoush, 100, 151; falafel, 3, 82, 93, 99, 100, 104, 151, 223; hummus, 1, 3, 5, 151; *knafe,* 17; in Megiddo Prison, 22, 157, 159–60, 161, 219, 226; sesame rings, 108; tabbouleh, 2, 3, 100, 151; tahini, 2, 3, 59, 100, 108, 151, 217, 219, 220, 223; *za'atar,* 108

Palestinians, 1, 3–4, 16, 17, 23, 75, 77, 78, 103, 106, 112, 146, 217; and 1967 War, 22, 23, 75, 80, 86, 146, 166, 167, 179; Abu Gosh, 3, 4, 5, 7, 8, 18, 150; *Al Arabia,* 3; Arab revolt, 1936–39, 75; Zuhair Bahloul, 5; Bedouins, 57–58, 103, 195–96,

199–200, 201, 215; Druze, 201; "good Arab," 242n7; hunger strikes, 13, 14, 232n16; Ibrahim, Jawadat, 3, 4, 5–6; in kibbutzim, 138, 241n16; occupied territories, 76, 151, 167, 179, 239n23, 242n7; Palestinian Authority, 151, 161, 226, 242n4, 242n5; peace talks, 6, 153, 179; political organizations, 157, 175; Second Intifada, 151; shawarma, 82, 151, 223. *See also* Megiddo Prison

Palmach: ethos, 57, 236n2; and barbecues, 57, 63; chicken stealing, 198

*pargiot* (spring chicken), 64, 65–67, 219, 223

pasta, 26; enlarged servings of, 30, 38, 96–98; imported dried, 86; institutional meals, 135, 160; popularity of, 85, 89, 92

Pearl, Yehudah, 1

periphery, 21, 23, 62, 88, 100, 103–4, 106, 108–9, 127, 194, 210, 222; Beer-Sheva, 44, 90, 95, 104, 113. *See also* development towns; kibbutzim; moshavim

pilgrimages, 57, 60–61, 236n9

pita bread, 2, 27, 40, 56, 59, 63, 137, 219, 223, 224; baked by prisoners, 157, 160; industrial, 217–18; and schnitzel, 218, 219, 220

pizza, 21, 82; and commensality, 93; in the periphery, 103–4, 106, 108–9; pizzerias, 82, 83, 85, 88, 93–94, 103, 104–5, 106, 108–9; in the United States, 85, 86

Poland: Jews, 209; trips to Holocaust sites in, 174. *See also* Ashkenazi; East European

pork, 51, 90–91, 110, 109, 240n8; substitution in schnitzel, 217; and Thai migrant workers, 194

portions, enlargement of, 21, 26, 29–31, 121, 165, 218, 224, 225, 226, 227; American, 34, 36; Diasporic hunger and, 46; of dim sum, 38; gourmet food, 35–36; Italian food, 96–98, 110; in kibbutz dining rooms, 140; McRoyal burgers, 41–42; and nonsuckerhood, 47–48, 98; *Ochel, Kadima Ochel* (Food, charge forward [Biber]), 31; and satiety, 21, 42, 44–45, 48, 218, 227; sushi, 39–41; tapas, 36–38, 42. *See also* cheap food

potatoes, 56, 57, 96, 115, 135, 136, 233n2;
French fries, 139–40, 217–18
prisons, 13, 22, 225, 226, 227; prisoners, 9,
54, 242n5. *See also* Megiddo Prison
*Pronto: Ochel, Tarbut, Ahava* (Pronto:
Food, Culture, Love [Rafi Adar]), 87

Rabin, Yitzhak, 153, 179, 211
Ramla, 103
Regev, Miri, 223
renters in kibbutzim, 115, 116, 119, 137,
140–41
reserve soldiers at Megiddo, 22, 148, 155,
157; escorting prisoners, 166; ex-Russian
army, 163; dissatisfaction with food, 155,
165, 168, 177, 227; Palestinian view of,
170, 176–77; resentment of MPs, 162;
victimization narrative, 160, 168–69,
170, 171, 174, 226
resistance, 9, 13, 14; food as, 12, 225–26;
hunger strikes, 13, 14, 232n16; nonsuckerhood, 47; Palestinians, 75; victimization narrative, 168–69, 170, 174; *Weapons of the Weak* (Scott), 8–9, 11
Rosnhek, Zeev, 180
Russian immigrants, 137, 172, 174, 209,
210–11, 220; former army, 163, 164. *See
also* Soviet Union

Sabbath, 202; meals, 45, 91, 119, 120, 125,
130, 134–35, 136, 141, 162, 233n2; during
military service, 162–63
sabra (also *tzabra,* native Israeli Jew prickly
pear), 1, 198
Sabra Foods, 1, 2
Sacher Park, 21, 55, 56, 57, 73–74, 79, 80–81,
224. *See also* Independence Day
barbecues
Sahlins, Marshall, 51, 53
Said, Edward, 224
salad, 21, 27, 63, 83, 135, 136, 217, 224; in
Jerusalem mix, 2; portions, 29; in Italy,
96; in hotel breakfasts, 32; in kibbutzim, 140; mozzarella, 83; in Megiddo
Prison, 151; salad bars, 29, 115, 166; in
schnitzel in a pita, 217; Thai papaya,
192
Salatey Miki, 4

satiety (*saveah*), 21, 42, 44–45, 48, 218, 227
schnitzel, 135, 160, 162, 163, 164; in a pita,
217, 218–19, 220; in sushi, 40–41
Schor, Alex, 85
Scott, James, 8–9, 10, 11, 150, 225
Sderot, 236n11
seafood, 37, 90
secular: citzens, 16; pilgrimage, 57; secularization, 89
self-service (*hagasha atzmit*) in kibbutzim,
113, 116, 123, 124–27, 128, 129–30, 134,
135, 143
Sephardi (Spharadim), 60; in Italy, 237n6.
*See* Mizrahi
sesame, 106, 107–8; in pizza, 109, 110–11.
*See also* hummus; tahini
shakshouka, 26, 233n2
Shaul, Anat, 32–33
Shavuot, 119, 141
shawarma, 82, 151, 223
*sherut miluim* (reserve service), 146, 151, 153,
160, 161, 168, 169, 170, 171, 172; behavioral sciences officer (BSO), 154, 155. *See
also* Israeli Defense Force; Megiddo
Prison
Sirkis, Ruth, 26, 233n5
socialism, 117, 143, 144, 212–13, 228. *See also*
Zionism
Society for the Protection of Nature, 201
South Africa, 53, 54, 55, 62, 74
Soviet Union, immigrants from, 76, 114,
137, 171, 172, 174, 209, 210–11, 220;
former army, 163, 164
Spain: tapas, 36, 37–38, 43
spices, 28, 50, 71, 107, 109, 163; in Arab
salad, 27, 61; cumin, 2, 106, 108, 109, 111;
*dag Mizrahi,* 107; *harif,* 107, 108, 138,
160, 217, 219–20, 224, 225, 226; harissa,
106, 108–9, 111, 219; in military dining
rooms, 241n17; in Thai-Isan workers'
food, 192, 193, 200
Spiegel, Haim, 33–34
Strauss-Elite, 1
suckerhood, avoidance of, 46–48, 171, 218,
224. *See also* victimhood
Sukot, 119
surveillance, 13, 119; Tower and Stockade
(*Homa u'Migdal*), 74, 75–77

sushi, 36, 39–41, 42, 43, 44; American modifications, 39; Boaz Zairi, 18
Syria, 60, 155, 157, 219

*Taam Ha'Ir* (Taste of the City), 29, 35–36
tabbouleh, 2, 3, 100, 151
tahini, 2, 3, 59, 100, 108, 151, 217, 219, 220, 223
tapas, 36–38, 39, 42, 43, 44
*Taste of Power* (Katherina Vester), 10
*Tasting Food, Tasting Freedom* (Sidney Mintz), 25
Tegart forts, 155, 156, 169, 242n3
Tel Aviv, 3, 29, 71, 90; cafés and restaurants, 26, 28, 29, 31, 37, 38, 74, 82, 83, 85, 87, 94, 99; culinary history of, 86; as gastronomic center, 103; parks, 56, 68; Taste of the City festival, 29, 35–36
terroir, 99, 100, 102
Thai migrant workers, 22, 186; dog-eating accusations, 180–83, 206, 207, 208, 203–8, 214; donkey-eating incident, 194–96; foodways, 189, 191–92, 195, 197, 199, 207; and hunting, 100, 178, 180–81, 183–84, 192, 193, 200–203, 206, 226; labor and living conditions, 187–91; placenta soup, 197
Thailand: Isan (northeast Thailand), 189, 191–92, 195, 197, 199, 200, 207; Israeli tourism in, 212; Vietnamese in, 187
Toukan, Miriam, 5
tourism, 100, 185, 238n21; in Eilat, 90; Thailand, 212; Turkey, 34
Tower and Stockade (*Homa u'Migdal*), 74, 75–77. *See also* colonialism
Trattoria, 87
Tunisian food: harissa, 108–9, 219; shak-shouka, 233n2
Turkey: food, 27; popularity as tourist destination, 34, 238n21
*tzabar* (sabra, prickly pear, native Israeli Jew), 1

Ultra-Orthodox Jews, 95, 103, 222, 224, 238n14, 239n23
United States, the, 4, 12–13, 34, 37, 39, 53, 74–75, 172; African Americans, 12, 212; American hotel breakfasts, 234n14;

Americans in Israel, 63, 73; ballparks, 142, 143, 144; barbecues, 53, 56, 58–60, 63; Chicago, 84, 85; dogs in, 214; food discourses, 8, 10, 12, 25–26, 27, 94, 219; Israelis in, 4, 59, 86, 220; Israeli perceptions of, 236n5; Italian-American food, 84–85, 86, 87, 88, 91, 92, 111; kosher in, 90; McDonald's, 36, 41, 42, 141, 142; Native Americans, 53, 74; New York Jews, 109–10, 111, 218; relations with Israel, 59–60; sushi in, 39–40; *A Taste of Power* (Katharina Vester), 10; *Tasting Food, Tasting Freedom* (Sidney Mintz), 25

vegetables, 39, 45, 88, 150, 193; at breakfast, 32, 44, 234n14; in cholent, 115, 129, 135, 136, 141; Israeli/Arab salad, 27, 151, 217, 270; in Megiddo Prison, 162, 168; omnipresence, 40
vegetarianism, 89, 91, 201; and feminism, 52–53; and gender, 52, 149; and Hinduism, 149–50; vegan, 89, 201; "except for schnitzel," 218
Vietnam, 15; dog meat in, 185, 186, 187, 206; ethnographic research in, 16, 17, 18, 19, 20
Vietnamese: immigrants in Israel, 211; in Thailand, 187; workers in Israel, 243n1
victimhood: and the Holocaust, 23, 45, 46, 48, 85, 174, 224; reservists vis-à-vis detainees, 168, 170, 171; suckerhood, 46–48, 171, 218, 224
Vivekananda, Swami, 150

*Walla News*, 3, 206
Wallner, Heimo, 18–20. *See also* illustrations
*Weapons of the Weak* (James Scott), 8–9, 11, 150
Weber, Max, 8, 9, 10, 12, 13, 225, 226; "iron cage," 113, 141, 142
West Bank, 23, 24, 76, 175, 176–77
women, 12, 144, 149; and barbecues, 52–53, 58, 64, 65, 67, 118; and chicken, 78

*yam-tichoniut* (Mediterranean-ness), 98, 100

Yefet, Orna, 36

*Yekes* (German Jews), 90, 120, 209

Yemeni Jewish, 60, 82, 209; spicy sauce, 219

Yom Ha'atzmaut (Independence Day), 49, 50, 78. *See also* Independence Day barbecues

Yom Hazikaron (Memorial Day), 57, 63, 65, 69, 73

youth: backpacking, 237n14; Bnei Akivah, 63; extended childhood, 95; Holocaust trips, 174; military service, 95, 240n5; movements, 57, 63; *noar hagva'ot,* 77; trekking, 57

*za'atar,* 108

Zairi, Boaz, 28, 39

Zehavi, Eitan, 86

Zeid, Giorah, 75

*Zen and the Art of Motorcycle Maintenance,* 172

Zionism, 12, 23–24, 75–77, 153, 210; and egalitarianism, 144, 211, 212–14; moshavim, 22; and nonsuckerhood, 47; and Palestinians, 167; youth trekking, 57. *See also* collectivism; kibbutz; State of Israel

Zohar, Uri, 208–9, 210, 211